WALKER
IN THE
FOG

The C. Henry Smith series is edited by J. Denny Weaver. As is expected to be true of many future books in the CHS series, Volumes 1 through 6 are being released by Cascadia Publishing House (originally Pandora Press U.S. , a name some of the earlier series books carry) and copublished by Herald Press in cooperation with Bluffton University as well as the Mennonite Historical Society. Bluffton University, in consultation with the publishers, is primarily responsible for the content of the studies.

WALKER IN THE FOG

On Mennonite Writing

JEFF GUNDY

Foreword by Hildi Froese Tiessen

For Gertrude
well met in
Bluffton!
Jeff
Oct. 2006

The C. Henry Smith Series
Volume 5

Cascadia

Publishing House
the new name of Pandora Press U.S.
Telford, Pennsylvania

copublished with
Herald Press
Scottdale, Pennsylvania

Cascadia Publishing House orders, information, reprint permissions:
contact@CascadiaPublishingHouse.com
1-215-723-9125
126 Klingerman Road, Telford PA 18969
www.CascadiaPublishingHouse.com

Walker in the Fog
Copyright © 2005 by Cascadia Publishing House,
Telford, PA 18969
All rights reserved.
Copublished with Herald Press, Scottdale, PA
Library of Congress Catalog Number: 2004027650
ISBN: 1-931038-26-0
Printed in the United States
Book design by Cascadia Publishing House
Cover design by Gwen M. Stamm

The paper used in this publication is recycled and meets the
minimum requirements of American National Standard for Information
Sciences—Permanence of Paper for Printed Library Materials, ANSI Z39.48-1984.

Grateful acknowledgment is made for permission to quote materials listed in
"Acknowledgments and Permissions" at back of book.

Library of Congress Cataloguing-in-Publication Data
Gundy, Jeffrey Gene, 1952-
Walker in the fog : on Mennonite writing / Jeff Gundy.
p. cm. -- (C. Henry Smith series ; v. 5)
Includes bibliographical references and index.
ISBN 1-931038-26-0 (trade pbk. : alk. paper)
1. American literature--Mennonite authors--History and criticism. 2. Canadian literature--Mennonite authors--History and criticism. 3. Mennonites--United States--Intellectual life. 4. Mennonites--Canada--Intellectual life.
5. Mennonites--In literature. I. Title. II. Series.

PS153.M35G86 2005
810.9'9212897--dc22

2004027650

12 11 10 09 08 07 06   10 9 8 7 6 5 4 3

To Joseph Joder,
poet and ur-lurker,
and to Mennonite writers and writing
yet to come.

CONTENTS

FOREWORD

Jeff Gundy's *Walker in the Fog* is, first of all, a record of the author's sojourn among the Mennonites of the American Midwest and beyond. Gundy is both poet and critic here, actor and observer. His diverse reflections, composed over several decades, are alternately meditative and probing, speculative and documentary, critical and playful.

Gundy is interested in Mennonite/s writing, in the nature of art, the artistic process, the communal reception of literature, and the character of interaction among writers, and between writers and their worlds. Art—literature in particular—is for him "the place where the communal memory is maintained and negotiated." For Gundy the communal memory concerns Mennonites. He is always after the Mennonite point of reference, the Anabaptist footprint.

Gundy has been captivated by particular authors and texts and points of view. Although he invites his readers to consider the words of figures as diverse as Plato and Kristeva, Blake and Pound, Rumi and Kierkegaard, he lingers over none of these. That is, while he engages these "outsiders" in passing, his attention settles always on what he calls "some sort of Mennonite connection." As he roams the Mennonite territories he knows, he attends not only to creative writers like Rudy Wiebe, Patrick Friesen, Di Brandt, Julia Kasdorf, Jean Janzen, and Keith Ratzlaff, but also to Mennonite critics, historians, sociologists, and theologians. The wide-ranging web of allusions and connections he plants and nurtures in his reader's mind traces the scope of his investigation, which is tenaciously oriented toward a focal center even as it leads ever outward.

Jeff Gundy, poet and critic, has participated in and observed Mennonite writing from the earliest years of its emergence as an area of performance and inquiry. As an engaging and perceptive commentator in the field, he draws on creative insights that are at once personal and passionate, lively and concrete. He interacts freshly and provocatively with the spheres he encounters, musing with insight and good humor on the cultural landscape he and the writers who draw his attention inhabit.

This volume, like Di Brandt's *Dancing Naked* and Julia Kasdorf's *The Body and the Book*, offers its readers a prismatic perspective on what it means to be a writer among Mennonites. Every one of these titles—including Gundy's own *Walker in the Fog*—reveals that these poets attend, first of all, to the sensory world. What all these poets have to say is rooted perhaps not precisely in what W. B. Yeats called "the rag-and-bone shop of the heart" but certainly in embodied experience, in lived encounters. The essays published here reflect those things that happen when one living force comes into contract with another. Here are salutations and embraces, questions and exclamations. Like Brandt and Kasdorf, Gundy is ever conscious of his place in every encounter, and his text, like theirs, is self-reflexive. Despite his claims to a peculiarly Mennonite humility, Gundy energizes his work by foregrounding his presence relative to the subjects he addresses and the figures he embraces.

Between the covers of this volume a reader is invited to travel with Gundy in the territory of Mennonite/s writing and to encounter, along the way, signs and allusions that suggest innumerable tracks to be taken off the main path of investigation. Gundy has named this book *Walker in the Fog* as if, as he remarks, to suggest that as individuals traverse the landscape he charts, their view must inevitably be obscured. As readers we would enhance our tour, he remarks, if we "listen to others' reports . . . very carefully." He proposes for us here a singular report on this terrain—the geography of Mennonite/s writing—and suggests to us a particular, luminous path.

—*Hildi Froese Tiessen*
  Conrad Grebel University College
  University of Waterloo

SERIES PREFACE

C. Henry Smith began his teaching career at Goshen College, 1903-13, and then taught history at Bluffton College (now Bluffton University) from 1913-48, except for the 1922-23 year he spent at Bethel College. The first Mennonite in North America to earn a Ph.D. and remain in the Mennonite church, Smith was the premier North American Mennonite historian of his era. He wrote many articles for Mennonite periodicals and was a central figure in planning the *Mennonite Encyclopedia*. He published five major works over thirty-five years, more full-length writings than any other Mennonite historian of his time. Also a church leader, Smith was on the publication board of the General Conference Mennonite Church and the Peace Committee of Middle District.

Producing the C. Henry Smith Series (CHS) with cosponsorship of the Mennonite Historical Society is one dimension of the service Bluffton University seeks to provide the Mennonite church as well as Anabaptists at large and the wider Christian tradition. Smith's historical expertise, commitment to pacifism and nonresistance, commitment to the church, and wide-ranging interests beyond the discipline of history all represent the values and interests that characterize the series bearing his name. Naming the series for an individual of multiple interests and talents signals a vision to publish works that use a variety of disciplines and modes of inquiry to serve Anabaptist and Mennonite churches.

Works in the CHS Series reflect the assumption that a peace church worldview holds potential to shape discussion of any issue. These books present no consensus view, however, since none exists. Instead, they address aspects of Anabaptist and Mennonite studies pertinent to the future of these churches. Precisely that future dimension compels CHS publication.

SERIES EDITOR'S FOREWORD

I am old enough to remember Mennonite writing before the development of the kind of Mennonite writing that is the subject of this book. Even though I was far from a young literary critic, what little Mennonite writing I recall from my early years did not exactly capture my attention for very long. Plots of novels or short stories were predictable—children got punished for doing the things we were warned against in Sunday school, where little boys might learn that it was more fun to dry dishes for their mothers than to play baseball with the neighbor boy who lived down the block. I was much more inclined to read books with real plots from the public library than to labor through—as a church obligation—whatever Mennonite literature was handed to me. If latent skepticism about the quality and character of Mennonite writing still remains, Jeff Gundy's *Walker in the Fog* should expunge such doubts.

Imagine Mennonite writing as an ever-changing, ever-rolling sea. Although it is a complete and connected presence, it still has currents that run in different directions and that at times may cancel each other out or end up in disastrous whirlpools. At times it is calm, with gentle swells. Other times it features boisterous waves with white caps and spray flying.

This book is Jeff Gundy's navigation of this sea. He marvels at its beauty, as he paddles us across its shining swells or sometimes decides just to sit in his canoe and drift where the current wills. Other times, Gundy adds to the sea's turbulence as his oar sharply cuts the water, or adds vigorous or playful splashes to the flying spray. And throughout the book is a sense that the beautiful sea can turn dangerous, and we see Gundy maneuvering to stay afloat amid the potential peril. It is a beautiful, sensual, humorous and venturesome cruise that anyone interested in Mennonite writing will want to take.

Gundy's chapters show us the sea. Each chapter can stand alone. But almost mystically each of them means more as a part of the larger "sea" that is this book. Although a number of these chapters previously appeared as individual essays, they cohere in this book so that the whole is clearly more than the sum of the parts—as a wave can be studied for its own power, volume and symmetry but is more meaningful when seen as a part of the sea.

Gundy says that this book is not a systematic survey of Mennonite writing—and he is of course correct. Nonetheless, this book navigates much of the length and breadth of Mennonite writing and Mennonite writers, and those who stay on board to the end will finish the voyage with a comprehensive sense of the people and the issues and the pleasures of Mennonite writing—and perhaps most of all with a sense of Mennonite writer Jeff Gundy.

It has been a pleasure to work with Jeff Gundy in producing this fifth volume of the C. Henry Smith Series. I trust that readers will discover that same pleasure in reading it. Much appreciation is due Steven L. Mullet and Jill Basinger Mullet for their generous support of the C. Henry Smith Series and of this volume.

—*J. Denny Weaver, Editor*
  The C. Henry Smith Series

AUTHOR'S PREFACE

Like most books, this one has been both a lonely project and one that would not exist without the help, suggestions, scholarship, creativity, and conversation of many friends and colleagues. J. Denny Weaver, my longtime conversation partner, was instrumental in convincing me to pay attention to Mennonite writing and in offering generous amounts of advice and information all along the way. Others have also served as listening boards and instructors on topics directly or indirectly addressed here.

The Bluffton community has provided me with a great deal of support; I am deeply indebted to Bluffton College (now University) and the Bluffton College Study Center, which have provided sabbaticals and summer grants, and to the Ohio Arts Council and Ohio Humanities Council for fellowships and speaking opportunities. Karen Bontrager helped greatly with the formatting and proofreading of the final manuscript. Among my many colleagues and friends, I must especially thank Mary Ann Sullivan, Lisa Robeson, Lamar Nisly, Judith Kingsley, Gregg Luginbuhl, Gerald Biesecker-Mast, Susan Biesecker-Mast, Perry Bush, Gayle Trollinger, Bill Trollinger, John Kampen, and Lee Snyder. Librarians and archivists Ann Hilty at Bluffton and Joe Springer, John Sharp, and Dennis Stoesz in Goshen have been patient and helpful with research questions.

Colleagues, friends and editors in the larger Mennonite world have provided feedback, publication, and inspiration over many years: thanks to Theron Schlabach, John Roth, Ervin Beck, John Fisher, Todd Davis, Ruth Krall, Ann Hostetler, James Juhnke, Ami Regier, Brad Born, Raylene Hinz-Penner, Carroll Yoder, Hildi Froese Tiessen, Paul Tiessen, Arnold Snyder, Marlene Epp, Victor Jerrett Enns, Pete Blum, Scott Hol-

15

land, and others I am surely forgetting. Thanks to Elizabeth Fricke, Erin Wahl, and Chad VanBuskirk for their invaluable help with the index.

Finally, I am most grateful for those Mennonite poets, novelists and writers who have become my friends, mentors, and fellow travelers: Julia Kasdorf, Keith Ratzlaff, Jean Janzen, Dallas Wiebe, Sheri Hostetler, David Wright, Di Brandt, Patrick Friesen, and many others.

—*Jeff Gundy*
  Bluffton, Ohio

INTRODUCTION

When I began trying to write about Mennonite literature nearly twenty years ago, the phrase was still nearly an oxymoron, at least in the United States. Over two decades after Rudy Wiebe's *Peace Shall Destroy Many* (1962) had supposedly ushered in a new era of Mennonite literary creativity, it was still difficult to find serious imaginative writing by Mennonites south of the long border. In particular, as I scratched around for American Mennonite poetry to write about I could find little more than slender chapbooks; I was reduced to the stratagem, only partly selfish, of also writing about some poems of my own which had been published only in magazines.

The essay I eventually produced on the work of Keith Ratzlaff, Eric Rensberger, and myself appeared in 1986 in the *Journal of Mennonite Studies*, though it now seems too dated to republish here. Shortly thereafter, however, an unprecedented flowering of creative writing, especially poetry, by U.S. Mennonites did begin. Paralleling the slightly earlier renaissance among Canadian Mennonite writers, the U.S. version continues to gain momentum.

This flowering has both made this book possible and complicated it. While I once imagined writing a more or less complete survey of significant Mennonite literature (at least in the United States) of the last twenty years or so, there are now too many fine Mennonite writers and texts to make that task within my means.

What I have done instead is something more personal, partial, and in places polemical—some readers, my editor suggests, might even discover traces of humor. This volume includes what seems most worthy from my prior work on Mennonites writing and over a hundred pages written since I conceived this project-much of it unpublished. Formally the pieces are varied; readers will find more or less conventional literary criticism, more personal and idiosyncratic essays, and even a few forays into the perilous territory of literary theory. As I worked on these pieces I was also writing poems and creative nonfiction, and all these chapters, no less than the more "creative" work, came out of my complicated and untidy existence. Be warned, then: their high seriousness may well lapse into whimsy, sarcasm, special pleading, and various other transgressions.

The book begins with an introduction which considers my own history as a writer in the context of other Mennonite writing and reflects on the necessary but difficult process through which writers—as well as others—construct stories of their own origins.

The next three chapters were all originally written in the late 1980s. First presented at the Mennonite Experience in America conference at Bluffton College in November, 1987, "Humility in Mennonite Literature" later appeared in *Mennonite Quarterly Review* 63 (1989): 5-21, with a response by Shirley Hershey Showalter. As later chapter titles and recurring considerations of this theme will make clear, I have been fascinated by the category of humility for a long time. One of the most complex and mixed terms in our lexicon of human attributes, it has often been used and sometimes abused among Mennonites; its meaning and proper function in contemporary Mennonite literature and culture remain hotly contested. This first look at the subject was also one of my first efforts at thinking carefully and systematically about contemporary Mennonite writing.

Chapter three, on Patrick Friesen, was written for a special issue of *The New Quarterly* edited by Hildi Froese Tiessen in conjunction with the "Mennonite/s Writing in Canada" conference held at Conrad Grebel College in May 1990, and was published in *The New Quarterly* 10, 1&2 (Spring/Summer 1990): 138-149. The first sections are relatively standard critical readings of Friesen's poetry collections *The Shunning* and *Flicker and Hawk*, paying special attention to his treatment of Mennonite situations and issues. The last few pages, more personal and reflective, begin to take up larger issues of poetics and how poets—Mennonite or not—can and should place themselves in relation to the world. As further chapters show, I have often returned to these questions as well, seeking to articulate my developing sense of the function of poetry and imaginative writing in this world.

While still in college I discovered the poet and teacher William Stafford's work, and was immediately drawn to his warm, subtle, firmly nonviolent voice. I wrote one chapter of my dissertation on Stafford's poems, and did further research on his life and work in the late 1980s, with the aid of a grant from the Bluffton College Study Center. Chapter four was the result; it argues that his work exemplifies strongly and beautifully what a poet in the Anabaptist tradition might be and do. The section on Stafford's *Down in My Heart* appeared as "Without Heroes, Without Villains: Identity and Community in *Down in My Heart*" in *On William Stafford: The Worth of Local Things*, ed. Tom Andrews. Ann Arbor: University of Michigan Press, 1993: 95-103.

The chapters that follow reflect an increasingly complicated engagement with issues of Mennonite writing and with the increasingly rich literary situation that began to develop among American Mennonites by the early 1990s. Sometime in the middle of that decade John Roth, editor of *Mennonite Quarterly Review*, asked me to write a survey essay on U.S. Mennonite poetry for a special issue on Mennonite literary topics. As I researched, corresponded with, and met emerging and well-established Mennonite poets across the country, I found myself considering the social and cultural factors that were enabling them to find their way into print and the developing sense of a Mennonite writing community. The lengthy piece that resulted appeared as "U.S. Mennonite Poetry and Poets: Beyond Dr. Johnson's Dog" in *Mennonite Quarterly Review* 71.1 (1997): 5-41. Chapter five of this book, it includes considerable historical and theoretical background as well as individual treatments of many poets.

Four shorter, more personal and polemical chapters follow, most of them written for particular occasions. Chapter six, "In Praise of the Lurkers (Who Come Out to Speak)" was composed for a plenary session of the 1997 "Mennonite/s Writing in America" conference at Goshen College and published in *Mennonite Quarterly Review* 72, 4 (Oct. 1998): 503-510. Drawing both on Mennonite writers and on others as disparate as Plato, Kierkegaard, Wallace Stevens, and Rumi, it attempts both to define and to celebrate one plausible role for Mennonite writers as "lurkers," figures who are within their communities without being entirely "of" them.

"At the Vision Conference" and "Black Coats, Pig-Headed Fathers, and Growing Souls" both deal with the figure of Harold S. Bender, whose life and work are so crucial to Mennonite life and thought throughout a good part of the twentieth century. The first was written after a 1995 conference at Goshen College in honor of his ground-breaking "Anabaptist Vision" essay, and was published in *Mennonot* 4 (Spring 1995): 17-19. (Because of its personal nature and style, I have petitioned my editors for an exception to the mighty "no contractions" commandment here and in a few other places.) The second was composed for a 1999 Mennonite Historical Society meeting in honor of Al Keim's biography of Bender and appeared in *Mennonite Life* 54.4 (Dec. 1999): 9-15. Readers of both essays will quickly note my equivocal and subjective sense of Bender and his legacy, which reflects my larger ambivalence about most authority figures and institutions. This trait, which is at least as temperamental as it is political, is further complicated by my own curious position as a sometimes grumpy critic of the Mennonite establishment and a longstanding participant in it. Like many Baby Boomers who came of age in the sixties, I have found entering middle age complicated, especially since I have not yet managed to convince myself that maturity is an entirely desirable condition.

"(In)visible Cities . . . ," with its coyly postmodern title, came out of a conference on Anabaptism and Postmodernity at Bluffton College in 1999, and continues my exploration of the actual and possible roles of creative writing and creative writers within the Mennonite sphere. It examines master narratives such as Bender's in the light of postmodern skepticism about those narratives, and suggests that, at the very least, Mennonite poetry and fiction can offer necessary complications and supplements to the stories we tell about ourselves. It first appeared in an earlier volume in the C. Henry Smith series, *Anabaptists and Post-modernity*, edited by Susan Biesecker-Mast and Gerald Biesecker-Mast (Telford, Pa.: Pandora Press U.S., 2000): 175-190.

Chapters ten and eleven, the first dealing with some key Mennonite terms and the second on four recent books of poems, were written specifically for this book and continue my wrestling with issues of narrative, control, and creativity that are not only "literary," but historical and sociological and even religious as well. How can and should Mennonite writers and thinkers operate? What are their responsibilities to transmit, redefine, and re-imagine Mennonite traditions and stories? What place do literary imagination and innovation have for a people in such rapid transition?

Chapter twelve, "If the Earth Is the Lord's, Do We Have to Hate the World?" explores the long contention among Mennonites about "the world" and our relation to it. It takes the first part of its title from John Ruth's recent history of Lancaster Mennonite Conference, *The Earth Is the Lord's*, and was written for the Festschrift in honor of Ruth—Mennonite historian, film-maker, preacher, and sage—titled *The Measure of My Days* and edited by Joseph Miller and Reuben Miller (Telford, Pa.: Cascadia Publishing House, 2004). The chapter reflects on both Ruth's life and his massive book, and especially on the long suspicion of education and intellectual pursuits among Lancaster Mennonites.

The most recently written chapter, "What Is It I Know?': Notes Toward an Embodied Gnosis," deals with ritual, subjectivity, and their role in poetic creativity, and argues that some aspects of gnosticism might have a place in a Mennonite practice and imaginative life. It was composed for the June 2003 conference on "Ritual in Anabaptist Communities" at Hillsdale College.

I have violated strict chronology once more to close with "Heresy and the Individual Talent," a quasi-serious manifesto written for the second Mennonite/s Writing conference held at Goshen College in October 2002 and published in *Mennonite Life* 57. 4 (Dec. 2002). An experiment in form as well as content, it led me into uncharted realms of thought and language, as I tried to imagine the possibility of an Anabaptist Surrealism-or perhaps a Surrealist Anabaptism. I hope that readers who make it that far will enjoy and forgive its extravagance and lack of proper Mennonite solemnity.

Crossing back and forth between the forms of literary criticism, creative nonfiction, and poetry, and transgressing the boundaries of academic disciplines as well, has come to seem second nature to me over the last twenty years of my writing life. This book reflects that eclecticism in both its form and content; chapters with a good deal of historical emphasis, especially numbers seven, eight, and twelve, and the sociological and cultural inquiries of chapter ten coexist throughout with literary analysis, creative prose, and even some poems.

Does this book have a thesis? If so, it is this: that imaginative writing, as much as any other human activity, is a gift from God. Like all gifts it may be abused or squandered, but I am convinced that much recent writing by and about Mennonites has been done with care, integrity, and joy, and that we can all be enriched by the gifts that have been given.

A secondary theme is to celebrate the range and variety of voices, themes and stories emerging from Mennonite writing, and to argue that such diversity actually strengthens and deepens Mennonite identity and culture by mapping its complexities more fully and accurately.

My original intent was that the previously published and presented essays would stand here much as they were originally written. But in addition to correcting some obvious errors, removing some repetitive sections, and smoothing out some stylistic lapses, I have rewritten sections of several chapters that seemed outdated or inadequate more substantially, and added some commentary and transitional material to help knit what were separate essays into a coherent book. Alert readers will note that the tone and style still range considerably; after much consideration I decided against trying to smooth everything in this book into a unitary style or a single particular tone. These shifts reflect the range of my own thought and feeling about Mennonite writing, and here (as elsewhere) it seems right to value accurate complexity over reductionist simplicity and multiple perspectives over arbitrary neatness.

Readers familiar with this territory will notice that I have written little or nothing about some of the better-known Mennonite writers, especially Canadian authors. Some, most notably Rudy Wiebe, have been extensively studied by critics much better informed than I am on their work; many others deserve closer and deeper study as well. A systematic and comprehensive historical survey of Mennonite writing would be an extremely valuable project. What I offer is surely neither comprehensive nor systematic, but an idiosyncratic gathering of observations and arguments. Taken as a whole, *Walker in the Fog* attempts to expose readers to some vistas of recent Mennonite writing, while also offering and reflecting upon my own forays into that ever-changing landscape. That it reveals as much about its author as it does about its ostensible subjects is, I have come to think, inevitable. Whether that is fortunate or not, readers must decide for themselves.

WALKER IN THE FOG

On Mennonite Writing

CHAPTER ONE

MYTHS OF ORIGIN AND ARRIVAL

Origins: The Bad and the Bland

Rudy Wiebe, Pat Friesen, Di Brandt, Julia Kasdorf—early books of all these quintessential Mennonite writers are driven by a powerful sense of ambivalence about the communities of their birth. *Peace Shall Destroy Many* (Wiebe, 1962), *The Shunning* (Friesen, 1980), *Questions I Asked My Mother* (Brandt, 1987) and *Sleeping Preacher* (Kasdorf, 1992), different as they are, all describe tight Mennonite enclaves whose communal warmth is deeply compromised by their authoritarian repression. All are places which will tolerate very little independence and destroy or force into exile those who question the communal order. All these authors did indeed leave those communities, though their particular trajectories and receptions have differed; all faced the fear of being scorned, chastised, shunned, even killed by their own people, and in varying degrees all have endured scorn and chastisement—along with considerable communal and public acclaim.

This story seems to be the Ur-myth of the modern Mennonite writer, the agonistic story of how the most visible and prominent cried out against communal repression and endured the costs. It is not a new story, nor one exclusively Mennonite; the "kiss-it-goodbye" story can be found emerging from many closely knit communities. In one way, strangely, it seems a variation of the Mennonite martyr myth, with the

25

community now in the place of the old authorities who tortured and burned our heroes for daring to speak their truths, and with the unspeakable narratives about patriarchy, repression, and hidden violence in the place of adult baptism and the refusal of the sword. The difference, of course, is that these martyrs, at least thus far, remain quite alive and active, lauded as well as lambasted by the Mennonites who remain a major if not primary audience for their writing.[1]

A powerful if painful motif, this story of the writer's emergence as a necessary separation and critique of "home" has fueled much of the best Mennonite writing to emerge so far. As a myth of origins, its variations have yielded many stories and poems that I would not be without. Yet I must begin with a strange sort of confession: The myth I have outlined above is not *my* story. I will try to demonstrate that there are numerous exceptions, and that however different their myths of origin, the trajectories of Mennonites writing at the turn of the twenty-first century do often converge. But first I must tell my own story, or at least one version of it.

My home church in central Illinois, Waldo Mennonite, was founded in the mid-nineteenth century as the Gridley Prairie Amish congregation. If I ever knew that it began as Amish I had thoroughly forgotten until about ten years ago, when I happened to be back on a Sunday when its history was revisited for a (typically modest) anniversary celebration. Hearing that my ancestors had named themselves Amish started me wondering what else I did not know about them, and I began to explore family and church history—a process that has led to two prose books about my Amish/Mennonite ancestors. In the last two decades many Illinois Mennonites have turned with renewed interest to their own history, emerging from a long period of near-silence about their own history as a specific people as well as part of the larger Mennonite world.[2]

But stories of our particular history were mostly not told in my childhood. We heard almost nothing about the first Amish settlers' arrival in the 1830s, relative late-comers from Alsace and the Palatinate and somewhat more progressive than their already well-established Pennsylvania and Ohio cousins. In the mid-nineteenth century these pioneer families in Illinois, including both my mother's and father's ancestors, were among the first to move out from the groves along rivers to the open prairies. They had broken the tough prairie grass with the aid of

John Deere's steel plow and established some of the first farms in the area.

I also heard nothing about the ministers' meetings or *Dienerversammlungen* of the 1860s and 1870s, one of the most divisive of them right there at Waldo, though my three-times-great uncle John Strubhar was one of those who spoke at that meeting. The more conservative Amish, not liking the drift of the meetings, stopped coming in the 1860s and became the Old Order Amish. The most progressive groups in Illinois, led by the charismatic Joseph Stuckey, went their own way after a split in 1872, modernizing and eventually joining with the General Conference Mennonite Church. Others, including the Gridley Prairie group, became acculturated more gradually and became part of the Old Mennonite conference, which eventually renamed itself, either simply or presumptuously, the Mennonite Church.

At Mennonite youth conventions in my teens I became confused when asked if I was a GC or an OM. I did not know what the terms meant, though once someone explained it to me I began to understand why the four Mennonite churches within fifteen miles of my home sent their youth to three different camps. Otherwise I could tell little difference between the Old Mennonite Waldo congregation and the nearby General Conference churches, Meadows and Flanagan Mennonite; my parents had relatives and friends in all three. As for the Evangelical Mennonites at Salem, well, we did know that *they* were different, though not much about how or why.

It would take me years to learn that all four churches had begun as one congregation. Flanagan and Meadows had split off from Gridley Prairie during the Stuckey Amish division. The Evangelical Mennonites separated around the same time, restless with traditional Amish quietism and desiring more emphasis on personal salvation and evangelism. Gridley Prairie, conservative enough that one wedding in the 1860s was stopped until the bridegroom took the part out of his hair, remained plain but gradually eased dress and technology restrictions; one of the last moves, sometime in the mid-1960s, was to make the coverings that women still wore to church optional. Quickly almost all the women abandoned them.

If a couple of paragraphs of these schismatic details make your eyes start to glaze—as mine tend to—perhaps that partly explains why such stories were seldom retold. They must have seemed water under the bridge, like the dispute in one of the churches over a small field bridge, which caused flooding in a neighbor and church-member's fields, so that the men of the second family tore down the bridge, so that the first family could no longer reach *their* fields, then . . . but the details of that small, painful feud must wait for another time.

The church of my youth, then, was plain but vigorous, sometimes boring for a restless boy, a little backward but not entirely provincial. The pews were filled with farm families and their many children; it did not occur to me, growing up, that the sons and daughters who went off to college did not often return. I never felt, to use the terms of Julia Kasdorf's "Bodies and Boundaries," that my individual body was encased within a singular Body of Christ from which it would be cast out if I offended (Kasdorf, *Body* 80). I did not grow up with much anxiety about being in or out; this was no Pennsylvania valley bounded by mountains, but an open plain with escape routes in every direction. The revival meetings and the Cold War of my youth combined to fuel plenty of anxiety about my personal salvation, but my worry was not that I would be punished for drawing too much attention to myself—except in school—or for telling the communal story in the wrong way.

Di Brandt speaks of thinking of Reinland as the center of the world, and Kasdorf says that though her family moved from Big Valley before her first birthday she "always regarded it as our real home" (Kasdorf, *Body* 4). While I have a similar attachment to the physical space of the Illinois prairie—where my mother's and father's families have lived for at least four generations—I never remember thinking that the prairie was *central* in any but a personal, private sense. Instead I assumed from early on that real life, even real Mennonite life, was somewhere else, perhaps in Goshen or Bluffton or even, out at the edges of my personal universe, Kansas or Pennsylvania. I was ambivalent about all this, as most midwesterners are; the prairie was flat and severe intellectually as well as physically. I loved it in my way, but from an early age I imagined living elsewhere.

It was clear quite early that I too would go off to college, and that once I was over the long horizon things would be different, though I had only hazy images of just how. I never thought much about being a writer before leaving for college, but I read constantly, and the reading served as an early way of separating myself from others, even from family, and of opening myself to a world of possible other lives. Amid the crowded living room I could fly through distant galaxies, triumph in the championship game, or explore the mysteries of bodies, while the rest of the family just thought that Jeff had his nose buried in a book once again.[3] They were vaguely suspicious of all my reading, and for good reason—in many ways, even in those days, I was not entirely *with* them, though I did chores and walked beans and prayed at table just like everybody else.

Going to college at Goshen—then the largest and, at least by its own lights, the flagship Mennonite college—reinforced the sense that I was making a dramatic break, leaving home for good. I left my letter jacket behind, and my high school jock status with it. My more-or-less steady girlfriend and I had drifted apart over the summer. I knew enough of my classmates from camps and conferences to ease the transition, and found the classes challenging but not entirely overwhelming. The strangest part was being surrounded by so many Mennonites, most of them (it seemed) better-connected and better educated than I was. What did it mean to be from Scottdale, or Lancaster County? I did not even know that they were in different parts of Pennsylvania, but I saw that my classmates from the east had a very different sense of their identity than I did. They lacked my sense of coming from the provinces; they gave the impression that even Goshen was merely an upstart western outpost, that true civilization was back east somewhere. (Many years later, when introduced by Pennsylvania Mennonite author and historian John Ruth at a poetry reading, I was bemused when he pointedly noted that "my people" had come to North America nearly two centuries after his.)

When people ask me how I began to write, this is the story I tell: I was at college, away from home for the first time, not desolate but a little lonely and trying to understand what to make of my new life. I met a beautiful woman (and this is the tricky part—every way of telling it is wrong. But these are the phrases that have become habitual) I thought she was really special, and she thought I was really ordinary. I had been turned down often enough before, but this time, impulsively, I went to the bookstore and bought a notebook. I began to try to put words into shapes that would somehow put my longing and desire outside of myself, give them a less tangled and more tangible form. I wrote about other matters as well—I had discovered, as young people do, that the world was unjust, and thought it might be my duty to distribute this discovery to the masses. And all else follows.

Our one date ended early, awkwardly, at the entrance to her dorm; men were of course not allowed in except on special occasions. "I guess I'll go read some poetry," she said.

Without planning it, I found myself answering "I guess I'll go *write* some poetry."

She gave me a sudden, surprised look. We said little more except good night, but I could tell that she was somehow impressed by my claim to be not merely a consumer of art but a creator, a writer . . . though insufficiently for my purposes at the time. We drifted apart, she married a nice guy who played soccer, I married a beautiful woman from British Columbia. Surely it was all for the best. I kept writing.

I have lived for a long time now with the sense that what little power and authority I may have in the world comes through words, through being able to fit them into creations that have some measure of beauty and force. Only years later did it strike me that this story of how I got started is another myth of my place at the margins, as someone negligible who must find a means to become worthy of notice. It makes of the woman a figure with power to put me away, to refuse me her notice, let alone her affection. Writing becomes, then, an alternate way of claiming, if not the body and soul of the beloved in all her mystery, beauty, and secret reserve, at least some small measure of her attention. It links poetry with love and power, where it belongs, although in ways that I have learned to suspect—for if the woman is made a figure of power she remains a *figure*, objectified and abstracted, not a full human being.

Thinking as a Mennonite, I marvel at how selfish, how lacking in humility, this story is. It has nothing to do with doing the work of the Lord or the blessed community. It tells no story but my own. It is in many ways a generic American myth—think of the poor Jay Gatz re-creating himself as the wealthy Jay Gatsby to win the rich woman that he thinks will make his life complete, and of Theodore Dreiser's *An American Tragedy*, about a penniless young man determined to rise in the world by marrying well. Perhaps it is a deeply Midwestern myth as well, though I doubt it belongs exclusively to that region.

This story is not the whole tale of my life, of course, but it is *there*. It has much to do with my writing poems that had almost no explicit "Mennonite" content for twenty years. I took up most of the classic subjects—love, death, nature, politics, the inner life—but except for some scattered incidents my childhood seemed too benign, even bland, to provide much material. I had nothing like the sort of trauma that has wounded so many Mennonite writers into voice, no urge to produce a confrontational or agonistic first book like those mentioned at the beginning of this essay.

Only in my late thirties did I begin to imagine writing a "Mennonite" book in prose. The impulse was more inquisitive and nostalgic than angry: I hoped to recover some of that obscure, nearly forgotten history of the Amish who came to Illinois and made a place for themselves on the prairies. Perhaps telling those stories for people who knew them only vaguely would be of service; perhaps, also, it would allow me entry into the place where the communal memory is maintained and negotiated. My aim was not to say *This was often cruel, whatever its intentions,* but *This has been ignored yet should be remembered.* And so *A Community of Memory* flirts with nostalgia, finds more to celebrate than to mourn, is an act of gratitude rather than critique. I meant it so not as a correction of those other, harsher works, but as a supplement, one more part of the story, not final either. And the telling continues.

Mennonite Literature and Mennonites Writing[4]

Given the conditions I have outlined here, it seems natural that I find myself fascinated and moved by the Mennonite writing now emerging and feel both deep identification and ineradicable difference as I read it. That is as it should be, I think. One theme of this book is the need for many specific, particular, even contradictory stories as supplements and counterbalances to the abstractions of theology and the generalized narratives of standard history—both of which require a reductionism that may impoverish as it simplifies.

The emergence of sophisticated writing by and about Mennonites and Amish in Canada and the U. S. in the last half of the twentieth century is part of the general entry of Mennonites (and to a lesser extent Amish) into the general culture. The changes wrought by higher education and migration to urban centers continue to transform Mennonite life, and a somewhat different pattern of pressures and social realities means substantial changes for Amish as well. Educated Mennonites like me are often distanced from our birth communities, but—for those of us with the inclination—higher education also provides research and writing skills to explore our traditions in new ways, and to preserve or re-imagine it in stories and poems. The increasing distance of many modern Mennonites from traditional communities, with their oral transmission of key stories and doctrines, has created both the need for new ways of maintaining identity and new tools to do so. (As I will discuss at more length, the work of artists and creative writers includes but is not limited to "maintaining identity.")

This new work creates tension when it seems to speak from "outside," to refuse older notions of accountability, and especially when it portrays traditional communities in unflattering ways. The long distrust of imaginative writing, especially among the Swiss/German Mennonites of the eastern United States, has multiple sources, but one is a very high view of the power of texts, and a corresponding fear that texts not produced under communal control might be strong enough to destroy the community. Thus "official" writing for centuries was required to have a clear religious or didactic purpose.

Even now, Mennonites are cautious about what they themselves put into print. The major Mennonite publishing house, Herald Press, restricts its list mainly to theology, history, peace and justice, and other nonfiction. The major exception is novels about Amish and conservative Mennonite life aimed at young and elderly readers, which sell well in the tourist shops of Pennsylvania, Ohio, and Indiana.[5] The privately owned and operated Good Books, a commercial enterprise based in the Pennsylvania Amish country of Lancaster County, publishes mainly glossy quilt, recipe, and children's books, although its list includes a few more literary novels and books of poems. In the last few years, Cascadia Publishing House has begun to publish serious Mennonite writing, especially poetry, with books by Ann Hostetler, Todd Davis, Dallas Wiebe, Shari Wagner, Julia Kasdorf, and Cheryl Denise, among many others, now on its list. Still, most of the still small but growing body of serious Mennonite imaginative writing has been published by "outside" presses.

To make a rather coarse distinction, then, "Mennonite literature" might be defined simply as work that seeks self-consciously and more or less directly to promote Anabaptist faith and practice. While it may critique minor elements and dramatize certain issues, the outcome will be relatively predictable. Much might be written about this work from a sociological point of view, but my attention here is mainly devoted to something quite different, less cohesive and predictable but more diverse and exciting, which I will call Mennonites writing.[6]

What is Mennonite writing, and who produces it? Such definitions are difficult enough that I am tempted to avoid them entirely, but let me note a few principles. First, I understand "Mennonites" here in a very broad sense: not only "birthright" and continuing members of Mennonite churches, but also those who grew up with considerable Mennonite influence but do not now think of themselves as Mennonite, and those who join the fellowship voluntarily at some point along the way.[7]

Another approach to definition might begin with Yeats's famous observation that we make rhetoric of the quarrel with others, but poetry from the quarrel with ourselves. Mennonites writing often resist taking doctrine and official narrative as either their starting or ending points. Instead they tend, like all strong writers, to deal with their own deepest questions, obsessions, and ambivalences, in ways which make the outcomes unpredictable. Their work is sometimes deeply celebratory of this or that aspect of Mennonite identity, sometimes just as deeply critical, sometimes thoroughly ambivalent.

Mennonites writing sometimes focus either deeply within what is traditionally defined as "the Mennonite community" or a long way outside it; in either case, their work may seem barely "Mennonite" at all. Among many possible examples I might offer two beautifully written and conceived novels by authors with some Mennonite connections. Janet Kauffman's *Collaborators* (and two later novels which form what she calls a "Mennonite trilogy") treats a Mennonite family in the tobacco country of Pennsylvania with sympathy and insight, but the focus is intensely interior and subjective, and "religious" issues as we usually define them are presented subtly enough that only quite sophisticated readers are likely to recognize them. I will discuss *Collaborators* more fully in a later chapter; here my point is only that to my knowledge it has created neither controversy nor celebrity for Kauffman in Lancaster County, mainly because it is a literary novel that happens to have Mennonite characters.

David Bergen's *See the Child*, a slightly different case, features a main character who has a Mennonite name and lives in one of those southern Manitoba villages so memorably described by Di Brandt, Pat Friesen, and Armin Wiebe. Yet as Bergen's unhappy narrator grapples with the death of his son, the breakup of his marriage, and a complicated relationship with his son's lover and a grandson born out of wedlock, there is only the faintest sense of religious community as either a resource or a source of oppression. The main character shows no discernible Mennonite consciousness, and church is no part of his present or, from what we learn, his past life. If Mennonite community means anything in this novel, it is only through its absence.

I do not mean these sketchy, inadequate descriptions negatively—both novels seem very fine to me as works of literature. My point is only that neither is meant to explain, justify, defend, or even wrestle with "core Mennonite values" in a communal context in any very explicit way, to use the terms with which John Ruth challenged Mennonite writers in his *Mennonite Identity and Literary Art*. The kind of cultural work they are meant to do is simply different. If they contend with values and issues and tell stories important to modern Mennonites, they do so in far less overt ways than, say, Joseph W. Yoder's classic *Rosanna of the Amish*[8] or Rudy Wiebe's *Peace Shall Destroy Many*.

If communal-religious issues become less central and crucial in such texts, other "environmental" factors may be more clearly revealed. During the time I was working on the prose narratives in *A Community of Memory*, I was writing poems that were collected in a volume titled *Flatlands*. Religion and family are important to many of those poems, but (as the title suggests) the most important factor is *place*—the flat, austere prairies of my central Illinois boyhood and the only slightly less austere farmlands of northwest Ohio where I have lived most of my adult life. My desire to make art that would explore and illuminate such places and what it meant to live there ran parallel, not opposed to, whatever might be called "Mennonite" in that book.[9] I am not alone in such interests—to cite only two examples, Jean Janzen's recent book of poems *Tasting the Dust* and "new Mennonite" poet David Wright's *Lines from the Provinces* also pay deep and sustained attention to place.

In groping toward an identity as a writer and a Mennonite in the Midwest, I encountered the quite different flowering of Canadian Mennonite writing around Winnipeg from about 1980 on. According to Al Reimer, this renaissance happened along with a wider development of the arts in western Canada. Mennonites were well positioned to help establish the literary identity of the area, Reimer says, "merely by writing out of their own Mennonite experience and exploiting their sense of ethnic difference." In contrast, he suggests, in the U. S. "Mennonite writers are for the most part anonymous voices lost on the vast stage of a much older, much larger, much more mature national literature"

(Reimer 21). If overstated, Reimer's description rang (and rings) mainly true to my own experience.

Another factor is even more personal. Reimer discusses some literary examples of problematic father-son relations within patriarchal Mennonite society: "The rebellious son is typically unable to come to terms with the all-powerful father figure until the father grows old or dies." Since this patriarch/father represents both church and family, Reimer argues, "the son's rebellion is accompanied by feelings of guilt, a sense of betraying his Mennonite heritage" (Reimer 39). He shows this syndrome persuasively in the work of leading Canadian Mennonite poets David Waltner-Toews and Patrick Friesen. In contrast, in a chapter on "The Re-Membering of the Mennonite Woman" Reimer suggests that women writers also must struggle with the father/patriarchy, but that women typically write out of a "strong sense of victimhood" while "the guilt is missing" (39).

I suspect this dualism is too simple, but Reimer offers a credible quick survey of writers such as Di Brandt, Audrey Poetker, Jean Janzen, Sarah Klassen, Sandra Birdsell, and others, and at least begins to note the individual differences within this broad scheme. As many others have, Reimer pauses within his survey to puzzle over the apparent difference between "angry" women such as Di Brandt and Audrey Poetker and the more tempered work of Sarah Klassen and Jean Janzen. At the risk of over-stating in my own way, I would like to offer another way of understanding these writers and the movement of their careers.

My theory also begins with biography. Say that a child grows up with some kind of major psychic wound—and my unscientific intuition is that many, perhaps most, do. That wound is very likely to be connected to family, especially to the father, and if the child grows up in church it is likely to be connected there as well. If the child begins to write, then, it is very likely that an early, pressing psychic need will be toward the healing of that wound by making it public, often by attacking the father and/or the community who inflicted the wound. The books I began with here—*Peace Shall Destroy Many, The Shunning, Questions i asked my mother,* and *Sleeping Preacher*—all seem to me clearly engaged in such work, though I hasten to add that much more is going on in each of them as well.

On the other hand, children fortunate enough to reach adulthood without such a wound may also begin to write. Their first work, in both psychological and literary terms, will not be to attack the father/church. It will be something else. Perhaps it will be to write the story of a more distant wound, as in Jean Janzen's case—she has often said that writing of her grandmother's long-concealed suicide was her first real work as a poet. I have been suggesting that in my case, merely to seek acknowledgement from another was the key motive. I am not sure I should be trusted on such matters, but it seems clear to me that I felt no great need to attack my father or the church. I think my father may deserve much of the credit for that, but I will leave that story for another time as well.

Instead I would like to speculate briefly about the trajectories authors take after their first books are published. In the case of many Mennonite writers, a first or at least early book critical of father/community is followed by others that leave behind that first wounding to explore more complex narratives and themes. Let me quickly sketch the pattern I have in mind in the four authors I have been following here.

Rudy Wiebe has written four "Mennonite" novels. The first, *Peace Shall Destroy Many*, criticizes the Harsh Father through Peter Block, whose efforts to control his community finally undermine the nonviolence he and the community profess. Next is *The Blue Mountains of China*, a wide-ranging historical epic which ends with a critique of Canadian Mennonite assimilation and materialism influenced by John Howard Yoder. The even later *My Lovely Enemy* is very different, an intense, sometimes magic-realist exploration of the varied forms and meanings of love and desire. His recent *Sweeter than All the World* returns to the historical saga of the Dutch/Russian Mennonites, mainly filtered through a worldly, wealthy modern Canadian Mennonite named Adam Wiebe, who is clearly a somewhat autobiographical character.

Patrick Friesen's *The Shunning*, a narrative poem which he rewrote as a successful stage play, was followed by several much more subjective, meditative books of poems including *Flicker and Hawk* and *Blasphemer's Wheel*.[10] (Since *The Shunning* was preceded by two collections of lyric poems, *The Lands I Am* and *Bluebottle*, Friesen's work fits the pattern I am tracing less neatly than the others.)

After *Questions i asked my mother* and *Agnes in the Sky*, Di Brandt's most "Mennonite" books, in the collections *Mother, Not Mother*, *Jerusalem, Beloved*, and *Now You Care* she has become increasingly concerned with the deeper ramifications of love, desire, and politics on many levels. And Julia Kasdorf followed *Sleeping Preacher* with *Eve's*

Striptease, a sequence of poems in which Mennonite issues are minimal and the main themes are desire, abuse, complication, and fulfillment.

I describe these books in such schematic, oversimplified ways only to note two points: First, each of these authors has moved toward themes of bodies, sexuality, and desire as their work matures. Second, in this motion they tend to converge with the work of other Mennonite writers who did not begin with the same kind of first books. Jean Janzen is one example; while her Russian Mennonite tradition and the suffering within it remains a constant thread in her later work, the strongest note of her work is a celebration of eros at work in the world, especially in human love. My own work may be another example, especially my book *Rhapsody with Dark Matter*, which I will discuss along with recent books of poems by Kasdorf, Janzen, and Keith Ratzlaff in another chapter.

It seems no accident that the true emergence of Mennonites writing has occurred in the same time period as the contemporary women's movement. In the emergence of U. S. Mennonite writing, women have been especially important; it is almost a truism to say that much of the energy of Mennonites writing today is women's energy. Freed (or at least freer) to speak in public, women have found that they have a great deal to say; able to step outside traditional roles, they have forged strong bonds with each other and, sometimes, with men as well.

Janet Kauffman's deep engagement with women's issues can be measured in the titles of her story collections *Places in the World a Woman Could Walk* and *Obscene Gestures for Women*. Jean Janzen's decision to return to school and educate herself as a serious writer in mid-life was clearly enabled by modern feminism, and the poems of Julia Kasdorf, Di Brandt, Shari Wagner, Juanita Brunk, Sheri Hostetler, Raylene Hinz-Penner, and other strong contemporary women writers just as clearly drink from the streams of feminism—in their very existence, but in their themes and concerns as well.

An important conference at Millersville, Pennsylvania, in 1995 brought many of these women together with historians and theologians and others. The performance piece *Quietly Landed*, composed by Carol Ann Weaver, Carol Penner, and Cheryl Nafziger-Leis with texts by many Mennonite women, provided an exhilarating collage of powerful, distinct, eloquent voices, no longer limited to quilts and gardens and teaching Sunday school, now speaking in public without apology or reservation.[11]

Talking with a male acquaintance after the performance, I discovered that we were both wondering when a similar group of Mennonite men would be capable of such bold, finely nuanced depictions of their inner and outer lives. Of those we knew, some preached, others taught, but few could have spoken in public with any kind of eloquence or precision about themselves or the deep conditions of their lives. Like most American men, Mennonite males still most often speak only from the practical and realistic parts of their bodies and their minds.

I say this with no interest in claiming a new victimhood for myself or my gender, but merely to register something rather obvious: The system of social and gender roles that some call "patriarchy" binds and restricts all of us, men and women, in ways that ought to be resisted and subverted. Even men, who benefit from patriarchy in many ways, must pay its costs in others.

This is not the place for a detailed analysis of gender roles, but let me mention instead a repeated memory from my childhood. From our frequent family gatherings and birthday parties with my nearby cousins, I remember this tableau: the women chatting freely in the kitchen while my father and an uncle or two sat in the living room, nearly silent except for widely spaced remarks about the weather, the state of the crops, prices, a piece of machinery. They were not uncomfortable with each other, as far as I could tell; they just did not have much to say.

I do not know when I first thought that the conversation in the kitchen might be more interesting, or at least faster paced. I do not know when I first drifted that way, to see if I might be welcome; usually I was, though if I settled in too tight I might draw strange looks. The women, I found, seemed to have a lower threshold of speech than the men in the living room; they talked freely of the most mundane events, of recipes and clothes, but also about children and other relatives, about people in the church and in town. Some of their talk seemed boring or trivial to me, and there was little of the free-ranging, sometimes lofty and sometimes profane conversation about art and life and great ideas I would later learn to love. But in those women's talk I began to sense ways toward speech that might be mine as well. I did not want to find myself as an adult in a room with my best friends and have nothing to say to them.

Ever since, but especially in the last decade or so, I have found myself seeking out the conversation of women. I have been grateful for the shifts in social patterns that make it possible for men and women, at least in the academic circles that I move in, to *have* such conversations with at least some freedom; it was far more difficult until quite recently, I think. For longer than that, I have taken pleasure in confounding my more conservative students by announcing to them that I consider myself a feminist and that all reasonable people of good will ought to do the same. But it has taken me a long time to get much beyond some glib generalizations about feminism and begin to understand that much of what I assumed I knew about the realities of women's lives was incomplete, if not just wrong.

I found myself drawn to such talk partly, I must admit, just because I enjoy the company of women, and not just because they often seem to have more to say than men. But through conversations with many strong, smart women—my wife, colleagues, students, relatives, and friends—I began to see how different the world looks from across the gender divide. Having managed to listen, at least for a while, I found myself—with typical male obstinacy, no doubt—also wanting to speak back, to register my own perceptions and reactions as a sympathetic yet undeniably male voice. To do so in this context meant taking on a perspective that was new to me—accepting that in their eyes, no matter how noble my intentions seemed to me, I was inevitably and rightly a figure of some suspicion. As a man, I was part of the patriarchy whether I wanted to be or not, privileged in ways that were often invisible to me until pointed out, a potential abuser as well as a possible ally.

Somewhere in all of this it struck me that the poems by women I was reading seemed much freer than those by men to speak about certain issues. These days every undergraduate English major learns about the embedded sexism of Andrew Marvell's "To His Coy Mistress" and many other classic poems and their tendency to objectify and mystify women. Many women, energized by these new understandings, have begun writing with anger and exuberance of their bodies and what they did with them, of their desires, of their physical and sexual joys and terrors. Male poets found feminism much less energizing for their work; how could they write about love and desire and sex without merely reproducing the old, sexist patterns? I saw some simply going ahead, but many others slipping into silence on such matters. And for a long time I wrote little about bodies and desire myself, except in oblique and distanced ways.

But eventually it seemed time to address these matters more directly, to try to speak of desire in ways that might be more honest and more worthy than I had managed before. I was hardly alone in this effort, of course. Jean Janzen, Keith Ratzlaff, and Julia Kasdorf, all of them among my closest friends, teachers, and conversation partners, have all also published books of poems during the last few years, and when I returned to their work with these ideas in mind, it struck me that in many ways our poems have been another avenue for these same conversations. The analysis in Chapter 11 of Ratzlaff's *Man Under a Pear Tree*, Janzen's *Tasting the Dust*, Kasdorf's *Eve's Striptease*, and my own *Rhapsody with Dark Matter* attempts to show that all of these books are driven by parallel efforts to address issues of gender, desire, location and vocation that obsess all of us.

If desire is one key to recent Mennonite writing—and I know how shaky and presumptuous a claim that is—perhaps it is because desire is both so fundamental to our lives and so underrepresented in earlier Mennonite literature and other texts. Although a certain earthy sensuality has always survived in Mennonite folk culture, especially in Low German discourse, it has been restricted to such "low" forms; the "higher" discourses of preaching, history, and theology were to be kept clean of such messy and emotional components.

While North American Mennonites were preoccupied with boundary maintenance and pacifism for most of the twentieth century—especially acceptance or refusal of military service—it is understandable that desire seemed a frivolous if not unnecessary category. But we are no longer living in the twentieth century. Even my oldest son, in his early twenties as I write, cannot remember the days of a military draft, though without my urging he wrote on his registration card that he considered himself a conscientious objector. For Canadian and U.S. Mennonites, even in a time of renewed warfare, the chance of being faced with military service is more remote than a dozen other tests of faithfulness.

What does it mean to be committed to nonviolence in such a situation? The question, I am convinced, is still important. Might the answer have to do with a far larger definition of nonviolence than Mennonites have typically practiced, one that encompasses every aspect of our social and sexual relations? What would it mean to compose a theology of nonviolent desire? Might such work be better done in poems than in rationalist treatises (including, alas, this one)?

The challenges and opportunities confronting Mennonites and the rest of humanity at the beginning of this new century are, I suspect, no more daunting than those faced by our ancestors in 1941, 1872 or 1525, but they are surely *different*. If it has ever been possible to "conserve" a tradition without any change—and I doubt that it has—clearly now Mennonites must find new ways of transmitting and even transforming what we believe and think we know. We must not, to use the image I heard recently, merely put the old wine in new wineskins.

But Mennonites writing remind us that there is no human activity not driven or colored, at one level or another, by desire. More easily than the rationalist discourses of theology and history, poetry and fiction can convey the always mixed and multiple nature of all our endeavors, including those we most wish to keep pure and pristine. To do so may mean celebrating the holy within the most physical acts, as Jean Janzen and Patrick Friesen often do; it may mean struggling to reconcile the aftershocks of abuse with the persistence of physical yearning, as Julia Kasdorf does. It may take a thousand other forms.

So the convergence upon desire is, in another way, a great opening. It involves a renewed attention to the vast spaces both outside and deep within the boundaries that Mennonites have for centuries drawn to keep their communities safe and their desires in check. It is still true, I think, that gathering together in community is a great and good thing. But for too long Mennonites have thought that the boundaries defined themselves. I remember the boy that I was, in a corner of the living room, vaguely aware of the television and the rest of the family in the room, watching or talking or browsing in their magazines and papers. My body was in the room, but my mind was wandering the wide world, following Tolkien or Heinlein or some other guide through a great range of adventures and wonders. As the song has it, *Die Gedanken sind frei*— even the strictest community cannot truly govern the thoughts of its members, nor insulate its members completely from the currents of feeling that run through all human beings.

In one way, speaking of desire is simply to speak of all that we do and think and say, for desire has many objects, from the most basic—shelter, security, food—to the most abstract and outrageous. The Anabaptist reformation was fueled by religious desires for a pure and renewed Christianity, surely; while we seldom use this language, both conservative and progressive Mennonites are driven by desire for particular visions of what the blessed community might be and do today. The placing of bounds and limits on some forms of desire is an enduring human necessity and difficulty; as we all know, many types of desire are not only wondrous and powerful but also dangerous, like fire or nuclear energy.

When we attempt simply to ignore or repress desire, it becomes even more dangerous. Inversely, if we fall too wholly under its spell it will surely destroy us. And strangely, some desires which go under other names—order, conformity, purification of the group—are especially dangerous when they lead to overt or covert violence. If rhetoric is will trying to do the work of the imagination, then repression is the superego trying to do the work of the part of us that desires purely and truly, trying to impose by force what is not entered into in freedom and joy.

Desire is large, indefinitely large if not infinite, and there lies the rub: what we yearn for must always exceed what we can have, just as the universe and God must always exceed our grasp of them. "Now it's fine if the truth is real to you," John Howard Yoder once remarked, "but if it's not, it's you that's left out and not the truth" (Yoder 5). This brilliant, provocative statement has haunted me for years, but it strikes me now that it cuts more than one way. What are the chances, really, that Amish or Mennonites or any one small group of human beings—*any* group of human beings, or all of us put together—might have the truth, in any sort of complete or exclusive way? Are we all not left out, yearning to understand the whole truth, to know as we are known, to see clearly, to commune fully with the Other outside and the Other within?

However strong my faith that in the story of Jesus lies the closest and clearest vision of truth that human beings have yet been granted, whatever constructions we assemble around or on that story are surely mere grass huts on the endless plains of reality. Beyond what is now real to us, I believe, is much more, hidden by the limits of our senses and our minds. Poets know that we cannot and should not blindly obey every whim and urge that comes to us from the vast and oceanic realm of desire. But, they tell us, we must not close our eyes and our ears to it. We must pay it and the rest of our lives the closest attention and learn everything that we can, lest we be left out of the truth we seek.

Why do we write if not to see more clearly, to understand less partially, by working our way through language into new spaces of the mind, new images that might be at least related to what is real and true? At the heart of all such work is the hope that, while we will always see through a glass darkly in this world, we may indeed see more clearly, find our way with a bit more confidence. To believe such about the imagination is, in effect, to believe in progressive revelation, the doctrine that God continues to act in the world and to reveal things to us.

In one of the more obscure passages in his *Autobiography,* Ben Franklin dabbles in the doctrine of progressive revelation. He quotes the Dunkers of his day (forerunners of present-day Brethren), who say that they refrain from publishing any "Articles of their Belief" because

> it had pleased God to enlighten our minds so far as to see that some Doctrines which we once esteemed Truths were Errors, and the others which we had esteemed Errors were real Truths. From time to time [God] has been pleased to afford us farther Light, and our principles have been improving and our errors diminishing. Now we are not sure that we are arrived at the end of this progression, and at the perfection of spiritual or theological knowledge; and we fear that if we should once print our Confession of Faith, we should feel ourselves as if bound and confin'd by it, and perhaps be unwilling to receive further Improvement, and our successors still more so, as conceiving what their elders and founders had done to be something sacred, never to be departed from. (Franklin 127)

This Enlightenment confidence in progress toward truth may seem naive, but Franklin suggests that in fact it indicates an unusual humility: "This modesty in a sect is perhaps a singular instance in the history of mankind, every other sect supposing itself in possession of all truth." Worth even more reflection is his suggestion that we all tend to think of ourselves "like a man traveling in foggy weather: Those at some distance before him on the road he sees wrapped up in the fog, as well as those behind him, and also the people in the fields on each side; but near him all appears clear, though the truth is he is as much in the fog as any of them" (Franklin 127).

Do we all imagine that we have the clarity others lack, when in truth we are all just walkers in the same fog? We might then determine to listen to others' reports of the weather and the landscape very carefully, to learn of that which is obscured in the fog from where we walk, but clearer from another point of view. We might be wary of taking our local clarities—and those of others, as well—as global visions or master narratives. We might gather as many of these local truths as we can, brace and balance them together, take more from some and less from others, using all the resources that we have to find our way forward.

CHAPTER TWO

HUMILITY IN MENNONITE LITERATURE

This might well begin with an apology, or a series of apologies: for all the things I still do not know about Mennonite history and literature, for daring to talk about literature at a meeting of historians, for all the books and articles I still have not read, or could not work into this essay, for all the ideas I have condensed and oversimplified to stay within my time limit, for all the confusion I still feel when I think about the issues I am attempting to explore here. That would be a style, and not an uncommon one.

Or I might begin without any apologies, perhaps tuck them away in a footnote, concentrate on what I do know, now, which is surely more than when I started. I might launch at once into my value judgments, praises and dismissals, and let the proverbial chips fall. That too would be a style, and a common one.

But a style is never just a trivial, exterior choice of one subset of language or another. A style defines a stance, a worldview, a way of thinking and acting, both in what it contains and in what it leaves out. To open with an apology, with a statement of humility in the terms of this essay, is to recognize and assert one's limits and accountability from the start. It may be no more than a defense mechanism or a ritual, of course, and if it is not followed by some sort of assertion I am probably in trouble.

Still, it feels right to me to make that statement, just as throughout my life I have found myself making similar statements, even amid loud, sweeping, and dogmatic generalizations about the true nature of the universe. Somehow I have learned at least the rituals, if not the reality, of humility.

This chapter is about humility in the Mennonite tradition and in Mennonite literature. First I want briefly to sketch out some of the roots of the humility tradition, looking mainly at the nineteenth century. I will then examine more extensively some recent pieces of Mennonite criticism and literature to see how they reflect, refract, or relate to that tradition. Finally, I will reflect on ways in which I think the humility tradition can enrich and deepen the ways we think, write and act in our current situation.

ROOTS OF THE HUMILITY TRADITION

Both Joseph Liechty and Theron Schlabach have suggested and documented the centrality of the humility theme for eighteenth and nineteenth century American Mennonites. Schlabach says that from the 1770s through the 1880s and 1890s, humility is "a far stronger note [in American Mennonite theology and outlook] than any other except perhaps that of salvation history" (Schlabach 228).

Similarly stating that "Humility was the foundation of Mennonites' religious outlook in the 1860's," Liechty focuses his attention mainly on that period, especially on the *Herald of Truth* and John M. Brenneman's life and writings. Using Brenneman's classic pamphlet "Pride and Humility" (1866) as his main text, Liechty identifies four levels at which humility informed Mennonite thought and behavior: as a literary style, as a guide to personality, as a more general regulator of broader aspects of life, and finally as a requirement for salvation. "Indeed, theirs was a gospel of humility," he adds (Liechty 12).[12]

Brenneman's pamphlet works from 1 Peter 5:5, "God resisteth the proud and giveth grace to the humble." Arguing that the world consists of "two entirely distinct classes of persons. . . . The proud constitute one class; the humble, the other," Brenneman locates the origin of pride in Satan, who deceived Eve into the prideful step of seeking her own wisdom (Brenneman 6, 9). He offers numerous examples of the proud whom God resisted and destroyed: Noah's compatriots, the builders of the Tower of Babel, the people of Sodom and Gomorrah, King Pharaoh, Nebuchadnezzar, Herod.

Humility, then, is for Brenneman both the way to salvation and a means of avoiding worldly disaster. As Liechty notes, however, other streams of American religious life were hardly sympathetic; they "taught what amounted to a gospel of religiously sanctified pride, for they were still obsessed with the notion of Christianity's role in America's manifest destiny, hardly an idea conducive to humility" (25). Yet Mennonites largely failed to see the strength and relevance of the humility theme outside their narrow borders. Schlabach also suggests Mennonites were too "quietistic and accomodationist" to make full use of the humility theme as a prophetic counter to American arrogance, instead using it mainly for nurture and social control within Mennonite groups (233).

The "Great Awakening" or "Quickening" of the late nineteenth century brought new vitality and energy to the church, but at the cost of a dramatic shift in language and emphasis. Phrases like "aggressive work" replaced humility, military analogies abounded; an "Onward Christian Soldiers" mentality challenged the older teachings on humility and nonresistance as Mennonites faced increasing pressure to blend into the mainstream of American Protestantism. "Worldliness" came to mean being unsaved as much as failing to be the people of humility and peace, and being "active in outreach" became as great an imperative as imitating the meek and lowly Jesus (Schlabach, *Gospel* 48, 226).

The tension between these two views of the Christian life continued and continues. Harold Bender's *Anabaptist Vision* reasserted some aspects of the humility tradition, emphasizing discipleship, brotherhood and nonresistance (Bender 16). Yet Mennonites continue to be drawn toward American evangelical and fundamentalist groups, especially in recent years the media evangelists. Without making a full critique of that group, I must mention my mother's recent comment on their dress, style, and general deportment, which suggests that the grassroots of the humility tradition are very much alive. She said, "They just do not seem very Mennonite, at least to me."

Mennonite Critics and Humility

I hope this brief and sketchy overview will suffice to establish some context for discussing my main concern, which is the ways recent Mennonite critics and creative writers have worked, consciously or unconsciously, within or without the humility tradition. We will see, I think, that the humility theme is important both as a persistent presence and a significant absence.

Two Mennonite authors who became well-known during the 1960s, Elmer Suderman and Warren Kliewer, tend in their critical writings toward a relatively conventional aesthetic framework which poses the artist's unique and independent vision against an audience and community who are grudgingly tolerant at best and hostile at worst. In a series of essays in *Mennonite Life* beginning in 1965, Suderman discusses both specific Mennonite works of literature and larger questions about what Mennonite and Christian literature might be and do. Generally, he insists on the need for artistic integrity and independence, the distinct demands and strategies of aesthetics, and the virtues of literature as a way of knowing individuals and communities.

Suderman never deals explicitly with the humility theme. Most of his work, in fact, seems to assume that the artist and his community must at best exist in a state of uneasy tension. Even when he calls for "discipline, sacrifice, suffering" (Suderman 26), he seems to make little of the Anabaptist insistence that such virtues cannot be realized except in a like-minded community.[13] In his essay "Controversy and the Religious Arts," Warren Kliewer takes a similar position. Insisting that "it is absolutely necessary for the artist to be controversial," he emphasizes the need for more tolerant and sophisticated audiences, especially within the church. Saying that "the church must learn not only to understand but also to accept the artist's need to destroy," Kliewer leaves final responsibility and power with the artist: "A responsible artist destroys only as much as is necessary to begin creating" (Kliewer 8).[14]

It is not hard to understand how such statements, no matter how well intentioned, would make some people nervous. John Ruth's *Mennonite Identity and Literary Art* (1978), which began as four lectures delivered at Bethel College, articulates a more distinctly Mennonite view of the artist's relation to the community. Ruth speaks quite explicitly from within the Swiss-Pennsylvania tradition, beginning with a keen analysis of the ironic results of the conservative-progressive struggles of the late nineteenth century. "Lowliness, humility, mutuality and obedience," he writes, were "replaced with an activist mood, chorales with Moody-Sankey songs, and youthful wild-oats-sowing with devotions and tract-distributing."

The vigorous outreach of the Quickening swept him into the church, Ruth reports, but did not "minister to . . . a hunger to know, in imaginative, concrete, narrative terms, the earlier stages of the stream I was swimming in" (Ruth 14). He finds "near total amnesia" regarding the story of his people in America, the product of a short-sighted concern for "utility" that is ironically worldly in its effects, as it cuts church members off from their own dynamic history.

Ruth calls for a Mennonite literature that grows directly out of a confrontation with Mennonite traditions:

> To *wrestle through* the issues in the artist's personal encounter with a special tradition—that is the challenge. It is far easier to walk away from that struggle, to overlook the opportunities inherent in the polarities and relativities of our tradition's scruples, then to blame the scruples themselves for our own lack of vision. (43)

Ruth places special emphasis on humility as a "once basic stress" which his own community has largely lost. He insists that to reject it as "a hangover from an age when people apparently didn't like themselves and were ashamed of being 'assertive'" is shortsighted: "a virtue once considered fundamentally important must have tied into reality somewhere" (56-7). Reclaiming and re-examining the humility theme, then, is part of the larger work of coming to terms with one's heritage. Arriving at a point beyond careless repudiation or idolatrous absolutizing of his or her identity, the artist becomes able to explore and examine the "positive mystery," as well as the weaknesses and failings, of his or her tradition.

I have spent this much time with Ruth's ideas because they seem central to understanding how Mennonite artists might make of the humility tradition both a positive incentive to produce art and a subject in itself. All too clearly, a tradition suspicious of individualism, pride, and the independence of vision that even the most community-minded artist must maintain can be a powerful suppressant of art of any kind. Ruth insists that such a tradition need not, and indeed must not, keep the artist from finding "the imaginative courage . . . to become involved in the very soul-drama of his covenant community" (70). Indeed, comparing his ideas with those of a Mennonite critic with different roots will show some striking divergences.

North American Mennonites in the Dutch-Russian stream, more urban and more prosperous than the Swiss through most of their Old World history, never emphasized the humility theme to the extent that the Swiss Americans did. One resulting literary stance is the almost exclusively aesthetic understanding of Mennonite art and literature by Canadian Mennonite critic Hildi Froese Tiessen.

Tiessen defines Mennonite artists in communitarian terms, as "individuals who were nurtured within a Mennonite community, who . . . had access to the inside of the *Gemeinschaft*" (Tiessen, "Role" 5). But she assumes that artists are lone, solitary individuals, stifled in the repressive world of the community unless they manage to re-imagine the mundane, commonplace community as art having a "newly acquired, aesthetically framed complexity" (9-10). For Tiessen it is a matter of the artist making the prosaic world interesting, not the artist responding to the community's intrinsic interest or value.

Even more explicitly than Kliewer and Sudermann, Tiessen views Mennonite history and culture as raw material for the artist to control, exploit, and transform into something worthy of "aesthetic" attention. Tiessen's list of motifs and themes in modern Mennonite literature and art includes the mythologizing of the past, the exploration of the role of language, the dynamics of cultural assimilation and passage, sexual repression, the isolation of the community, and the fall from innocence. Striking in their absence are concerns such as nonresistance, discipleship, community as nurturing rather than isolating, and of course humility. Obvious and easily manipulable cultural markers like Lowgerman and Zwiebach seem to become central, and art beckons as a means of "escaping one's fate by embracing it aesthetically" (surely a doubtful proposition) rather than a means of engaging it.

One further point of contrast between Ruth and Tiessen deserves attention. Ruth speaks quite clearly from a sense of the poverty of the Swiss-Pennsylvania literary tradition, bemoaning the lack of "full-voiced artist[s]" within that tradition and noting that "readers of Russian Mennonite background do have, in Rudy Wiebe and the earlier Warren Kliewer, literary artists who have demonstrated the capacity for depth access to their own story" (24). Ruth mentions very few other Mennonite authors, although he cites or quotes Wallace Stevens, Hawthorne, Melville, Yeats, Irving, Cooper, Austen, Scott, Tolstoy, Dickinson, James, Faulkner, and Eric Erickson.

Tiessen discusses both Wiebe and Kliewer and adds nearly a dozen other Canadian Mennonite writers and artists, with liberal mention of their prizes, public successes, and high positions in the Canadian literary establishment: "member of the executive of The League of Canadian Poets and founding president of the Manitoba Writers' Guild . . . executive director of the Saskatchewan Writers' Guild, where his annual budget of close to half a million dollars is used to encourage new and established Saskatchewan writers . . ." (6). Simply the tone of this litany of worldly accomplishment was enough to make this Swiss Mennonite boy hang my head when I first heard it, feeling a complex mix of respect, jealousy, suspicion, and other emotions I have not yet sorted out.

Someone once told me that Mennonites do not know how to take compliments; it seems clear to me that these Canadian Mennonites have learned a straightforward willingness to celebrate their own successes that still seems foreign to me, and I suspect to many American Mennonites. One of the great ironies of the humility theme is that it has itself militated against its free and confident expression, although Ruth argues that it need not, and one purpose of this chapter is to show that it has not always and should not now.

MENNONITE LITERATURE AND HUMILITY

One underlying assumption of this chapter is that no artist is truly an isolated individual. Whatever the particular relation to the community, both artists and their works are inevitably and complexly linked to their social and physical environment. Anabaptists have traditionally claimed that valid interpretation and discernment take place within the community of believers, not in isolated individuals. The modern school of thought known as "social constructionism" goes one step further, to claim that the community is the prime location of all meaning and knowledge. Kenneth Bruffee summarizes the basic theory this way:

> A social constructionist position in any discipline assumes that entities we normally call reality, knowledge, thought, facts, texts, selves and so on are constructs generated by communities of like-minded peers. Social construction understands reality, knowledge, thought, facts, texts, selves and so on as community-generated and community-maintained linguistic entities—or, more broadly speaking, symbolic entities—that define or "constitute" the communities that generate them. (Bruffee 774)

The Mennonite literature I wish to discuss, though widely various in theme, style, and stance, displays a focus on and fascination with the Mennonite community that I believe justifies my discussing it in terms that draw on social constructionist thought. In searching for traces of the humility tradition in these works, we will learn not only about them and their authors but also about the communities out of which they come.

Most Mennonite literature falls into one of the two categories suggested by Ruth: "narrow rejection" or "fascinated attraction" to the larger society, with a reciprocal acceptance or rejection of the Mennonite community (60). Large numbers of the first sort of novel exist, mainly sentimental and often aimed at a juvenile audience. Somewhat more interesting, although also tending toward the formulaic, are what I sometimes call the "kiss-it-goodbye" novels: most often these are semi-autobiographical and written by authors on their way out of the Mennonite community. Just the title of Dallas Wiebe's novel *Skyblue the Badass* (1969) suggests its orientation. Gordon Friesen's *Flamethrowers* (1936), which like Wiebe's book centers on a sensitive young Mennonite who leaves his Russian Mennonite community in Kansas, is even more hostile. As Suderman writes, Friesen's Mennonites "are stupid, sickening, repulsive, and obnoxious, living in a 'world of grotesque unreality!' They are deceitful, vicious, dull, apathetic, cruel, and greedy, and the reason, in part, is that their doctrine and disciplines make them so" (Suderman, "Mennonite Character" 126).

Curiously, it is the pride and arrogance of the leadership of these communities that drives the sensitive youths away. An even clearer example may be Ingrid Rimland's *The Wanderers,* also about the Russian Mennonites. It begins with the lines "When Johann Klassen communicated with his God, he always did so in High German . . . a mighty and impressive language that wielded power and determination and was as sharp and cutting and as upheaving as the blade of his plow which furrowed his land" (Rimland 9). Power, determination, might, cutting, upheaving: the language is meant to convey a sense of masculine force that is far from humble. The novel ends with Karin, the youngest of the main characters, preparing to leave for an uncertain destination, but one driven by her own "purposeful, intelligent ambition" and her need for a "new, fertile, bountiful life" which the Paraguayan community, with its stiff insistence on conformity, simply cannot provide (322).

The Wanderers seems to me less than great literature, but it does fix in a compelling and representative way the traditional dualism between a close, pious, but restrictive group and an individual seeking greater autonomy and freedom. From the humility perspective, the solution to such a dualism clearly does not lie in the individual abandoning the community as occurs in all these novels. Yet in each of these books the community itself is seen as guilty of a spiritual pride in its own inflexibilty and conviction of righteousness that engenders the characters' rebellion. Friesen's and Rimland's Mennonite patriarchs contain elements of caricature, certainly, but also elements of truth.

Rudy Wiebe is the best-known contemporary Mennonite novelist, and his novels *Peace Shall Destroy Many* and *The Blue Mountains of China* attempt more complex depictions of Mennonite communities in Russia and Canada. Wiebe has striven hard throughout his career to remain in the difficult position of critiquing his tradition without rejecting it, and has himself weathered much criticism for doing so. He deserves credit for having largely avoided the simplistic dualism of repressive community/creative individualist in his novels about Mennonite history and themes, and those novels reveal an increasing concern for something very like what I have been calling the humility theme.

Wiebe's first novel, *Peace Shall Destroy Many* (1962) centers on a Mennonite community in Canada during World War II and the strains that develop as their pacifism and isolationism are threatened. As in the other Russian Mennonite novels, the humility theme is only dimly present in this book, then mainly in terms of submission to the church's authority, which is patriarchal, rigid, centered in seclusion from the world and unswerving adherence to the tradition as defined by the church leadership. The main character, Thom Wiens, is torn between his pacifist tradition, his sense of guilt at letting others fight so that his people might live peacefully, and his increasing awareness of his own capacity for violence, which finally emerges when he strikes a man during the book's climactic scene. Out of all this emerges a somewhat vaguely defined determination to persist: "If in suppression and avoidance lay defeat, then victory beckoned in pushing ahead. Only a conquest by love unites the combatants. And in the heat of this battle lay God's peace" (238).

The Blue Mountains of China (1970) is an ambitious novel on the Mennonite migrations from Russia to Canada and Paraguay, epic in scope but episodic—almost fragmentary—in structure and Faulknerian in the style of its leaps across time and space. In the last chapter, "On the Way," a whole assortment of Mennonites meets on a highway where one of them, John Reimer, is walking across Canada with a cross on a "kind of walk of repentance." Some have denied their Mennonite identity altogether, some become caught up in the business world; in a scene that reads almost like a parody of the Mennonite game as it is played among Mennos meeting anywhere in the world, they discover that they are all in some way related, held together by their common heritage and the stories and blood they share.

Reimer is a prophetic figure, calling for others to "have a new attitude toward everything, toward everybody." His view of Jesus' call resonates strongly with the Mennonite vision of the "Gospel of Peace":

> you show wisdom, by trusting people;
> you handle leadership, by serving;
> you handle offenders, by forgiving;
> you handle money, by sharing;
> you handle enemies, by loving;
> and you handle violence, by suffering. (225, 227)

If Reimer is a voice of humility, suffering, and peace, however, he is a marginalized one. The urbanized professional Mennonites leave him quickly, and only the old Jakob Friesen, who lived through the revolution and has just come to Canada for the first time, walks on along the road with Reimer.

In its balance of reality and idealism *Blue Mountains of China* is perhaps Wiebe's best-rounded novel with explicitly Mennonite characters and themes. His third, *My Lovely Enemy* (1983), is certainly his most provocative.[15] The story of a lapsed Mennonite and university professor who has an affair with a graduate student, it is first of all frankly sensual, not extraordinarily explicit by the liberal secular standards of the 1980s, but not bashful either. What to me makes the book even more adventurous and intriguing is its clear attempt to discover a way of living together in community that demonstrates both Wiebe's fascination with something very close to what I have called the humility theme and his sense of its absence in his own tradition.

The book shares many themes with Wiebe's earlier work. After his adulterous affair with Gillian has begun, James Dyck muses on his lack of a firm community, even a harsh one. He realizes that no one at the university would react strongly to his becoming a Christian or to his having a mistress—a far cry from Wapiti, the village in *Peace Shall Destroy Many,* where all conduct is subject to the community's scrutiny and judgment. He can scarcely believe he is "being tempted by Christianity? In what possible way? By the image of a minister who dominated two hundred families with a formulaic simplicity of ultimate salvation, finally all groans and prayers gone into that other silence, inert and flat like sod?" (Wiebe 167)

This image of the church is typical of Wiebe's novels: it is authoritarian, repressive, simplistic, harsh, humble only in what it expects of its members. What Dyck is groping toward, though, *is* a religion, or at least a religious sense, more humble in its claims to utter truth, more open to the welter of human experience and emotion, more oriented toward a community of loving relations. "The certain temptation of Gillian drives me to the possible temptation of the personal Jesus. The temptation not of formula but of a singular certainty" (169).

My Lovely Enemy, then, goes considerably beyond the dynamic of authoritarian repression versus individualistic freedom which we saw earlier. It begins with James Dyck having rejected his tradition, but ends with him trying to re-imagine some way of living together more communitarian than his present life but less repressive than his remembered past.

As the novel continues and the strain on Dyck's relationships intensifies, the form becomes less and less realistic. Jesus makes several nocturnal visits to discuss the nature of love with Dyck, and there is a long scene in a coal mine/restaurant which culminates in Dyck, his wife Liv, Gillian and her husband Harold having a long discussion on a "beach" lined with snow. Their conversation is intellectual, paradoxical, exhilarating, too rich to do full justice to here. The main thrust of it and of the rest of the novel, however, is toward unity and acceptance, away from the negative emotions of ownership and jealousy even within those areas where we typically hold them to be valid and inevitable. "Nobody ever owns anything," says Gillian, insisting that their story is not about jealousy, but about love. "Love is trust beyond all possibilities," Liv adds; the women here are remarkable for their refusal to react in the ways we might expect, and they keep pulling James into revelations he does not anticipate. The section ends with a lyrical celebration of this sort of unconditional love:

Was it possible for them all to endure this and live; all of them knowing the unimaginable for which they had all always longed? To love totally, without debauchery. Nothing heals like it, as the man said. . . . they dreamt they were free at last from the necessity of both want and freedom and were only good, and found themselves unimaginably happy in that; at last. (229, 235)

A subplot of the novel concerns Dyck's mother, who represents the heritage he has tried to abandon. Near the end of the novel she dies, and the book's final scene, which takes place at her funeral, also shifts suddenly from realism into fantasy. Dyck goes down into the grave as the coffin is about to be covered, opens it, and his mother opens her eyes and smiles: "'Well, that is nice,' she said, and sat up. 'Is this bottom half fastened down?'" (253, 257)

Dyck, his mother, and Liv and Gillian and the mortician go out into a wheatfield with a cluster of the grandchildren. They meet a farmer who gives them the remains of his lunch, and sit together to eat potato salad and drink ice tea from the "seemingly bottomless thermos," sharing the cup and the fork. They talk, again groping toward a vision of unity beyond social divisions and dualisms. James Dyck sits there surrounded by the women he loves, his wife and mistress and mother and daughter and sister, and when they finish eating his mother asks him if he has something to say. The introduction to "what he has to say" closes the novel:

For a moment he could not quite gather what he wanted to say. . . . My soul waits in silence. To teach stones to speak. Be still and know. . . . And he heard a corner of that silence that was before the world began, called out by the living voice of his mother and he was empty of all his ravaging words, his pre-inspired words were quite gone, he wanted to listen his loved ones into life, now, even the ones who were no longer there. . . . he prayed to see them all at once and know them all, not distinct and separate, even himself, but all one. For he understood they all together had to speak or he could never say what was ready to be if only it would be spoken. So he opened his mouth to make that. And much more. (261-2)

There is a great deal of humility language here: listening his loved ones into life, losing his old, ravaging, pre-inspired words, losing his individualistic arrogance to "say them all together." Yet this is certainly not the traditional Swiss Mennonite view of humility. Wiebe is too broadly educated, too versed in Indian lore and literature and linguistics and history and philosophy, to forget the wisdom he has found in those realms. And in one sense, as Suderman notes, it is arrogant to assume that Mennonites, or Christians, have a corner on truth, and important to "listen humbly" to what contemporary writers and other traditions have to say about the world and ourselves ("Religious Values" 23). What James Dyck seems to learn in this novel, more than anything else, is to listen to others, especially to women, to resist his professorial urge to be constantly telling others and to let others tell him.

Yet however appealing this vision is, it clearly and perhaps deliberately leaves many questions unresolved. Looked at more skeptically, beneath its spectacular technique and insistently visible learning it seems a rather elemental, even childish wish-fulfillment fantasy. Dyck ends with everybody ready to listen to him, with his wife, mother, mistress, and daughter all gathered round him and reconciled to each other. By finding this new and humble stance, he is somehow granted everything he wants, all at once, while giving up only a few outdated attitudes.

The magic realism and fantasy elements allow Wiebe to present all this with a certain diffidence; he can expect of us the suspension of disbelief and leave us there in the wheatfields with the potato salad, while the wife and the mistress exchange great-hearted aphorisms and the mother raised from the dead seems ready for another twenty years. He can evade dealing with the more usual sorts of outcomes, the pain and bitterness and jealousy he wants to dismiss as remnants of an outmoded religious repression.

It is surely true, as Catherine Hunter has suggested, that this novel is an "exploration of the possibilities of love," and of the mysteries of "the infinite passion that cannot be understood or expressed on a literal level" (Hunter 50). I admire not only Wiebe's artistry but his courage in shaping such a strange and beautiful vision of a group of people discovering that they can love each other more completely than most of us would believe possible. Yet I find myself yearning for a return from the vision, the way Frost's birch-swinger must return to the earth, to touch the ground again, to discover what the vision means for life in this world.

A novel still closer to the humility tradition both in style and theme is Armin Wiebe's *The Salvation of Yasch Siemens*. Written in a hilarious mixture of Low German and English, it is the episodic narrative of a Manitoba Mennonite farm boy as he searches for love and happiness and somehow becomes romantically involved with the plump Oata Needarp. Yasch finds his life seeming to be one lesson in humility after another. Circumstances push him into working for Oata and her father, and, after her father dies, into becoming engaged to her. During harvest she does the threshing and goes to town for parts, leaving him to do the dishes. Even his mother contributes to teaching Yasch humility:

> I am really bedutzed now. My own Muttachi telling me that she won't make me something to eat and that she won't come to help me and Oata. It sounds like it's maybe the second coming or something. Maybe I should go to Preacher Janzen's place and tell him that it must be the end of the world. But my stomach is hanging crooked and it's growling and I know I have to go back to Oata's if I am not going to die from hunger. (155)

Yasch's "salvation" comes not through the Brunk Tent Crusade, which comes through when he is young but which he remembers his father saving him from. It comes not through being pious or demonstrative; after a memorable testimony, the rest are content that he goes to church as a "good place to rest after a week's hard work." It comes from his accepting his lot, farming conservatively but well, raising children with Oata, who slowly gets thinner while his friends' thin wives are getting fatter. "I guess you could say that I am one of the still ones in the land," Yasch says; the final anecdote has him almost buying a television dish:

> But then I thought that if I brought [it] home . . . they wouldn't be satisfied with that 11-inch black and white no more and be after me to buy color, and that's just too much. In these troubled times you have to watch out. (167-68, 176)

This novel is true to the genre of comedy in its ending with successful marriage and the integration of its characters into an ongoing society. The terms of that integration for Yasch show that something like the humility tradition does exist among Canadian Mennonites. The rousing success of the novel as sheer entertainment, which I have barely hinted at here, also suggests that more writers might work the vein of Mennonite comedy.

Yet Yasch's humble version of salvation is clearly drawn as a minority position in this novel, one that comes to him despite his community rather than because of it. His neighbors *are* buying satellite dishes, fancy pickups, automatic barn cleaners, and the rest, some of them going broke in the process. Their wives *are* getting fat. Yasch learns to accept living more with less not because that stance toward life is his tradition but because his particular situation and experience teach him lessons most of his peers seem uninterested in learning.

A Mennonite novel which draws still more explicitly on the humility tradition is Sara Stambaugh's *I Hear the Reaper's Song*. Born in Lancaster County, Pennsylvania, Stambaugh tells the story of her great-aunt Barbara Hershey's death in a buggy-train accident in 1895 through the voice of her grandfather, Silas Hershey. Occuring amid the Quickening, the accident served as a focal point for the growing controversy in the church over revivalism, mission outreach, and progressivism; ministers used the incident in revival messages, suggesting that the two who died might not have been saved and pressuring young people toward immediate conversions. In Stambaugh's fictionalized version, men like Bishop Eby

> said it was a terrible thing to think that any one of us could be cut off and be changed any minute from joy and beauty to something less than clay that people turned their faces from. . . . we should all pray that God wouldn't cut us off before we were ready, just as we should pray for Him to show mercy to Barbie. (Stambaugh 149)

In her afterword, Stambaugh writes that her interest in the story was partly to "give a voice" to the Lancaster County conservatives, to "articulate the opposition to the revival which existed in the county at the end of the last century" (220). Silas Hershey's brother Hen makes an outspoken critique of the progressives' use of the accident:

> "It's hard to believe my own sister would go along with those revivalists," Hen said, and he spit out "revivalists" like it was a swear word. "They're like a bunch of vultures flocking in to feed off the dead, taking advantage of Barbie and Enos being killed and using them to work up every featherbrained girl in the county." (182-83)

In this novel the progressives end up looking a little like stereotypical modern fundamentalists: they are arrogant, opportunistic, and manipulative, preying on the shock of the accident to force impressionable young people into premature, emotional decisions and, Silas Hershey suspects, scaring as many people out of the church as they bring in.

The theology of this novel is not very complex or nuanced, as the conservatives are not very educated. Yet their perspective is appealing, at least to farm-born, university-trained intellectuals like me who are also suspicious of *Gottseligkeit* (piety) and revivalism. In this novel the conservatives, the humble ones, are also those who can tolerate sowing of wild oats, the ones who are willing to wait for their children to come to the fellowship through a mature decision rather than through fear and emotional coercion. That willingness is risky, of course; some do not join at all, some feel the need for more emotional heat and find it elsewhere. That humble stance can yield stagnation and decline. But in its willingness to trust and its refusal of emotional coercion it has a modesty and a peaceable equanimity that I think we lose at considerable peril.

John Ruth may be right that no Mennonite writer has yet fully dealt with the humility tradition both as a heritage and as a worldview full of contemporary relevance, although *The Salvation of Yasch Siemens* and *I Hear the Reaper's Song* are worthy beginnings. The most sustained, subtle, and successful exploration of the stance of humility that I know, however, comes from a writer who is closely related to the Mennonites. William Stafford was born in Hutchinson, Kansas, in 1914. He did CO service in Brethren camps during World War II and wrote a memoir entitled *Down in My Heart* about those experiences. Stafford is best known, however, as a poet and a teacher, and in both vocations has worked persistently from a stance of humility. (Chapter four will look more closely at his pacifism and poetics.)

In a recent essay Stafford says "Imposing my will on language—or on a student, or on the citizens of a country—was not my style. I wanted to disappear as teacher, as writer, as citizen—be 'the quiet of the land,' as we used to designate ourselves in CO camps" (Stafford, *You Must* 21). In an essay on writing poetry he speaks explicitly of humility:

> In its essence, poetry, like other sustained human endeavors, is done best in a condition of humility and welcoming of what comes. The exploration of what the materials of life can yield to us, and the discovery of what is implicit in human experience, will work best for one who is turned outward, with trust, with courage, and with a ready yielding to what time brings into view. This practice can be the opposite of egotistical. (70)

Stafford consistently emphasizes that writing is an *outward* search, into the riches of the language and the "materials of life." In a poem called "Vocation" he writes that "Your job is to find what the world is trying to be" (Stafford, *Stories* 107). In "Parentage" he speaks wryly and, I suspect, with tongue partly in cheek, of his prototypical, almost fanatical humility:

> I want to be as afraid as the teeth are big,
> I want to be as dumb as the wise are wrong:
> I'd just as soon be pushed by events to where I belong.
> (*Stories* 67)

Stafford also suggests the final point I want to make here, which is that humility is more than an optional way of looking at things, perhaps intriguing or useful but only one of the smorgasbord of philosophies, worldviews, religions, self-help programs, and cults our society bombards us with. Stafford writes "I have found it natural to assume that no human being can perceive well enough or reason surely enough to grasp things as they are. We are ultimately so limited as to make any vaunting irrelevant, foolish, misguided. Limited as we are, humility befits us" (Stafford, "Personal letter").

The vision of humility, Stafford suggests, is valuable because it is ontologically accurate, or, to speak more humbly, because it is true. I think that some North Americans are beginning to see the need to rediscover a vision which is a great deal like the one our ancestors had. At an early Mennonite Experience in America conference,[16] Joyce Clemmer Munro quoted from the last chapter of *Habits of the Heart*, where Robert Bellah and his fellow scholars speak as though unwittingly repeating the words of John M. Brenneman for a new situation:

> Above all, we will need to remember our poverty. We have been called a people of plenty . . . yet the truth of our condition is our poverty. We are finally defenseless on this earth. . . . It would be well for us to rejoin the human race, to accept our essential poverty as a gift, and to share our material wealth with those in need. (qtd. in Munro 11-12)

If Bellah et al. speak for poverty, defenselessness, and responsibility to our neighbors as social and political realities, the social constructionists suggest that the interdependence and mutuality essential to the humility tradition are ontological realities as well. I quoted Kenneth Bruffee earlier on the social constructionist claim that everything we call "reality" is a product of community dialogue and discourse. This view suggests a way of avoiding many of the traumas and difficulties that our habitual dualistic thinking (inner and outer, spirit and flesh, subjective and objective) has created. If we assume that "the matrix of thought is not the individual self but some community of knowledgeable peers and the vernacular language of that community," if we accept that "knowledge and the authority of knowledge [are] community-generated, community-maintaining social artifacts" (Bruffee 777), many things change.

The most fascinating aspect of this way of thinking is its affirmation from a secular, scholarly, philosophical framework of something very much like the Anabaptist worldview, not as a deliberately chosen or rejected alternative but as the way the world works whether we like it or not. It offers an implicit critique of the novels that pose the repressive community against the individual's need to be "free": as long as those are the horns of the dilemma, frustration and loss are inevitable. And, even more significantly, it suggests that humility, defined as a stance toward the world that recognizes our interwoven responsibilities and needs for each other, our limits and poverty and defenselessness, is far more than an obsolete notion of a few fanatics. It is responsible, healthy, sustaining, fertile, and worth all the distribution we can manage.

Near the end of his little pamphlet, John M. Brenneman wrote "Now, dear readers, having seen the great difference between the proud and the humble, what will we do?" (40). That, of course, is always the question. Taking action that is based in humility rather than pride, creating art that engages our tradition without either sentimentalizing or caricaturing it, will never be easy. We remain fallible and prideful beings, whose worst failings are probably the ones we do not even recognize. "Right has a long and intricate name," Stafford has written (*Stories* 78), and perhaps the most dangerous error of all is that of presuming we can say that name easily or quickly. I think Mennonite literature (or what, in the terms of this book, I would prefer to call Mennonite writing) has begun to unfold for us some of the syllables, words and phrases that make up our rich and equivocal tradition of humility, and to imagine the directions that tradition may be guiding us. And I would humbly suggest that humility, as a literary and existential and prophetic stance, belongs as an integral part of our art and our scholarship and our living together.[17]

CHAPTER THREE

VOICE AND HISTORY
IN PATRICK FRIESEN

In the last chapter I surveyed authors who, whatever their quibbles, are more or less willing to claim a religious identity, although not all of them would be equally at ease with the language of humility that I employed there. In Patrick Friesen, however, we encounter something different. Of all the contributions to the 1988 anthology *Why I Am a Mennonite*, Friesen's is perhaps the most ambivalent. He suggests that whatever Mennonite identity he has is largely due to happenstance (his piece is titled "I Could Have Been Born in Spain") and describes his feelings toward his tradition as a mixture of shame, pride, and confusion: "Religiously I'm not Mennonite. In other important ways I am. Some days I feel Mennonite, other days not. It doesn't really matter" (Loewen 105).

These mixed feelings are apparent throughout Friesen's poems as well. Despite the final sentence above, his work shows that being and feeling Mennonite or not-Mennonite, whatever those terms mean, does matter a great deal to Friesen, and that a struggle to define that tradition and himself in relation to it runs through his work. I want to explore that struggle in two of his books, examining some of the formal strategies Friesen has adapted and the stances he adopts toward material that clearly has tremendous emotional force for him. In the long narrative poem *The Shunning*, journal entries, dramatic monologues, and narrative in which the presence and personality of the narrator are deeply concealed take us into a Mennonite family whose relations to the church community are deeply troubled. In the more recent and personal volume, *Flicker and Hawk,* the central strategy is the use of an extravagant, many-faceted lyric voice through which the poet, his life and his tradition can be explored, deconstructed and reconstructed.

The Shunning traces the lives of the brothers Peter and Johann Neufeld and their families. Peter is a dreamer, a thinker, a kind of proto-poet who even as a child is given to extravagant description: He tells his brother that swallow's nests are "purses holding golden coins/ to pay the hawk as rent" (19). Shunned for daring to speak his unorthodox thoughts about the incongruity of hell and a loving God, Peter suffers vividly through his isolation. We occasionally hear his voice and thoughts but more often see him through others, including the midwife who helps at his birth, the doctor who fills out the papers after his suicide, and especially his wife Helena. She loves him but seems unable to follow his theological torments, and unhappily obeys the church leaders' demand that she shun Peter also. The elders, who periodically invite him back into the fellowship if he will only recant, seem more interested in asserting their authority than in understanding his feelings or helping him grapple with them; they want surrender, for him to "cry uncle" as the epigraph puts it.

Finally Peter kills himself with his .22 rifle. In the aftermath the local doctor puzzles over the case for a moment and then forgets about it; Peter's brother Johann remembers their being boys together, and Peter "thinking you could bring night" by shooting out the sun. The section ends with a mourner, apparently Helena, standing at Peter's grave and lamenting "Peter/ who wanted so much what wasn't/ if love could clothe his bones in flesh" (52).

Peter's short, traumatic life is counterpointed by Johann' longer, less dramatic one. The epigraphs to each section are revealing; Peter's is "some praise God/ some cry uncle," a dualism of unreflective praise or unwilling submission that seems to leave him no way out. Johann' suggests a more equable, even idyllic, life: "For thou shalt be in league with the stones of the field: and the beasts of the field shall be at peace with thee." And indeed Johann lives without Peter's theological agonizing, even through the death of his first wife Caroline and the burning of his house. Both his mourning her death and his celebration of their love are cast in sharply physical terms; he suffers, but his personal losses do not lead him to Peter's intellectual speculation or rebellion:

snow fluttering against glass
and I'm wondering how hard the earth
shovels flashing at noon iron strike iron
how they lowered her then
snow and dead leaves wheeling across her casket
I lie facedown on her side of the bed
the warmth the musk of her
this I cannot bear. (63)

Johann is much closer to a stereotypical Mennonite farmer in some ways: He is hardworking, loving, practical, more or less content to live within limited horizons. As "time happens" to him, however, we see that his relations to the church are distant, even suspicious. He finds himself singing "Amazing Grace" in the spring after Caroline's death, but when later asked about Mennonites, his response is mixed. He describes his daughter who is "always doing what she thought was best for others" but also his son who is a shiftless farmer as well as "sharp" businessmen who "pay their workers dirt. Who live in their big houses and say God has blessed them" (87). He says that for him Menno Simons is just like J. J. Fast, the blacksmith who wanted above all

that no one put himself above the church. And you never saw someone who could hide better. Behind the preacher. Behind the Bible. Behind God. Yes if you know that man you knew something about Mennonites. Not everything mind you. (90)

No doubt driven by lingering resentment about Peter's fate, Johann does share with Peter this view of church leaders past and present as primarily concerned with preserving their own authority. Although his response is withdrawal rather than open rebellion, certainly Johann has no more sense than Peter of the church as an egalitarian community of worship, a "priesthood of all believers." When he is taken away to a nursing home, old and soon to die, his religion is listed in the medical record as "Protestant," with "Mennonite" crossed out. The book ends with brief lyrics remembering Peter and Johann; the speaker is not clearly identified, but speaks of "the flames [Johann] endured the iron in him" (97):

johann remembered his brother
who tore the curtain and went blind
who taught johann fear and not fear

that the child dies no matter what
and a man carries his funeral with him
you never know how many people you bury with a man
nor how many are born again
come said johann let's go back to the house
ruth bakes bread today
it's good when it's still warm and the butter melts
listen he whispered
that rasping sound that's a yellowhead
see it over there near the creek
and I saw
a blackbird with a sun for its head. (98)

Johann's willingness to settle for simple pleasures, for fresh bread and butter, is clearly posed against Peter's "tearing the curtain" and being destroyed for it. The book ends with a last little twist, however: the hymn line "*O dass ich tausend Zungen hätte*" (Oh, for a thousand tongues to sing), which suggests an exaltation, a willingness to praise, that is somewhat difficult to identify with either of the main characters or to find a base for in the rest of the book. Neither of the options the brothers' stories offer seems especially attractive. It seems one must either be destroyed for daring to think independently, for refusing to cry uncle—or must settle like Johann for a life of stoic endurance and simple pleasures until time happens.

Perhaps that last line is better read as the voice of the narrator, as a lament for the inadequacy of his "tongue" to do justice to these characters and their stories. Still, in the hymn the yearning for voice is to sing of God, not of men. The initial epigraph, "some praise God/ some cry uncle" suggests that praising God is on Friesen's mind, at least as a possibility, but in *The Shunning* such praise tends to be muted and muffled, expressed largely through natural images with a whiff of the miraculous, such as "a blackbird with a sun for its head."

In chapter two I analyzed the dualism in Mennonite literature between authoritarian community and rebellious individualism and argued that this dualism is especially strong among Canadian Mennonite writing, for a variety of historical reasons. I also suggested, following John Ruth, that for Mennonites the third option should be the aspiration to a redemptive, nurturing, supportive community. Ruth asks how often we have seen

an aesthetically serious representation of our ethos in its classic issues—obedience, simplicity, humility, defenselessness, the questioning of progress, the maintenance of identity? How often have
these ideas received aesthetic representation from a full-voiced
artist, that did not veer into sentimental advocacy or irritable expose? (*Mennonite Identity*, 23)

Certainly no one can accuse Friesen of lacking aesthetic seriousness,
nor of engaging in "sentimental advocacy or irritable expose." It does
seem the case, however, that *The Shunning* finds precious little to celebrate in what Ruth lists as the classic Mennonite issues; in this society
they are either absent or hardened into their destructive extremes. Even
Johann' simplicity is presented as a personal virtue, one unconnected
with any explicitly Mennonite ethic or theology. Finally, I think that in
social terms we must read *The Shunning* as a lament for a would-be community that proves unable to keep and to nurture not only its most independent and inquiring children but its moderates as well.

Flicker and Hawk is quite a different work, lyric and reflective, a unified collection of poems rather than a single narrative. The book does
show a kind of narrative movement, however, beginning with memories
of a Mennonite childhood, following its poet-protagonist into adulthood, tracing a continuing struggle with religious questions and values.
The dominant note is one of uneasy maturation and return to origins,
including even an equivocal and unconventional sort of worship.

The first section, "water burial," is set in a community closer to us in
time but much like that of *The Shunning* in its closed, restrictive nature.
"sunday afternoon" describes the fathers in town asleep, dreaming "of
old days and death," mother reading "a book a true book of someone
else's life," and the speaker as one of the youths driving around, "wondering how to get out of town": "in nightmares angry lords walked
through my room/ it took my breath away how ferocious love could be/
sometimes jesus hung on the wall or was it the shadow of an elm?" (3).
The poem ends almost desperately, with the claim "I got out I'm getting
out I'm getting out," immediately countered by the realization that
"what I left there the child" is still "waiting for the next time and another
town."

The driving force of this part of the book is memory, with numerous relatives and townspeople and events remembered, for the most part
affectionately though equivocally. Some of the poems are in various al-

ternate points of view, but near the end of the section the voice and style
typical of the rest of the book become dominant. "water burial" gives us
that abrupt, insistently interior first-person voice; it seems to come directly from the poet, and constantly swings between concrete observation and metaphysical meditation, continually refining and correcting
itself:

> whether it's a july afternoon
> and you're swimming off patricia beach
> knowing this is the inheritance you were born to
> or you're listening to the blue ridge rangers
> singing you toward the home you imagine
> or you're stealing an afternoon from necessity
> you are on your way to salvation
> if not already there
> on the other hand
> how easily the body drifts away sometimes
> dreams or disease mishap or sloth (23)

The poet remembers sitting naked in water, "thinking as usual of
words to bring this surrender ashore," until nothing is left, "until all the
voices I'd been/slipped through the sky's blue hole in my head/ and there
was no saving me" (23).

This loss or abandonment of the body, of voice, of identity, is a typical stage on a spiritual journey; here, especially in the implied contrast
of "water burial" with water baptism, it suggests a failed or incomplete
conversion, one that ends not with the establishment of firm identity in
a tradition but in existence without identity. That sense of being somehow absent from one's self continues in part two, "nothing in the mirror," as the title itself suggests. This section is a long poem in fourteen
parts, an elliptical narrative of a search for love and relationship in which
the pursuit of an elusive woman takes on archetypal proportions. The
woman is mother, lover, fortune-teller, whore, wife, and the feminine
part of the speaker, the part he glimpses occasionally in the mirror. In its
oblique presentation, dreamlike juxtapositions, and indeterminacy
"nothing in the mirror" is determinedly contemporary, although its
conclusion celebrates a memory of togetherness:

> I am remembering
> how the blouse slipped

> from her shoulders
> there is no other comfort
> a dream of winter in her eyes
> she puts her finger to my lips
> a top hat at her feet (41)

If there are hints here of continental films, with their moody fatalism and silent, doomed lovers, there is also a curious hint of Matthew Arnold's "Dover Beach" in the key line "there is no other comfort": The idea that comfort, love, and assurance are to be found in the context of sexual love runs throughout *Flicker and Hawk*. Friesen comes close in some poems to Arnold's sense that the world is merely a darkling plain where ignorant armies clash by night, that the "Sea of Faith" has ebbed for good, and that only love offers shelter. Yet if Friesen sometimes appears to pose sexual love as an end in itself, he also sometimes treats it as a means of passage to transcendent love. At any rate, this poem begins the book's turn from a past that has proven inadequate, at least in personal terms, to a search for a present sense of relation in which lover and God are repeatedly connected and sometimes merged almost beyond distinction.

The initial poem of part three, "black river," returns to images of rivers and women, and thematically also returns to the concerns of "water burial," though it takes us one step (or stroke) further:

> I'm dreaming a dream of the black river where I can't swim I'm
> dreaming my last breath I'm dreaming how things are almost
> over I'm dreaming a possible swimmer with powerful arms to
> hold me
> the river is cruel and cold I would drown for warmth
> my legs dangle beneath me in the water my hands perform circles
> my lips are open for a kiss who will kiss them?

This dream-state appearance of a "possible swimmer" reminds me of the protagonist of Rudy Wiebe's *My Lovely Enemy*, who also encounters a "possible Jesus" in a dream-vision (169). That vision is crucial to both books; here the speaker begins to imagine the possibility of something like hope, something like salvation, although hardly conventional in its appearance or its source:

> my love take me away all the way to where my lies are true
> take me beneath your umbrella of water that will be good

enough
for me to stand in the rain dreaming the dreams of the dead
and living dogs barking in backyards remembering the love
and terror that brought me here
my beauty lay me down and take me all the way I'm dreaming
the dream of my death or someone is it doesn't feel like me
anymore
he's gasping the river is in his ears he's banging at the window
he wants to break into the swimmer's dream he wants another
another (45)

Love and death and rebirth: Do we find them within or outside?
How do we imagine and experience God? How approach truth through
the "lies" that all our language must be, in its puny and inadequate efforts to do justice to experience and emotions too powerful to be more
than hinted at? The rest of *Flicker and Hawk* is less an "answer" to these
perennial questions than a depiction of one man's ongoing contention
with them. There is no meek retreat to orthodoxy here. Friesen is not
about to return to the idea that "a true book about someone else's life"
can contain the wild, essential paradoxes of experience, and so rather
than avoiding or concealing his interior confusions and contradictions,
Friesen makes them his main subject matter. Gradually, though, the
poems move toward a willingness to declare a sort of allegiance:

give me ropes and water I will place them in my shrine
I will learn the love that tears me open
give me celestial burial my body spread-eagled and dispersed
throughout the world
I will be your fool in the talons of an iron bird I will be free in the
horrible sky (47)

At this point a key shift of imagery takes place: from now on air,
flight and birds replace water and swimming as the dominant motifs.
The title poem celebrates a strong but not simple love that endures
through all anger and division:

lord this love is strong even when it's on the edge when we find
others to make us whole we're not everything to each other
we're everything else and that's the juice you can't get every day. . . .
we have learned the odds and embrace them
we come together fire and water flicker and hawk this is what
we know of love (49)

"What we know of love," then, is that it is complementarity rather than identity, embracing rather than merger. It calls for acceptance of the other as a whole being, an acceptance Friesen is not sure he can expect from the lord:

> I'm asking can you take me straight on? I'm a lion some days a
> rabbit I'm not anyone else. . . .
> I want to be everyone
> I am with you
> when I'm lewd or unruly can you laugh? when I'm tender what
> then? (53)

In the last poem of *Flicker and Hawk*, Friesen writes "I hold no hope beyond our embrace in the doorway" (70). "one time around" is perhaps the most energetic, certainly the most affirmative, poem in the book: "hey ma it's not the end times I've got hot feet and next to nothing to say." It seems appropriate and satisfying to end with this sort of unreflective revelry, breaking free from thought and speech after so many words, so much struggle. Having spent my own time in such struggles, and been nowhere near this successful at getting them into poems, I am enormously grateful for the vitality and accuracy of lines like "my devotion to the lord is imperfect there's some fight left in me I may be hooked I am not landed. . . . I want to redeem love before it does me in" (67). I know the feel of that hook in the mouth, and having read the poem I know also that I am not alone in that feeling.

The voice of this book makes me feel that it is absolutely uncensored, that no emotion or experience is being held back, and more than many books of poems this one inspires trust, leaves me believing that the experience it recounts is entirely authentic. We might call these poems "confessional" for their psychological concentration and complexity, but for all their ambivalence they are finally much less agonized and neurotic than the work of poets like Robert Lowell and John Berryman. In fact, the breathless quality created by the lack of punctuation, the tendencies toward a generic, archetypal vocabulary and a sense of baffled worship, also remind me of the work of W. S. Merwin, who has never been called a confessional poet. Here is part of Merwin's "For the Anniversary of My Death":

> Then I will no longer
> Find myself in life as in a strange garment

Surprised at the earth
And the love of one woman
And the shamelessness of men
As today writing after three days of rain
Hearing the wren sing and the Falling cease
And bowing not knowing to what (133)

Friesen's work is much thicker with the things of day-to-day modern life than Merwin's: place names, typewriters, postcards. Yet thinking
of the two poets together has helped me see that Friesen's work is not
quite as inclusive as I first thought. What is hard to find in *Flicker and
Hawk* is a sense of the public world, of the environmental and political
realms that are central to poems of Merwin's such as "The Last One" and
"Caesar." Friesen's lyric poems, at least those in this book, oscillate between the home and the infinite, between the private self and the nuclear family and God, without much attention to the world between.
"I'm here where I live and wrestle where I'm father for my children and
everything I can be for love," "private ceremonies" concludes, and I find
these lines compelling and beautiful on several levels. Yet some faint un-
reconstructed puritanical Sixties-style social consciousness part of me
hears a resonance, probably unintentional but still uncomfortable, between "everything I can be for love" and the "be all that you can be" re-
cruiting slogan of the most expensive and powerful organization in
recorded history for threatening and killing people at short, medium, or
long range.

I am a Yankee of course, and somewhat more compelled than my
Canadian friends to recognize the dark side of my government, which
provides me with personal freedom, interstate highways, a flag to worship, and the opportunity to contribute to the construction of weapons
of unparalleled destructive vigor. I treasure the craft and feeling of Pat
Friesen's poems greatly, and know that I have little right to expect anything more, or anything different, from them. And yet that little voice
will be heard.

What kept me always at least tenuously connected to the Mennonite church, what drew me back almost despite myself, was the sense
that the church I grew up in was at least mainly on the right side of the
social questions of our time. Having given up its German long ago and
lost its ethnic foods to middle-American fried chicken and apple pie, my
home church's identity was fixed for me by subtler markers. The middle-

aged men told stories of their times as COs in CPS during World War II in lieu of military service, letting me know in the late sixties that my resistance to war was part of a long and honorable tradition. The Sunday school teachers told stories from the *Martyr's Mirror* and wanted to know if we were ready to die for our faith. (I did not know then, and I do not now.) The women stopped wearing coverings when I was in grade school, and in high school we were allowed to go to the rather sedate dances at homecoming and prom. But the idea that we were different from those around us in some mysterious but fundamental way, that more was expected of us, that we should expect to find ourselves taking a stand for peace and faith sooner or later, somehow made its way to the center of my being. No matter how corrupt and compromised the church seemed to me at times, how hidebound some of its theology or how rigid some of its spokesmen, how slowly and painfully the hymns were sung, I never really doubted that something there deserved my respect and allegiance.

I read both *The Shunning* and *Flicker and Hawk* several times before I realized that what for me is most distinctly Mennonite, the notes of peace, service, and community I heard struck over and over through my childhood and college years, are almost entirely absent from both of them. Peace and service have meaning for Friesen in terms of family and of God, perhaps, but he rarely if ever connects them to his town or county or country; there is unstinted loyalty to family, more equivocal loyalty to God, but very little sense of membership in an intermediate community that is either in concord with or in resistance to the larger society. I do not know how to make judgments about such matters without hopelessly confusing people and poems, so I will not try; I only offer this as what I have seen, and a few thoughts more.

I began with the statement that being Mennonite, or not Mennonite, mattered. I am still not sure what "being Mennonite" means, or that what it means for me and for Patrick Friesen overlap very much. I am tempted to think, as I told a friend during my first year in graduate school, that it has to do merely with believing that there is a true nature of the universe and that our task is to try to glimpse it, that the struggle to recognize and worship what is truly worthy of our devotion distinguishes us from the secularized masses. That is surely no more than partly true; Mennonites have no corner on spiritual earnestness. Beyond that? Certainly the differences of experience, language, and outlook even among North American Mennonite writers indicate some of the multiplicity that by now makes talk of a single Anabaptist vision seem more and more a wistful illusion.

I am sure we can still talk to each other; I have faith we can listen to and learn from each other. There may be better fates, but there surely are worse ones. The deeper we plumb the past, I think, the less hopeless the present looks. With all our compromises and adjustments, our complaints and accusations and rationalizations, we at least are carrying on the discussion. If we want guarantees we can always go to Sears for snow tires. Otherwise, we had just as well figure on this world remaining as Pat Friesen shows it: puzzling, often painful, sometimes tragic and occasionally joyful.

Beyond that, I do not know. We all could have been born in Spain, or Ethiopia, or Flanagan, Illinois, but we were not: we grew where we were planted, and became what we are out of that particular soil. We share a heritage that fits and does not fit us, a rich and terrifying mystery that we will never plumb once and for all. Our tradition is not everything, but it is the ground of our lives, no matter how unequal we are to it or how like the blind men describing the elephant we sound in our trying to name it.

This is not meant as complaint. I am grateful just now for being shook out of my own tendency to weary, predictable, apocalyptic moping. Hey, Ma, it's not the end times. I've got hot feet, and no more to say.

CHAPTER FOUR

ALMOST ONE OF THE BOYS: MARGINALITY, COMMUNITY AND NONVIOLENCE IN WILLIAM STAFFORD

Continually the forces of war incited frustrations and enmities that led easily to personal rebellion; but for us a personal rebellion against other human beings became a capitulation to the forces we held to be at the root of war. We perceived this hazard poignantly, because to avoid participation in the large violence of our immediate society—and thus to stay true to a larger society—we found it necessary to act in such a way as to arouse the antagonism of our neighbors.—William Stafford, *Down in My Heart (8-9)*

But the trees not carved and walls undefaced
mean "Not even Kilroy was here,"
and millions of us haven't killed anyone,
or a bear, or even an hour. We haven't
presumed. And—who knows?—maybe we're saved.
—William Stafford, *An Oregon Message (45)*

The century just concluded was a great one for violence, war, and other assorted disasters. It was also, and not coincidentally, one in which peacemaking became more than a fringe occupation. As our means of mass destruction multiply, so the need to avoid using them escalates.

Einstein's remark that nuclear weapons have changed everything except our way of thinking has the force of truism, but in important senses it is not true: our ways of thinking *have* changed, and continue to change. The question now is whether they will change quickly enough, and meaningfully enough, to avert the many potential disasters which confront us.

The long career of William Stafford takes on particular significance against this backdrop. From his early *Down in My Heart*, a memoir of his experience as a conscientious objector in World War II newly reissued by Bench Press, to his recent collection of poems *An Oregon Message*, Stafford's commitment to nonviolence has undergirded all his work. Yet Stafford's work is important not for any doctrinaire anti-war rhetoric, although that can be found in places, but for its exploration of how a stance of consistent nonviolence develops and is repeatedly tested through contact with individual and social forces. Exploring these two books in particular reveals that his particular brand of nonviolence is based in his sense of membership in a marginalized but supportive alternative community, and that for Stafford the real test of nonviolence lies in establishing positive and peaceable relations with the larger world even at the expense of an abstract purity of principles.

His education slowed by the Depression, Stafford was in his middle twenties but still a student at the University of Kansas when World War II reached the United States. As he tells it, "within two weeks, carrying a copy of *The Journal of John Woolman* given me by my landlady, I was on my way to a camp for conscientious objectors in Arkansas" (*You Must* 11). Somewhat older than the average draftee, he was in his early thirties by the time Brethren Press published *Down in My Heart* in 1947. Although it served as his master's thesis at the University of Kansas, and is written in a laconic, impressionistic prose rather than the poetry for which he became better known, the book is considerably more than apprentice work. Unlike many first works, it is not an introspective *Bildungsroman*; the narrative includes lightly fictionalized versions of Stafford's own encounters, but the narrator serves mainly as observer, only occasionally as participant. The narrative more often focuses on group experience and its significance than on merely personal feelings, and the overall design is to present, as the introduction says, "a series of incidents, purposely planned to give the texture of *our* lives" (*DIMH* 10, emphasis added).

Stafford depicts a group whose principles are constantly challenged on very human, immediate levels. Having declared themselves conscientiously opposed to fighting in a popular war, they must face the antagonism of neighbors and superiors, working with them while defusing the threat of personal hostilities that would be "a capitulation to the forces we held to be at the root of war" (*DIMH* 9). Their stratagems vary:

> "When the mob comes," George would say, "I think we should try surprising them with a friendly reaction—take coffee and cookies out and meet them."
>
> "As for me," Larry would say, "I'll take a stout piece of stove wood, and stand behind the door, and deal out many a lumpy head—that's what they'd need."
>
> "Well, I don't know about you all," Dick would say, "but I intend to run right out of that back door and hide in the brush— 'cause I don't want my death on any man's conscience." (*DIMH* 13)

As these characters suggest, the men in the camps are hardly homogeneous and far from being saints. Each of these plans of action seems understandable and even defensible, though we might expect Larry's pacifism to go deeper than it evidently does. George's coffee-and-cookies hospitality looks forward to some aspects of the active nonviolent resistance of the civil rights and anti-Vietnam War movements to come. Yet he is also in a tradition of generous response to enemies which goes back at least to the Old Testament: "If your enemy is hungry, give him bread to eat; and if he is thirsty, give him water to drink; for you will heap coals of fire upon his head, and the Lord will reward you" (Prov. 25:21-22, RSV).

Dick's plan to hide, to avoid putting "my death on any man's conscience"—if we accept his reasoning—also involves more than the cowardice we may see at first glance. He is typical of traditional conscientious objectors of the religious, as distinct from the political, sort, whose aim has been not only to avoid doing harm to others but to stay as clear of systems and situations of violence as possible. It was, in the beginning, to avoid military service that large numbers of the historic peace churches (including Stafford's Brethren, as well as Quakers and Mennonites) migrated to the New World. Only after a considerable history of persecution, imprisonment and struggle with civil authorities during American wars did the peace churches achieve full legal recognition of conscientious objector status and permission to do "alternative service" during World War II.[18]

Down in My Heart makes clear that such service—often in forestry, sometimes in mental hospitals or other situations "of national importance"—was not merely an easy way out. Abruptly distanced from everything familiar, the men are not quite prisoners in the work camp but do hard physical labor in confined and penurious conditions. They are treated as traitors, cowards, or at best shirkers by many that they encounter. In the first chapter, several of the men in service (often called COs) go to a small town near the camp on a Sunday afternoon and are drawn into a half-comical, half-threatening exchange with the townspeople. Ideas about cowardice, war, art, and poetry that does or does not rhyme fly back and forth (the narrator has *Leaves of Grass* under his arm, and a companion has been writing a free-verse poem critical of the town). The COs manage to remain "quiet and respectful," partly because they do not know what else to do, and the authorities finally arrive and send them back to camp, keeping their pictures, poems and letters as "evidence." Stafford's narrator muses that "almost always the tormentor is at a loss unless he can provoke a belligerent reaction as an excuse for further pressure or violence" (*DIMH* 20), but the chapter closes with a warning from the camp director about the difficulties their "little society within a society" faces:

> Don't think that our neighbors here in Arkansas are hicks just because they see you as spies and dangerous men. Just remember that our government is spending millions of dollars and hiring the smartest men in the country to devote themselves full time just to make everyone act that way. (22)

In the context of daily life, the task of the COs is not to "resist war" in some lofty, abstract sense. It is to work at being a distinct society within but not removed from the larger one, at living out their convictions in the face of both natural suspicion and all the propaganda resources of modern government, at building understanding and common human feeling between themselves and the officials, citizens, and others they encounter. This task—to be a witnessing, nonviolent community in but not of the world—is one that the Anabaptist ancestors of modern-day Brethren and Mennonites have been talking about since the sixteenth century, when they emerged in Switzerland and Holland as a sort of third wing of the Reformation.

The first Anabaptists wanted to free Christianity from the worldly entanglements they saw in both the Catholic and Protestant churches of their day. They looked to the Sermon on the Mount, to the life of Jesus, and to the vision and practice of the early church, especially its sense of separation from earthly powers, as models of what their lives should be. And they saw the Emperor Constantine's transformation of Christianity into a state religion as having led to disastrous compromises of those models, particularly in the sanctioning of violence in the service of the state.[19]

In a peculiarly modern way, then, Anabaptists have long struggled with that questions of worldly involvement and withdrawal, of practical effectiveness versus ethical purity, that Stafford's COs encounter. His understated, subtle style itself models both the calm humility Anabaptists have sought and the urge to find distance from the public world. The occasional passages of poetry especially model these qualities:

> Far up the canyon where the salmon leap
> and splintered sunlight nails the forest floor
> the people without houses put their feet.
>
> And often here below we drag a breath
> of something from the wind we missed, and steeply
> think: The place we built to live is too near death. (*DIMH* 37)

The withdrawal from the world yearned for in this passage is seldom possible for the men; even their isolated camps provide no escape from the thinly veiled racism and nationalism that drove the war spirit of the time. Many episodes turn on the tensions and ironies created by unlikely conjunctions of people. On one fire-fighting trip, for example, three men sit at a campfire: a serviceman with a purple heart for killing Japanese, a Filipino prisoner sentenced to a life term for killing a Japanese man "out of season," and the narrator, "who's up because he refused to kill Japs" (*DIMH* 53). The incident is simply recorded, in Stafford's typically laconic way. But here and elsewhere his irony serves a much different purpose than, for example, that of Robert Lowell's superficially similar poem "Memories of West Street and Lepke." Remembering his own World War II experience as "a fire-breathing Catholic CO," Lowell recalls the jail where he was thrown with "a Negro boy with curlicues / of marijuana in his hair," the "fly weight pacifist" Abramowitz, and Czar Lepke of Murder Incorporated (Lowell 91).

The irony of Lowell's poem is that the murderer is the privileged one in the prison society, allowed a radio and crossed American flags on his dresser. But Lepke is merely glimpsed, described, and dismissed (in Lowell's typically caustic terms) as "flabby, bald, lobotomized"—a telling emblem of the murderous stupidity that Lowell sees suffusing American life, but an emblem only.

Stafford makes a far greater effort at sympathy for those outside his own circle; virtually every person in the book, including those most hostile to him and his position, is presented as capable of growing beyond stereotypical attitudes. Many years later he restated directly this Gandhian distinction between opponents and enemies:

> In a world like the one we face, we are an opposition; it has to be. Caught in a world center of power, we scramble for footing. But we are a loyal opposition, for our concern happens to be people, and there are no "enemies." Redemption comes with care. In our culture we can oppose but not subvert. Openness is part of our technique. ("Making Peace" 12)

Numerous incidents in *Down in My Heart* demonstrate such efforts at careful, open dealings with opposition. A small group, sent out on a trail crew with a hostile boss named Eric, runs into trouble with his abrasive, profane ways. Ken, the cook, bears the brunt of Eric's hostility, and finally types out a list of conditions: he insists that Eric stop beating on plates, griping about the food, calling him "Chink," and so forth. When the other COs back Ken, Eric berates them for a while, then says he will cook himself. The others do not accept this "settlement," however, and convince Eric to look carefully at Ken's statement, working at each part of it through "a reading, a pondering, a group decision" (*DIMH* 35). By the district ranger's visit two days later, Eric reports that everything is "just fine": "He looked around at the society he lived in at Anapamu Creek. 'I was off my feed for a while, but going good again. . . . How's everything with you?'"

Not every situation in the book is so neatly resolved, and not only the Erics of this book find themselves changing. With a few exceptions, Stafford's COs have little of the smugness of those convinced of their own righteousness. Their intense study and discussion during the sparse time off work are repeatedly mentioned, as is their interest in the inner life and mystical experience: "Our thoughts in those wartimes were peculiarly susceptible to Ken's kind of [mystical] philosophy, for we met continual frustration; and every magazine, newspaper, movie, or stranger was a challenge to convictions that were our personal, inner creations" (*DIMH* 37).

Spurred by this interest, some of the men spend a week-long furlough at a retreat center in California led by Gerald Heard. Heard, almost unknown today, was something of a mid-century forerunner of 1960s guru Alan Watts; Stafford describes Heard as member of a "flourishing California group of mystics" that also included Allan Hunter and Aldous Huxley. His many books include meditations on the Lord's Prayer and the Beatitudes, mystery novels, and a number of works of the sort of *The Human Venture*, an attempt to render "the inward story of man's understanding and ordering of his own life" and to offer an integrated understanding of life by drawing on Western, Chinese, and Indian religions (Heard xi).

Heard serves as mentor for the group, and for the narrator in particular, who remarks that his own attempts at meditation were unremarkable but that he made up for it by jotting down some of Heard's key phrases: "illumined spirit, inwardly profitable, the way of wonder, alert passivity, anonymous memories, the love offensive, divine incarnation. . . . Suddenly everything is lit with a terrifying heightening of significance" (*DIMH* 45). These phrases, I think, will sound familiar to anyone who knows Stafford's work, and suggest that a deeper investigation of his links to Heard's thought would be a worthwhile subject of research.

A particularly crucial idea comes in response to a man who asks how he might prove he is not merely cowardly or dumb for refusing to fight:

> "Do not attempt to do so," said Gerald Heard. "We are each of us fallible, cowardly, and dumb. We can say, as great men have said before, 'Yes, it is true, I am a frail vessel in which to transport the truth; but I cannot unsee what I see. . . .'" (*DIMH* 45)

This simultaneous insistence on personal humility and steady refusal to "unsee what I see" becomes a central theme of Stafford's work. In practice its apparent simplicity demands a constant, subtle process of negotiations and decisions: the commitment to rigorous nonviolence leads toward just the sort of confrontations which break relationships, while the commitment to maintaining dialogue can all too easily lead to compromise and mere accommodation. And in less political terms, it connects directly to Stafford's famed hospitality and generosity as a teacher, and his openness to a wide range of influences in his writing; when I interviewed him in 1988, he talked in almost the same breath of his unstinting admiration for both Nietzsche and Cardinal Newman (Gundy, "If Struck" 48-49).

For all this tolerance, and his oft-repeated willingness to accept whatever impulses or ideas occur in the process of writing, there is a countervailing steadiness running through all that he has written; I would suggest that one of the origins of that steadiness is here, in his experience at maintaining an unpopular position without surrendering to mere alienation.

In the last chapters of *Down in My Heart*, these issues are explored through the mounting tension between the narrator's efforts to pursue a middle course and the more radical and uncompromising position of the character named George. George is unmoved by the celebrations at war's end, unable to forget the injustice and oppression that remain. He asks "How can we join in the celebration of the atomic bomb?" (81) and insists "We've got to stay out to be consistent—no nationally advertised brands for us—of toothpaste, or soap, or salvation" (82).

The narrator feels the force of George's alienated vision, sees with him the hapless, materialistic citizens in their unreflective festivities. The men go back to camp after the celebration in a sort of limbo, still bound to their segregated camp, feeling "more foreigners than ever" (85). George soon leaves the camp illegally, having decided "You've got to draw the line against conscription—complete refusal to take orders" (90). We are told he "had found the exhilaration of making a complete decision that ended uncertainty and the need of making other decisions" (90). But while such absolutes also appeal to Stafford's narrator, he cannot accept George's once-for-all decision as either practical or right; as he says, "I want to change others, not alienate them." The book ends with the narrator visiting George as he lies, silent and unresponsive, in a prison hospital bed where he is on a hunger strike. "I'll keep on saying those things we learned," the narrator promises:

incidents without heroes and without villains, and with no more
than a hint of that sound we heard during those war years, a
memory of our country, a peace we looked for down in our hearts
and all around us. (95)

What he and George have learned are quite different things. Yet
while Stafford himself clearly has chosen the narrator's path, his narrator
also grows restive at being kept in the camp rather than freed to begin
the real work of peacemaking. He also feels his isolation from mainstream life, even while he is immersed in it, and the cost of the stance he
has taken:

> No one is watching you. You are the person beside the aisle. Peo-
> ple who wave are waving at another person, someone behind you.
> On the street no one calls your name; but despite not talking to
> anyone you are learning everyone's language—more than ever
> before. You are going to a big school, with halls that go every-
> where. It costs everything you have to attend it. Its books are all
> over the world. (87)

The narrator seems to become more isolated, less caught up in the
group identity, as the book ends and the camp members go separate
ways. Yet the promise to "keep on saying those things we learned" implies a continuing commitment to both the community of memory that
the camp now forms, and the outside community to whom the stories
may be told. That commitment may be seen in Stafford's lifelong involvement with the Fellowship of Reconciliation, with other peace
groups, in his teaching, and of course in his writing. Many years later,
Stafford reflected on his choice of the narrator's path, at the risk of being
accused of compromise and inaction:

> There were people who were framed into this adversarial position
> against society, for whom it became an addiction, and they just
> couldn't live without being in contention with the society around
> them. They were professional and life long "aginners," and I was
> always looking for those places, those bridges, those possibilities
> [for reconciliation]. That's my intellectual position. ("If Struck")

The last disclaimer is an important one. In all his efforts toward reconciliation, Stafford never forgets that evil does exist, that no commitment to peacemaking eliminates the need for hard choices. His poems

continually demonstrate and reflect upon the challenges of living peaceably, often in unexpected, "ordinary" situations. His best-known poem, "Traveling Through the Dark," is a good example. The speaker discovers a dead deer along a narrow mountain road and stops, thinking "That road is narrow; to swerve might make more dead." It is a doe, with a still-living fawn inside. He hesitates, and we can imagine along with him the possibilities of dramatic, heroic action: a caesarean section with a pocketknife? Haul the mother to the vet, twelve miles away? Yet the poem ends without such heroism:

> The car aimed ahead its lowered parking lights;
> under the hood purred the steady engine.
> I stood in the glare of the warm exhaust turning red;
> around our group I could hear the wilderness listen.
>
> I thought hard for us all—my only swerving—,
> then pushed her over the edge into the river. (*Stories* 61)

Not many American poets would be willing to present themselves with this particular sort of vulnerability; Stafford has almost to himself this steady, stoical acceptance of his capacity to be less than heroic. The poem recognizes the moral ambiguity of all such action, refusing platitudes and confronting the costs of whatever commitments we make. Even the primary human allegiance to "us all," Stafford suggests, is not so marvelous that we should forget its price to those outside the pale.

Many of Stafford's poems take a point of view outside the "normal" human one, probing for unexpected political and moral significance. His little poem "B.C." would probably strike few readers as explicitly political, certainly not in the mode of Shelley's "Men of England" or Robert Bly's "The Teeth Mother Naked at Last":

> The seed that met water spoke a little name.
>
> (Great sunflowers were lording the air that day;
> this was before Jesus, before Rome; that other air
> was readying our hundreds of years to say things
> that rain has beat down on over broken stones
> and heaped behind us in many slag lands.)
>
> Quiet in the earth a drop of water came,
> and the little seed spoke: "Sequoia is my name." (*Stories* 76)

Characteristically, the voice here is small, quiet, and speaks in and from the earth. It is, however, a voice of ultimate, patient triumph, set in contrast to the sunflowers "lording the air" but soon to be gone and the "broken stones" the rain merely beats down on rather than "meeting" and germinating. In an interview with Peter Stitt, Stafford remarks,

> I've always felt that the conscientious-objector beliefs—all the alternative life-style ways of dealing with society—are like that little sequoia seed. They're quiet, but they're going to last. My political position is nonaggressive, and it makes me jumpy to have doctrinaire positions and forensic stances. I think my poems are consistent with this—I would rather have them be nonapparently political than apparently political. (Stitt 93)

This underplayed nonviolence has puzzled many critics. Sanford Pinsker's comments on Stafford's "Parentage," which repudiates heroism and ends "I'd just as soon be pushed by events to where I belong," take on a note of perplexity:

> Nothing could be more straightforward . . . and, at the same time, more dependent on its elusive quality of tone. Is the speaker being "serious" here? Or, if one drops the New Critical strictures against biographical interpretation, is this Stafford, the conscientious objector during World War II and a lifelong disciple of passive resistance, holding forth? (25)

Some of this perplexity, I think, stems from the ease with which Stafford's pacifism can be seen as mere passivity, standing outside of events and avoiding conflict. Some comes, as Pinsker notes, from Stafford's characteristic tone, which is playful sometimes to the point of coyness. More importantly, though, many literary critics are not used to thinking of nonviolence as a full worldview rather than a "political" stance relevant only to international issues; thus they are unprepared to recognize the full implications of a rigorously nonviolent stance.

In the course of an interview with Peter Stitt, for example, Stafford handed him a pamphlet from the Fellowship of Reconciliation, a veteran pacifist organization, and said "This explains pretty much what I believe." The pamphlet begins "The F.O.R. is composed of men and women who recognize the essential unity of mankind and have joined together to explore the power of love and truth for resolving human conflict."[20]

Yet although Stitt states that Stafford's lifelong pacifism is important to understanding his work, and is generally a sympathetic and acute
critic, in reading Stafford's poems he turns back to the shopworn literary
idea of the pastoral as an organizing principle. For Stitt, Stafford is

> a wisdom poet who uses the world of nature as a means to an
> end—he is in pursuit of a truth higher than those customarily
> perceived by ordinary men leading ordinary lives. Thus, in those
> poems mentioned above wherein nature's power to destroy is em-
> phasized, the lesson is one of *humility* for mankind. . . . This tru-
> ism is very much in line with the general pastoral vision, which
> locates delusion in man's works and cities, while the real, the ele-
> mental, the essential and true, is to be found in the less-peopled
> places of earth. (66, emphasis added)

Stitt is right to see the centrality of humility in Stafford's outlook.
Yet to reduce this humility to mere geography and pastoralism is at best
condescending, at worst misleading; although Stafford's vision is con-
gruent with many elements of the pastoral, I think I have already shown
that the origins and bases of that vision are quite different. His mode of
resistance to majority life may be more like John Chapman's than Daniel
Boone's or Jesse James's, but it is no less thoroughgoing for its modesty.
The poems of *An Oregon Message* (1987), perhaps more systematically
than earlier collections, show this mode at its finest.

The brief preface, "Some Notes on Writing," connects his ethic of
humility and nonviolence to the act of writing itself, refusing tight control and predetermined ends in favor of "giv[ing] the language its own
freedom and confidence," expressing a blend of modesty and confidence regarding the self as "a fallible but susceptible person. I must be
willingly fallible to deserve a place in the realm where miracles happen"
(10).

While Stafford's poems persistently seek to celebrate the miraculous, however, he is less interested in "success" than in what seems like
failure, which "A Life, a Ritual" among other poems here explores:

> There are people whose game is success, but others
> hear distance: guided, often betrayed,
> they wander their lives. Their voices go by
> every day, outside of history, outside of importance.
> They ritual whatever they do.

> My mother is nothing now. Her child—
> wide gaze like hers—remembers the blanket,
> and the song that taught how to lose. Oh, shadow
> that came large on a wall, then face that recognized
> mine: this distant song about failure
>
> Is for you, is for you. (15)

The first stanza above presents typical anabaptist separation; a sense of feeling unlike "the world," betrayed by the successful, unimportant. Yet clearly the "failure" the poem ends with is neither the glorious disaster of an Oedipus or Hamlet nor the grinding pathos of a Willy Loman. It is connected, I believe, with the sense of being "outside of history," in a position which may be quite tolerable, even fulfilling—"they ritual whatever they do"—but also produces the sense of distance, almost guilt, described in "Confessions of an Individual":

> I let history happen—sorry. When Muslims and
> Christians fought in the Crusades, I didn't stop it;
> the Egyptians and Jews clashed and my efforts were not
> sufficient to prevent that. Remote effects from these
> disasters still exist, and I have not erased them.
> My ancestors were busy cutting hay, planting potatoes,
> and so on. . . . (20)

The compensation for this sense of distance from the great events of history is in concentration on local events, things directly perceived, small dramas in which large issues are contested. Often the context is one which presents a "little society" committed to peace and justice existing uneasily and ambivalently within a larger society less concerned for those issues, if not actively hostile.

Stafford's sense of membership in a "little society" goes back to his boyhood in small-town Kansas. "Serving with Gideon" takes us to a prewar village where, as in *Down in My Heart*, the speaker stands between the general society and a sub-group. He remembers a segregated drugstore where the black elevator man cannot buy a Coke, and the Legion hall, whose leaders were generous to "their sons or the sons of friends":

> Look down, stars—I was almost
> one of the boys. My mother was folding
> her handkerchief; the library seethed and sparked;
> right and wrong arced; and carefully

I walked with my cup toward the elevator man. (35)

Strikingly, Stafford does not make much of this speaker's isolation nor directly suggest anything heroic about his decision. The ambivalence of being "almost one of the boys" is poignant, but finally the boy's position is not to be pitied. The menacing "blue fist" of night and the dark "deep as war" fade before the sense of a narrow escape from conventional complacency and prejudice. Against the natural, powerful longing to be "one of the boys," the last stanza evokes a web of compensatory relationships—with the natural world, as seen in the stars, with his mother, with the larger culture (the library), with the elevator man—against which the small, careful gesture of "serving" stands as a marker of entry into an alternate community where right and wrong have an integral place, and where it is possible to grow beyond boyhood.

Robert Pinsky's *Poetry and the World* poses closely related questions of how poetry can and should relate to "the world of worldliness," the social world with its power and attraction, its seaminess and corruption, "its almost identical powers to divert us and to jade us." Pinsky celebrates Elizabeth Bishop's poems for their

> insistent, credible enactment of a human soul that is in the World, but not entirely of it, outside of the World, but not entirely apart from it. Her poems suggest that when we write, we need not be limited merely to the spinning-out of the filaments of memory and autobiography, on the one hand, or on the other hand merely to idly shifting the diverting kaleidoscope of imagination. Without neglecting the pleasures, interests, urgencies of the communal realm, she stays true to the way the mind itself craves something beyond that realm. And she does that without sanctifying either realm. (3, 16)

With some differences in emphasis, these terms fit Stafford very well. Pinsky is especially acute, I think, on the advantages for poetry of this stance of being in but not of the world, of engaging it while maintaining a certain reserve, and of thus avoiding the limiting dualism of simple nostalgia or idle imagination. Stafford's particular stance allows for unconventional, even startling explorations of this theme, such as "A Memorial for My Mother":

> For long my life left hers. It went
> among strangers; it weakened and followed

foreign ways, even honesty, and courage. It found
those most corrupting of all temptations,
friends—their grace, their faithfulness.

But now my life has come back. In our bleak
little town I taste salt and smoke again.
I turn into our alley and lean
where I hid from work or from anything
deserving of praise. Mother, you and I—

We knew if they knew our hearts they would blame.
We knew we deserved nothing. I go along
now being no one, and remembering this—
how alien we were from others, how hard we chewed
on our town's tough rind. How we loved its flavor. (105)

Nostalgia undergoes fascinating and frightening changes here, as
the poem remembers and evokes not the comforting sense of belong-
ing and being convinced of one's own goodness, but of feeling alien
and unworthy, tolerated only because the town's regulars do not see
past the external conventions. Stafford's evocation of a society that is at
once feared and loved, mistrusted and envied, chewed like a rind for
what small nourishment its leavings might provide, resonates intriguingly with Pinsky's discussion of ways of treating one's community in
literature:

To mythologize or inflate a community, or even to make anecdote (or allegory) of it, is both to submerge one's identity partway
into the communal identity, and to assert one's importance. To
make one's native place illustrious is an acceptable, ancient form
of claiming personal significance. As a kind of impersonal boast-
ing, it raises the great conflict and accommodation between self
and community, figure and background. (Pinsky 147)

As I have been suggesting, Stafford's mythologizing of place departs
from the standard self-versus-community or self-in-community patterns to include a subgroup resistant to the majority community and
supportive of the self. Including that third term or "little society" also
makes the claim to significance more than individual, enlarging and
deepening the potentials for complex interaction and conflict and mul-
tiplying the possible outcomes beyond the standard ones of rejection or

acquiescence. In the title poem of *An Oregon Message* Stafford provides an especially intriguing variation on this theme:

> When we first moved here, pulled
> the trees in around us, curled
> our backs to the wind, no one
> had ever hit the moon—no one.
> Now our trees are safer than the stars,
> and only other people's neglect
> is our precious and abiding shell,
> pierced by meteors, radar, and the telephone.
>
> From our snug place we shout
> religiously for attention, to hide:
> only silence or evasion will bring
> dangerous notice, the hovering hawk
> of the state, or the sudden quiet stare
> and fatal estimate of an alerted neighbor.
>
> This message we smuggle out in
> its plain cover, to be opened
> quietly: Friends everywhere—
> we are alive! Those moon rockets
> have missed millions of secret
> places! Best wishes.
>
> Burn this. (60)

There is no sense here that changing the world at large is possible or even desirable; here the network of "friends everywhere" persists despite the sense that if the majority society understood what "we" actually were it would quickly attack. Given Stafford's tradition, such a sense is not hard to understand.

Anabaptist history has been a long series of removals, migrations across most of the earth in search of a place to be left alone. The Mennonite martyrs of the sixteenth century are still remembered, as are the conscientious objectors who were jailed or interned during every American war; but when possible most Anabaptists have quite naturally tried to avoid controversy, to be the "quiet in the land," to find places where the authorities would at least tolerate their quirky insistence on taking the hard sayings of Jesus seriously.

Now those migrations have in large part ended; in the global village, there is no place left to be truly alone. The community must exist within the world, yet either by adapting to its norms or by persuading the world that it should be tolerated. How can this be done? Stafford suggests, intriguingly, that to "shout for attention" has become less dangerous than silence or evasion, that a carefully chosen message may lull the others into paying no attention.

The "message," however, is more than mere camouflage. If it does not presume the ability to save the world, it does insist that a spark is still alive: that if we can remain alert, preserve tradition and memory, recognize the limits of the human and the magnitude and magnificence of the rest of the universe, and continue to speak to each other, we can continue to live, even thrive, in the places that the rockets miss. The conspiratorial "Burn this" of the last line suggests a quiet but continuing resistance and determination to persist.

Stafford's tendency, as I have noted, is to try to find the best even in his adversaries, to reserve judgment and regard no one as irredeemable. "Graffiti" suggests the limits of his generosity, reserving some of his harshest words for those who presume the right to make absolute and final judgments:

> "Kill the tyrants," lovers of mankind say,
> and the religious write firmly, "Jesus saves."
> "A wall for not writing on" and "I waited an hour"
> are two that commuters must read. And—remember?—
> Daniel Boone "kilt a bar" on a tree.
>
> But the trees not carved and walls undefaced
> mean "Not even Kilroy was here,"
> and millions of us haven't killed anyone,
> or a bear, or even an hour. We haven't
> presumed. And—who knows—maybe we're saved. (45)

The serpent tempted Eve with the knowledge of good and evil. Stafford returns here to a stance very like Gerald Heard's in *Down in My Heart*, and in doing so touches on a crucial reality of the nuclear age: the danger of "presuming" an absolute knowledge that justifies doing violence to other humans, to the non-human world, even to ourselves, in the name of a cause. Here it is precisely the refusal of presumption, the willingness to leave the world unmarked by our passage, that may be saving, if anything is. The characteristic hedging of the final claim is essential to the particularly humble variety of nonviolence Stafford is pursuing; to claim confidently that this is the path to salvation would be merely to indulge in a new variety of arrogance.

All well and good, we might ask, but is all this irrelevant or even dangerous in the so-called real world? How do we cope with the Hitlers and Pol Pots, the Bin Ladens and Husseins, without force and the threat of force? Even if we agree that nonviolence as an ethic would make the world considerably more pleasant, what do we do until our enemies are converted? At times Stafford's response to such questions seems disconcertingly quietist, as in "Austere Hope, Daily Faith":

> Even a villain sleeps—atrocities
> are intermittent. We assume few saints
> among us—and inattention or fatigue
> is what we like in our great leaders.
> Some days Hitler didn't kill anybody. . . .
>
> In any town, or field, or forest,
> or on the sea, wherever you are,
> you may find a bird or fish, or maybe
> a stray dog, to help. And that little act
> will carry your name all the way to the stars. (129)

Poems this minimal in their claims may seem troubling as stances toward life, even granting Stafford his habitual playfulness. Being kind to animals seems to belong to the world of Raisin Bran commercials and chain-bookstore "poetry" sections rather than that of Realpolitik. Yet this insistence on the unheroic is, at the least, consistent; much earlier in his career Stafford wrote "It is time for all the heroes to go home/ If they have any" (*Stories* 193), and he is fond of quoting Thomas Mann's maxim "A national hero is a national calamity." In fact the very austerity and smallness of the claims here, the insistence that small gestures must be enough, are paradoxically part of the magnitude of the rethinking of our lives and values he calls for. One implication, as we have seen, is that expecting to save the world all too easily leads to excess and violence; another is, as Stafford puts it, that

> the real work of a pacifist is done in peacetime, beforehand. I mean, you're *noticed* when the war comes, but you're doing your work all the time. . . . it's the daily things that you do and not

those spectacular things that are crucial. . . . We can't just justify ourselves by saying "Well, when things get to a certain state count us out." We should be trying to keep things from getting to that state. ("If Struck")

It is the trying, not the final tally, that matters most to Stafford. Nothing is more central to majority American society than our fascination with winning, with keeping score, with statistics and judgments and litigations. And of course the desire to win, to overcome the enemy, to impose our will, to rejoice in our own power and the weakness of others, is a universal human one. Yet just as the Sermon on the Mount flies in the face of our "natural" inclinations, insisting that we re-envision all our relations with others and refuse simply to follow our instincts, so Stafford demands a rethinking of the drive toward success:

Learning How to Lose

All your years learning how to live to win,
how others judge you, who counts—you know
it's wrong: but those habits cling that brought you
this freedom. You know how to earn it but
you don't [k]now what it is—a friend that you
make is conquered, like an enemy.

Somewhere you'll rest, have faith, even
lose sometimes, accept the way you are, say
easily to the world: "Leave me alone, Hours.
I'm just living here. Let Now win." (30)

One of the delights of Stafford's writing is his sudden shifts from one level to another, his abrupt revisions of conventional categories. Here the relentless, habitual pursuit of success means that even freedom, that most sacred of American abstractions, has a wrongness about it; even friends are "conquered," and nothing, especially ourselves, can be accepted for what it is. To break that cultural conditioning demands another learning process, one that involves reconciliation to reality and loss, turning away from the "Hours" which are measured, designated and appointed by human beings and toward the eternal Now.

The extent of Stafford's effort to question the fundamental ways by which we organize and meet our experience has seldom been fully treated by critics. Some have tried to domesticate him into a poet of Nature and Childhood and acceptable sentiment. Reviewing *An Oregon Message for Poetry*, Vernon Shetley speaks highly of Stafford as a "celebrant of recaptured innocence or remembered youth" but dismisses his more public poems as "forays into psychopolitics" involving "a vision of unnamed manipulators whose business is that of stifling humanity" (109). Shetley likes best those poems whose "ambitions are limited," which are "touching and fine" rather than challenging or even resistant of the existing order. Other critics have been harsher, describing Stafford as "wise, dull, bewildered," or objecting to his "smallness" and passivity.[21]

In what I take as the best spirit of Stafford's work, however, I do not propose to argue directly with his critics here but to think along with him, as Stafford does in "Thinking About Being Called Simple by a Critic":

> I wanted the plums, but I waited.
> The sun went down. The fire
> went out. With no lights on
> I waited. From the night again—
> those words: how stupid I was.
> And I closed my eyes to listen.
> The words all sank down, deep
> and rich. I felt their truth
> and began to live them. They were mine
> to enjoy. Who but a friend
> could give so sternly what the sky
> feels for everyone but few learn to
> cherish? In the dark with the truth
> I began the sentence of my life
> and found it so simple there was no way
> back into qualifying my thoughts
> with irony or anything like that.
> I went to the fridge and opened it—
> sure enough the light was on.
> I reached in and got the plums. (29)

This poem seems to me a remarkable venture at evading instinctive human defensiveness. It enacts a kind of active nonviolence, particularly the willingness to put aside "winning" to listen to and learn from one's adversaries. And it does so without the kind of obnoxious stage-humility that crops up from time to time, most notably in the Puritans and the excesses of confessional poetry, where the competition to prove oneself a more lowly worm groveling in the dust or a more thoroughly miserable person than all the rest becomes merely another form of pride. Here a calm acceptance of the self, with both its weaknesses and its plums, carries the poet through.

The sort of humility Stafford finds is curiously impersonal, despite the folksy tone and realistic detail of the poem. In accepting his own simplicity he connects it with "what the sky feels for everyone"—a sense of human limits which in he connects to the *Pensées* of Pascal, no doubt with this famous "two abysses" passage in mind:

> For in fact what is man in nature? A Nothing in comparison with the Infinite, an All in comparison with the Nothing, a mean between nothing and everything. . . . he is equally incapable of seeing the Nothing from which he was made, and the Infinite in which he is swallowed up. (17-18)

In a letter, Stafford emphatically accepts this sense of human limitations and the partial nature of all human understanding: "I have found it natural to assume that no human being can perceive well enough or reason surely enough to grasp things as they are. We are ultimately so limited as to make any vaunting irrelevant, foolish, misguided. Limited as we are, humility befits us." This point of view runs counter to the standard Western and particularly American myths, of course; we have liked to think that we can know and do and be whatever we want to badly enough. Yet to recognize human limits while continuing to think and act in the world is hardly a sentimental or a naive perspective. It offers a levelness in encountering a hostile review in the mail or the plums waiting in the icebox which carries rich rewards of its own.

This perspective does not come naturally, no more so to long-term peace activists and poets than to generals or professional wrestlers. Our instinct is to strike back, to defend ourselves, to justify and explain, and of course in its unassuming way Stafford's poem is a quite firm justification of his poetic stance and strategies. But its receptivity and capacity to accept and incorporate criticism also reveal an unexpected magnitude. It not only evokes William Carlos Williams' "This Is Just to Say," but Walt Whitman's willingness to acknowledge, include and even celebrate his own contradictions and weaknesses, to find in them a measure of our common humanity, our common insistence on disagreeing with one another, and our capacity for living with such disagreements.

When I asked Stafford about the incongruity of his attraction to both Nietzsche and Cardinal Newman, he asked if I had read *Thus Spake Zarathustra*, "the passage about the death of God? That's really trenchant. Zarathustra is the one—they think he's crazy, because he says, 'you *see* what's happening? Nobody knows what's down, what's up, what's in, what's out, everything's up for grabs.'" Yet almost in the next breath he was praising Newman for his "locating and justifying himself," for his analysis in *A Grammar of Assent* of "what process the individual goes through to arrive at belief" and of the "illative sense," through which belief persists even in the face of logical argument ("If Struck").

The capacity to appreciate and to learn both from Niezsche's great attack on illusory belief and from Newman's reassertion of the possibility of belief even when it is not rational or provable, let alone fashionable—to incorporate insights from both of them while recognizing the tensions between them—indicates the startling, adventuresome openness beneath Stafford's surface calm. He has remained in conversation with a very wide range of voices, continued to listen carefully and to accumulate insights from many sources without simply rejecting or being taken over by them.

Allen Bloom's *The Closing of the American Mind* invokes Nietzsche in considering how, in the exhaustion of old values, great men might generate new ones:

> The self must be a tense bow. It must struggle with opposites rather than harmonize them, rather than turn the tension over to the great instruments of last manhood—the skilled bow unbenders and Jesuits of our days, the psychiatrists, who, in the same spirit and as part of the same conspiracy of modernity as the peace virtuosos, reduce conflict. Chaos, the war of opposites, is, as we know from the Bible, the condition of creativity, which must be mastered by the creator. (198)

Bloom's dismissal of psychiatrists and "peace virtuosos" as weak reducers or evaders of conflict strikes me as just the sort of ambitious wrong-headedness to which Stafford has been responding so beautifully all his life. For the pursuit of peace is itself a constant struggle, as all real peacemakers know. Stafford encounters opposites without simply loosening the bowstring or claiming that conflicts can all be resolved, mediated, or managed, but he also refused to melodramatically inflate the "creator's" struggle. Stafford works instead by remaining within those tensions; surely he would reject Bloom's description of chaos as "the war of opposites" as far too easy a surrender to an impoverished metaphor. The chaos and the promise of our world deserve more complex, more generative, and more accurate images.

To move among the things of that world requires for Stafford a "mastery" quite unlike that envisioned by Nietzsche or Bloom: an amalgam of humility and assertion, of receptivity and conviction, of security and risk, of responsibility and freedom, of identification with a minority community and interdependence with the widening circles of the living:

> O citizens of our great amnesty:
> We might have died. We live. Marvels
> coast by, great veers and swoops of air
> so bright the lamps waver in tears,
> and I hear in the chain a chuckle I like to hear. (OM 143)

CHAPTER FIVE

BEYOND DR. JOHNSON'S DOG: AMERICAN MENNONITE POETRY AND POETS

"Russian Mennonites . . . write vivid disturbing poetry. Swiss Mennonites . . . don't." —Craig Haas and Steve Nolt, 1993

"Sir, a woman's preaching is like a dog's walking on his hind legs. It is not done well, but you are surprised to find it done at all." —Dr. Samuel Johnson, 1709-1784

For most of the twenty-some years I have been writing poems, I have seen an American Mennonite audience for poetry as a contradiction in terms. I published many poems in literary magazines, and even a few (rather tepid) ones in church periodicals. But it seemed clear that much of my work was too restless, sardonic, or oblique for the church press, and that Mennonites at large were no more interested in poetry than other Americans. I found outlets for my work elsewhere and tried not to think about it too much, though I occasionally thought wistfully about the lively Canadian Mennonite literary scene, with its high-profile and controversial writers. I found the poets who meant the most to me mainly outside Mennonite traditions, although a few, like William Stafford and Janet Kauffman, had some sort of Mennonite connection.

In the few years since Haas and Nolt—with tongues partly in cheek—concluded that Swiss Mennonites just do not write "vivid, disturbing" poetry, things have changed, some. If they made that statement now, at some semi-intellectual Mennonite gathering, someone in the group would be likely to know of at least one Swiss Mennonite poet—Julia (Spicher) Kasdorf, probably. A real enthusiast in the group might come up with a few more names. It would be too strong to call the recent emergence of American Mennonite poetry, from both the Swiss and Russian streams, an explosion or even a renaissance.

Yet as poets such as Jean Janzen, Julia Kasdorf, and a number of others publish poems in national magazines and presses, win awards, and become recognized in the American poetry network, Mennonite recognition has followed. Poets are invited with increasing frequency to read, speak, and work with students on Mennonite campuses. It has become almost de rigeur, even at standard academic conferences, to include some writers and artists and to schedule a session or two of readings or creative presentations.[22] Magazines such as *Mennonite Life* and *Mennonot* (the latter now expired) have begun to publish more innovative and risky poetry than the general-circulation denominational magazines. Even *Mennonite Weekly Review* noticed when Jean Janzen won a $20,000 fellowship from the NEA, and Julia Kasdorf's poem "Mennonites" was the subject of a *Gospel Herald* editorial in 1995 after it was included in the MacMillan college text *Many Worlds of Literature*.

At least among the American Mennonite intelligentsia (a phrase whose ironic qualities I recognize) there is a clearly developing, if sometimes uneasy, sense that poets and other creative artists may have important things to tell us. Scott Holland, himself a controversial figure in the Mennonite community, puts it this boldly:

> I believe that our Mennonite and Brethren artists, poets and creative writers have more to teach us than our theologians and preachers about the ambiguity of desire, the enigma of the flesh, the deceitfulness of the heart, the goodness of grace and the mystery of God in the world. ("Communal" 19).

Most of Holland's key terms—ambiguity, desire, enigma, deceitfulness, mystery—are ones not often invoked, at least approvingly, by mainstream Mennonite church leaders. When they invoke poets, it is likely to be in less threatening terms. Lorne Peachey's editorial pays much closer attention to the teacher's guide for the anthology than to Julia Kasdorf's poem itself, noting with considerable satisfaction the statements in the "discussion notes" that Mennonites have "a single-minded devotion to God" and "seem to actually practice what they preach" (16). Both Peachey and the anthologist seem oblivious to the understated but radical irony of the poem, which begins by noting that "We [Mennonites] hoe thistles along fence rows for fear / we may not be perfect as our Heavenly Father. / We clean up his disasters." The poem proceeds to speak of "our" loving the gory engravings of *Martyrs Mirror*, of loving our enemies as well as the Nazi soldiers who "led the last cattle cars [filled with Mennonite refugees] rocking out of the Ukraine" and are thus, strangely enough, regarded as heroes. The poem ends with images that, read carefully, are deeply disconcerting:

> This is why we cannot leave the beliefs
> or what else would we be? why we eat
> 'til we're drunk on shoofly and moon pies and borscht.
> We do not drink; we sing. Unaccompanied on Sundays,
> those hymns in four parts, our voices lift with such force
> that we lift, as chaff lifts toward God. (*Sleeping Preacher* 34)

As any good Mennonite farmer could tell us, chaff is not worth much; it is what falls back to be left on the threshing floor or to blow aimlessly in the wind. Here the farm imagery is closely connected to those other primary markers of Mennonite identity, hymn-singing and ethnic foods, that run through both Mennonite history and, we shall see, Mennonite poetry as well. But the images here threaten to dissolve, to be inadequate against the gathering sense of lack of worth or identity: "what else would we be?" In its quiet way the poem raises fundamental questions about who and what Mennonites are; it challenges the very complacency that Peachey attempts, perhaps unwittingly, to restore.

Like many poets and artists and artists before her, Kasdorf lives and finds her art in the difficult space where faith, doubt and real, lived experience cohabit or collide. Therein lies much of the tension between artists and religious power structures, which are conservative by nature. Given that such structures must function to maintain the community and transmit core values from generation to generation, they and the people who represent them must inevitably resist whatever challenge and critique seems to threaten the authority and stability of the existing order. This is obviously not wrong; no tradition can survive without those who conserve and transmit it. On the other hand, no tradition survives for long without change, and sometimes painful story-telling, image-making, and critique are necessary both to healthy change and to discerning and preserving what is worth nourishing of the past.

If contemporary Mennonite are indeed telling us things about our past, present and future communal life that we badly need to hear, it remains to be seen what will happen if they are more often admitted into the center of our communal life. Will they merely become part of a rampant worldliness that is driving the liberal wing of the Mennonite church over the cliffs of modernity? Might they indeed help to both maintain and transform Mennonite thought and doctrine and practice, preserving the best of the old and helping us to break free from the worst? Or will they simply be assimilated, co-opted, their work made over into more support for an institution that remains stubbornly human, temporal, and interested in its artists only as they help ensure the survival of its power structures?

What happens will very likely be more complicated than any of these formulaic questions-as-prophecy, of course. Poems, like other forms of creative expression, do not simply affirm or deny credos and dogmas. They resist conclusion, they supplement, embroider, contend, amplify. They probe areas that the credos leave untouched, they insist that all experience and all feeling deserve attention, they work toward the messy inclusiveness of life itself. They resist being instrumental the way hymns and sermons and prayers are, instead insisting on their right to simply be, regardless of their usefulness or (un)orthodoxy. They may indeed, of course, be useful and/or orthodox, but often in peculiar ways. Poets resist the "adult" demands of those who would make all expression instrumental and functional; they insist on playing, long after the Apostle Pauls of the world insist it is time to put away such things. Robert Frost demanded that poetry be "play for mortal stakes." Yes, such practices are both vital and threatening.

In a 1986 essay on three little-known American Mennonite poets (myself included) I quoted Ezra Pound's statement that "Artists are the antennae of the race" ("Separation" 67), and wrote that "As we seek to invent and imagine what it means to be Mennonite in these yeasty and perilous times, we can little afford to ignore anyone whose antennae may be more sensitive than our own" (69). I am convinced that both statements are still true; the difference, ten years later, is in the number of substantial and significant poets and poems that have emerged. It seems worthwhile, then, to attempt some general observations about the state of Mennonite poetry in the United States near the end of the century, and to offer descriptive summaries of the poets who are writing and publishing most actively.

What follows will not be an exhaustive or encyclopedic survey of American Mennonite poets. I will not discuss the many fine Canadian Mennonite poets (except for a few comparative remarks); they are relatively well-known, at least in Canada, and serious discussions of their work already exist.[23] Mennonite fiction and essays are also not considered here. I have chosen, for space reasons, to deal almost entirely with poets who have published at least some work in competitive literary journals and presses, and to do no more than mention those who write mainly for a church audience, though this meant excluding some worthy poets and poems.

I have tried to write descriptively, rather than evaluatively, but of course any writing such as this involves many implicit judgments. In my case, the problem of judgment is further complicated—I know most of the people of whom I write and count some of them among my closest friends. It has been a pleasure to study and write about their work, to talk and write about the issues this essay takes up. But I am not an objective observer, if indeed anyone is.

DEFINITIONS, TENSIONS, PROPOSITIONS

What is a Mennonite poet? A Mennonite poem? Individual poets of Mennonite extraction have radically varied experiences—almost one per writer, I am tempted to say. For Julia Kasdorf "Mennonite" might mean black and orange buggies, women's talk in the kitchen, a valley in Pennsylvania with a firm ring of mountains defining its borders, as in "Vesta's Father":

> those mountains that rise dark and silent
> as old Mennonites standing in pews—
> black-stockinged women on one side,
> black-suited men on the other—
> those mountains so high they slow the sunrise
> and hurry the night. (*Sleeping Preacher* 5)

For Jean Janzen, being Mennonite might mean the dusty plains of Saskatchewan, *borscht* and *zwiebach*, stories of the terror in the Ukraine that her ancestors endured, and images like these from "Mennonites in Russia: The Photographs":

> Bodies in a long row of wooden boxes
> lined with linen, tiny vines
> bordering Elizabeth who was raped
> again and again. The murderers
> are resting in the burned wheat field,
> their hands steady as they light
> cigarettes. In the hazy distance
> the village, the mills broken and silent,
> the church with boarded windows
> like eyes that have closed. (*Three Mennonite Poets* 21)

My own childhood images of "Mennonite" are of small white churches on the flat Illinois prairie, sweltering revival meetings, small towns where the Mennonites look and eat just like everybody else, the older men telling stories of their CPS days. I could go on listing these sorts of particulars, and I suspect that Mennonite readers could all add their own. My point is that, given such diversity even among North American Mennonites, it makes sense that Mennonite artists and critics should continually seek to define themselves and their work and should just as persistently disagree. In fact, Mennonite artists seem as compelled as any to offer definitions, counter-definitions, proposals, and manifestos of what they are doing and why.

The two most sustained and important recent efforts to define Mennonite writing are previously mentioned books, John Ruth's *Mennonite Identity and Literary Art* (1978) and Al Reimer's *Mennonite Literary Voices Past and Present* (1993).[24] Ruth and Reimer, coming from quite distinct historical streams, clearly represent two very different views of Mennonite community and Mennonite writing as well.

Ruth's concern for community, tradition, and discipline clearly reflect his roots in and commitment to the Swiss Mennonite tradition and its Pennsylvania branch. He recognizes the dangers and limits of art that merely seeks to propagate communal values, but he emphasizes the importance of art as a way of keeping a tradition alive. "Access to a meaningful past is mediated via story," he writes (10), and Mennonites need to tell their own story "from that unique center of covenant-conviction where we stand" (13). Ruth insists that a true Mennonite artist must remain in close engagement with that tradition, "*wrestle through* the issues in the artist's personal encounter with a special tradition" (14, italics his). He calls for—though he clearly, in 1978, did not find it within the Swiss tradition—"an aesthetically serious representation of our ethos in its classic issues—obedience, simplicity, humility, defenselessness, the maintenance of identity" (23).

Al Reimer, a Canadian Mennonite novelist, critic, and professor, responded quite directly to Ruth's ideas fifteen years later in a series of lectures/essays first delivered at Bethel College. Reimer grants the appeal of Ruth's vision as a "desideratum," but says it has not been fulfilled, perhaps cannot be. Responding to Ruth's image of "wrestling through," Reimer asks, reasonably enough, "How can the artist do that fully and honestly without facing the possibility that after wrestling through the issues she may find herself in fundamental disagreement with the prevailing ideology of the community[?]" (62). He insists that "What the artist creates should come from the power of his imagination and be guided only by his sense of artistic integrity, that is, the degree of personal commitment he is prepared to make, the extent to which he is willing to accept or reject the values of the community" (63).

These two positions—communal responsibility on the conservative/Swiss side, independence and artistic freedom on the liberal/Russian side—have been argued for a long time. Indeed, one of the clearest and most direct statements of the issues is now thirty years old; Warren Kliewer's 1965 essay "Controversy and the Religious Arts," still rings true in disconcerting ways. Kliewer insists that art, if it is alive, will always be controversial, given that audiences always lag behind artists. While he emphasizes the need for more tolerant and sophisticated audiences, especially within the church, Kliewer says that the tension between artist and community is finally both inescapable and necessary. It must be "nurtured," "for the religious community is re-discovering that it needs the serious artist" (11) who provides for the necessary critique and renewal of the tradition:

> The first half of the creative process is destruction. If the church's new interest in art is genuine and serious, the church must learn not only to understand but also to accept the artist's need to destroy. A responsible artist destroys only as much as is necessary in order to begin creating. (11)

Put so flatly, this argument for destructive as well as creative artistic freedom is fraught with hardly concealed risks for the community: to whom, or what, is an artist "responsible"? To art, to a particular church, to a larger community, to God? Will the artist recognize any other claims? How does the artist decide how much destruction is "necessary," and what happens when others disagree?

On the other hand, it is difficult to imagine a successful artist giving a community, no matter how sympathetic, final control over his or her work. When Ruth writes sardonically that in traditional Swiss Mennonite communities, "What was not allowed was for the tail of [the artist's] personal satisfaction to wag the dog of the communal spiritual purpose" (37), this reader stirs restlessly, hearing an echo of the vanished bishop's voice, mocking and deprecating any view that might challenge his (I use the pronoun deliberately) authority.[25]

Elmer Suderman, one of the most experienced Mennonite literary critics and poets, rightly points out that many of these tensions arise not from some unique Mennonite hostility to the arts, but from the deep structures of human societies, which typically favor predictability, organization, and stability over the eccentricity and playfulness of art. He calls us back to literary texts themselves, away from our seemingly endless preoccupation with individual/community relations, saying that writers should write freely, critics should be generous but stringent, and readers should discover compassion and playfulness ("Mennonites" 25).

In broad terms, I agree with these conclusions. Yet I also think that such formulations of the individual/community model miss something crucial: the role of communities in *forming* individuals and individual values, in generating both artistic impulses and artistic tastes. Almost always in an artist there is some element of rebellion or resistance to communal values, of course; that resistance is often the origin of art. Yet is there any writer whose engagement with her birth community does not shape her even as she seeks to critique it, reform it, even leave it?

I believe that the artist's "self" (a term I use with all due caution) is in part a creation of that birth community, and that even within the self and within the art work the contention between different forces goes on continually. I also believe in a very wide range of expression and in the freedom of the artist to use any means necessary to achieve that expression. Yet surely it is naive in these postmodern days to imagine that the artist's "self" is some sturdy, indivisible, unchanging essence which can ever be either utterly "free" to create or totally restricted by the community. All of our selves are complex, changing, elusive entities whose impulses and qualities are beyond complete calculation. Within us and without us, the dialectics of identity and difference, conformity and rebellion, solidarity and distance, coalesce into the selves we think of as our own, the ones we present to the world, the ones that inhabit our poems and essays and letters, the ones that are identified as the "authors" of the words we claim as "ours." None of those selves would be as they are without our specific, individual, grounded experience of place and community and family. Yet that experience falls well short of explaining or defining any individual; something in each of us is not reducible to place and community.

In 1990 I began the family history project that eventually became *A Community of Memory: My Days with George and Clara*, a book of stories and meditations about my Amish and Mennonite ancestors who settled in Illinois in the nineteenth century. I did so with the sense that my other creative work—mainly poems, a few brief personal essays—had not really come to terms with my personal and religious heritage. I wanted to address those areas more directly and if possible in a way that would reach a wider Mennonite audience than I had so far. I decided to try working in prose, with real people and incidents from the lives of my paternal great-grandparents and their ancestors.

I could say many things about this project, but one or two points seem most relevant here. First, as I wrote I had a strong sense of two distinct readers, one seeming to look over each shoulder. One could be represented by my father, an intelligent but not literary man, a lifelong Mennonite farmer whose interest in the project was keen but hardly objective. The other could be my dissertation advisor, a slightly younger man, sympathetic but worldly, a sophisticated reader, also keenly interested but for very different reasons and with different standards.

At many points I despaired of ever finding a prose style, a way of telling the stories, that would please both readers. *I don't quite get that*, my father's voice would say in one ear, and a moment later my adviser's voice would say *My, that's a simple-minded sentence. These people were that good?* my adviser would mutter, and then my father would say, *Well, surely Grandpa wouldn't have said* that. In many ways it was the hardest writing I have ever done. It might have been paralyzing, and sometimes it very nearly was. Yet after struggling for years to satisfy both of them, I believe that having both of those readers looking over my shoulders was absolutely essential to finishing the book.

In a recent letter, poet Shari Wagner uses almost the same image: "I feel that I'm writing for two audiences, really—those rather sophisticated readers who buy literary magazines and then others who rarely read poetry, including my own extended family. Although she died more than a decade ago, Grandma Mishler is still one of my critics and she decides which of my poems she will tape to her refrigerator (if there are refrigerators in heaven)."

In thinking through these issues I have been helped by the recent work of Julia Kasdorf, whose poems about the tensions between her Amish/Mennonite heritage and her urban life have been widely celebrated. Kasdorf has thought long and hard about her own relation to her community, and in her dissertation proposal she offers this provocative definition:

> A work of Mennonite literature renders (often in its absence, from memory) the exterior boundaries of the community as they are marked by language, dress, custom, history, family relationship and other outward signs, as well as the inward boundaries as known through dialogue with collective memory and belief. The author gives form or *embodies* the communal body, makes it real, concrete, and present to itself by tracing its boundaries and its situation in relation to the larger world." (28)

Kasdorf compares her situation as Mennonite poet to Patricia Hill Collins' description of African-American intellectuals who "manage to inhabit both contexts but do so critically, using their outsider-within perspectives as a source of insights and ideas" (29). If poets and other artists must find some distance from their original communities in order to create, then, they may well remain very closely connected in some ways even while distanced in others. To render those exterior and interior boundaries, Kasdorf implies, one must have trespassed them to some degree. In a letter, she writes of the ways such boundaries can be internalized:

> When I was growing up, I think my mom and I believed we knew what the community demanded, clear and simple. . . . My family was so close to the Ordnung *in their heads*[,] which was the trouble, because there was no visible bishop to enforce it. There are many crazy stories to illustrate this, like the fact that when my mom finally cut her hair in her early 30s, she had the hair made

into a bun which she pinned on her head every time we visited
Big Valley. . . ." (emphasis hers)

As Yeats insisted, "We make out of the quarrel with others, rhetoric,
but of the quarrel with ourselves, poetry." The quarrel with ourselves—
again, "selves" is the slippery term—is the source of most worthy Mennonite poetry and probably of most worthy art. Yet as Kasdorf makes
clear, that quarrel is typically part of a larger sense of marginality, of simultaneous distance from and attachment to community. Such marginality is often personally uncomfortable, but it is also very often a stimu-
lating and productive state for the creation of art. Out of the wrestling
with the tradition, with the self, with God, comes the sort of art that
strikes us as authentic. It is work in which the outcome is not predetermined, and in which the stakes often seem to be very high, even in a
poem on a very minor subject. My friend and mentor Nick Lindsay used
to quote Robert Frost on this subject: "It's not serious," Frost liked to
say. "It's just a matter of life and death."

HISTORY, PERSONAL AND OTHERWISE

The first waves of Mennonites to enter higher education held onto
a great deal of the old utilitarianism even while they were breaking with
the traditional distrust of too much book learning. Especially in the
Swiss tradition, I think, this was so. Where is there space for imaginative
writing within the confines of Harold Bender's Anabaptist Vision? Fo-
cused on discipleship, nonresistance, and community, Bender provided
a restatement of Anabaptist themes which was orthodox enough to
make it possible for Mennonite historians, theologians, and educational
institutions to resist the onslaught of repressive Mennonite fundamen-
talism in the middle of the twentieth century. Yet the very clarity and
concreteness of his version of "the" Anabaptist vision reinforced the
long-standing Mennonite insistence that individual action and expression must be answerable to community doctrine and practice.

It has become a truism that much in traditional Mennonite—and
Christian and western—doctrine and practice has tended to stifle and
silence women. But in many Mennonite communities much potential
expression by both men and women was restricted and silenced, especially if it might threaten the community. Men were free to become pastors and teachers, if they kept what they said within acceptable bounds.

But both male and female Swiss Mennonites, in particular, have been discouraged from the kind of unrestrained exploration of their own consciousness and of the aesthetic world that leads to full-fledged artistic creation. Until quite recently there was very little significant poetry or fiction being written by Swiss Mennonites in the U.S., and very little by the Russian Mennonites of the 1870's migration who settled in the Great Plains.

There is no space here to look more closely into all of the reasons for that dearth or its gradual end. In the late 1960s some Mennonites, most notably Elmer Suderman, began to pay more attention to poetry and fiction; at about this time Nicholas Lindsay became the first poet-in-residence at Goshen College. But it seems clear that the drought truly began to break in the 1970s, when a few Mennonites, including Keith Ratzlaff, Jean Janzen and me, began graduate study in creative writing at secular universities.

We should not underestimate the importance of the systematic and sustained study of the craft of writing poetry that such programs allow. As with any complicated and demanding human endeavor, it is hard—though not impossible—to educate oneself to be a poet. Just like the best Mennonite chemists, historians and theologians, the most successful American Mennonite poets have advanced degrees from well-established graduate programs. These programs also provide sustained contact with serious poets of all varieties of religious and other convictions, without which Mennonite poetry would probably have remained provincial and amateurish. Going to graduate school makes it much more difficult to believe that Mennonites are *central*, in the way it is possible to believe that while living in Goshen or Harrisonburg or Lancaster County.

Perhaps the most remarkable aspect of the current situation among American Mennonite poets is their geographical scattering. Jean Janzen lives in Fresno, Elmer Suderman in Minnesota, Leonard Neufeldt in Indiana, Keith Ratzlaff in Iowa, Julia Kasdorf in Pennsylvania after many years in Brooklyn. Just as Mennonites are thinly spread across a very large country, poets are even more thinly scattered. Something of a network among American Mennonite poets does exist, especially in the last few years, but contacts are made and maintained largely through the mail, meetings at conferences, and in magazines like *Mennonite Life* and the much-missed *Mennonot*. I have been known to theorize that poets are somewhat like cougars or other large predators, requiring a vast number of "ordinary" people (prey, in this uncomfortably violent analogy) to support each one. There is nothing like an American Winnipeg, with tens of thousands of Mennonite in a large urban setting with high visibility, major representation at the universities, and relatively easy access to respected literary publishers.[26]

The Mennonite colleges all support Mennonite writers and artists, and in general institutional support seems to be increasing somewhat. The English departments at all of these schools, I believe, genuinely work at encouraging creative writing by their students, and all devote resources to visiting writers and student publications. Goshen College's long-running PinchPenny Press accounts for over half of the books of poetry listed in the *Mennonite Encyclopedia* bibliography, including first books by a number of writers who are still active, among them Julia Kasdorf, Don Yost, Barbara Esch Shisler, Lauren Friesen, Shari Wagner, and me. Its Broadside series provides visibility to poets and poetry on campus, mingling work by the famous and semi-famous with that of students.

Other Mennonite colleges have less active publication programs, but most have a student literary magazine of some sort, and offer some classes in creative writing. Jean Janzen taught part-time at Fresno Pacific and Eastern Mennonite University, Raylene Hinz-Penner and others have been offering creative writing courses at Bethel since at least the 1970s, and Bluffton offers courses in poetry and fiction writing (and, as of fall 2003, the first writing major at a Mennonite college).[27] All of these colleges also bring visiting writers to their campuses with some regularity.

On the other hand, it is only fair to recognize the limits of even the most active of these programs. PinchPenny Press produces only chapbooks with limited runs and almost no distribution outside of Goshen. The presiding poet at Goshen for twenty years was Nicholas Lindsay, a great man, a fine poet, and a marvelous teacher, but beginning in the mid-1970s he has spent only a few weeks per year or less on campus. Even the famous Mennonite frugality has had its own costs. Just after World War II Bethel College could have hired William Stafford, a CO and lifelong pacifist with Brethren roots. But the Bethel salary offer was half that of Lewis and Clark College, where Stafford taught for the next forty years and became one of the most beloved and respected American poets of the last half-century.

It is only realistic, I think, to say that poetry and creative writing in these places remain, as they are in American society in general, somewhat marginal endeavors. It has also been true, though it may be changing, that budding writers at Mennonite colleges have had few Mennonite examples to follow and very little curricular exposure to Mennonite writers. Only in the last few years have American Mennonite writers achieved enough status that the colleges have begun to invite them for readings and lectures. Ervin Beck at Goshen recently taught what is evidently the first course in Mennonite literature to be offered at a Mennonite college in the U.S., though Anna Juhnke began a similar course at Elizabethtown College a few months earlier. After years of planning, Goshen College hosted a conference on "Mennonite/s Writing in the U. S." in October 1997 and a second, international conference co-sponsored by Conrad Grebel College in October 2002—clear signs that the American Mennonite literary scene is approaching maturity.

The magazine and book publishing scene is likewise a mixed one. *Festival Quarterly* published a few poems (almost all with explicit ethnic Mennonite markers) each year. Until their demise, *Gospel Herald* and *Christian Living* published some poetry, most of it quite conventional, and *The Mennonite* continues to publish poems and occasional reviews. Among the more adventurous magazines has been *Mennonite Life*, where Raylene Hinz Penner has begun to edit a yearly arts issue with generous spreads by several poets or writers, often accompanied by reflective statements or short essays. Even more unfettered was *Mennonot*, the self-described magazine for "Mennos on the margins" published from 1993 to 2001 by Sheri Hostetler and Steve Mullet, which released a range of poems in every issue, as well as interviews with and essays by poets. An emerging outlet for poetry and other imaginative works at the book level is DreamSeeker Books (an imprint of Cascadia Publishing House) and at the magazine level *Dreamseeker Magazine*, edited by Michael A. King and published in a print edition as well as online (see www.CascadiaPublishingHouse.com/dsm).

The denominational publishing houses have done little with poetry. Faith and Life published *Born Giving Birth* (1991), a pleasant but rather tame anthology of poems by Mennonite women. Herald Press published Barbara Keener Shenk's luxuriously produced coffee-table style book of sonnets about women of the Bible, *The God of Sarah, Rebekah, and Rachel*, in 1985. The privately owned Good Books published *Three Men-*

nonite Poets, with poems by David Waltner-Toews, Yorifumi Yaguchi, and Jean Janzen, in 1986, then no more poetry until Jean Janzen's *Snake in the Parsonage* in 1995. As noted earlier, Cascadia Publishing House has moved rapidly into publishing poetry by Mennonite writers.

Still, the ongoing shortage of publishing opportunities within church-related circles has meant that serious poets must look for outlets outside the church, where magazine publication is not unduly difficult but the competition for book publication is almost surrealistically intense. Publishing a PinchPenny book at Goshen is relatively easy, but in the outside world any press that actually publicizes and distributes books of poetry is inundated with manuscripts. Julia Kasdorf's book *Sleeping Preacher* was chosen for the Pitt Poetry Series from over 900 first-book manuscripts; my second book was one of four chosen by Cleveland State out of 911 submissions to its yearly contest. Keith Ratzlaff's *Man Under a Pear Tree* was a finalist in no less than five national contests before being chosen as the winner of the 1996 Anhinga Prize competition. Jean Janzen's *Snake in the Parsonage* was accepted for publication only after she won a fellowship from the National Endowment for the Arts; just over two percent of the applications were successful.

"Humility" takes on very strange and complicated overtones under such conditions. All but the most talented and/or persistent writers tend either to fall silent under the pressures of the marketplace, to resign themselves to writing for less-than-sophisticated audiences, or to accumulate more and more unpublished work. Writers who have managed to persevere and to publish under such conditions deserve our attention, and it is to them that we will now turn.

Representative Poets

The structure of this section is very loosely chronological, moving from poets who have been publishing for a relatively long time toward those still emerging. It begins with three pairs of poets: Elmer Suderman and Dallas Wiebe, two elder statesmen with roots in Kansas; Jean Janzen and Leonard Neufeldt, both Mennonite Brethren and immigrants from Canada; Keith Ratzlaff and me, midwesterners and products of the 1960s. With Julia Kasdorf even these loose pairings break down. The writers who follow are mainly women and still emerging, but to impose any scheme on them would be mainly an arbitrary academic exercise.[28]

I have also resisted the impulse to fit these writers into some large thematic scheme. While I will note some of the plentiful connections and contrasts among them, their work seems to me too various and, in many cases, still too much under development to justify making any such scheme into a controlling metaphor. In these thumbnail sketches, brief and inadequate as they are, I have deliberately chosen to generalize briefly about the poets' work and to give at least one extended sample of that work; to quote any less seemed to me to claim too much authority as critic and interpreter. I hope that readers will seek out that work, and that others will undertake more detailed analysis and criticism than I can provide here.

Elmer Suderman

Elmer Suderman's essays and poems have been part of the Mennonite scene for years, as well as appearing in a wide range of other magazines and journals. Like a number of other Mennonite intellectuals, Suderman has remained in touch with Mennonites through his work and personal contacts while living and working largely "outside"; he taught for most of his career at a Lutheran college (Gustavus Adolphus) and served as a Methodist lay preacher. His poems, many of them published in *Mennonite Life*, tend toward the nostalgic, but are tempered by their clarity and a certain gruffness. Here he writes of his father's claiming land in the Oklahoma land rush:

> That night, Father found the north star.
> The creek was his, drought-dry, but later, when
> it rained, not often, providing badly needed water.
> . . . .
>
> Unsettled, he looked to the north star
> for something to hold on to.
> That was a long and lonely night. ("Father . . . ," 9-10)

Suderman's approach to standard Mennonite issues such as generational tensions and higher education tends to be genial, self-deprecating, and not too anxious, as in these stanzas from "My Mother and a Ph.D.":

> My mother came to see me once
> when I was working on my Ph. D.
> She did not understand why.

"It won't help you plow the land
your father homesteaded.
It won't help you heal the sick.
It will make you sick in the head."
. . . .
She worried about the two-room
upstairs apartment in which we lived.
"Too small," she said.
"Too many houses here and
too close together. Where do you
plant potatoes?"

She was glad that they at least had had
enough sense to build the university
on a hill. "You couldn't raise wheat or corn
or alfalfa either on that sand.
Too steep to plow."
She was right about that.

Dallas Wiebe

Dallas Wiebe's main work has been in prose; his youthful novel *Sky-blue the Badass*, a semi-autographical *Bildungsroman* written in an experimental 1960s prose style, deals memorably if caustically with his Kansas boyhood and subsequent flight from the Mennonite community into graduate school and an academic career. In his long writing career he has produced several fine collections of short stories and an impressive novel, *Our Asian Journey*, about the trek to central Asia in the 1880s by Russian Mennonites who believed the Second Coming was imminent. Although he has always resisted being identified as a "Mennonite writer," he does acknowledge that "In retrospect, I now see how much of [my] writing has some religious reference in it. Many of the ideas in my writing are 'Mennonite' ideas. Certainly many of the attitudes are. 'Gelassenheit' is everywhere. Or is it just plain laziness?" ("Personal correspondence").

Wiebe's only published collection of poetry, *The Kansas Poems*, is a delightfully wry, sardonic group of "minimalist poems for a minimalist state," as he describes them. Many midwestern Mennonites will resonate with their ambivalent attitude toward the prairies and the prairie way of life. Nearly sixty tiny poems, each titled "Tornado," run at the bottom of each page: "The baby was here / The last time / I looked," reads one, "I hope it hits the church. / I'm tired of sermons" is another. The poems at the top of each page are nearly as brief and pithy; "Elegy VII," with its finely balanced feelings, is typical:

> All that hate and envy.
> All that rage and sorrow.
> All that praying and singing.
> God,
>   it was wonderful. (59)

Leonard Neufeldt

Leonard Neufeldt and Jean Janzen both emerged from the Russian/Mennonite Brethren stream that has generated so much "vivid, disturbing poetry" in recent years. Their own poems, however, have much less hostility toward that tradition than those of the best-known Canadian Mennonite poets. Much of the difference, I have come to understand, stems from their life histories. Leonard Neufeldt grew up largely in Yarrow, British Columbia, although he lived in Indiana and taught at Purdue University from 1978 until his recent retirement. His work makes clear that his childhood was mainly free of the rigid, patriarchal abuses of power that so trouble Di Brandt, Patrick Friesen, and others. Neufeldt's poem "The tree with a hole in our front yard" is a direct response to that anger, dedicated "For Di Brandt, and to those who were angry." The poem describes a flowering chestnut tree in the Mennonite Brethren town of Yarrow, British Columbia, its "roundness so dark and unconditional" it is unquestioned until a drunken cousin from Oregon tears down a branch, creating "holes gaping with disbelief." The tree does not die, though its healing leaves a new awareness of imperfection and doubt:

> Some of us stood in the emptiness
> long after it had healed over,
> trying to remember
> word for word what Father said,
> as if a child's wonder or a father's answer
> are magic. They are more like trees
> or the sky trying to heal itself. (*Yarrow* 35)

Neufeldt's work, as this poem suggests, tends toward a nuanced acceptance of his tradition and the world, although not without edginess and grief. His style tends toward a clear, vivid, mainly conventional free verse. *Yarrow* closes with the title poem, and its lyrical, elemental, nostalgic, almost sentimental language seems to me representative:

> *If not overcome by water,*
> *you will live among blue mountains*
> *and green trees. The fields start here,*
> *bending suddenly up*
> *from the water, like young boys at nightfall*
> *finding their clothes in the high grass,*
> *certain they hear voices calling.*
>
> Something to catch the sleeves
> of those who remember the path to tables
> by the stream—
> uncertain of their places
> and the words of the psalm others begin
> in four parts and a descant rising together
> like birds to fields beyond. (55)

It does not take long, sometimes, for places of exile to become homes remembered with this sort of longing, as those raised in them are in turn exiled to new places. Yarrow is for Neufeldt something like Chortitza for the Russian immigrants of the twenties, an idyllic, pastoral landscape to which he can return only as an uneasy visitor.

Jean Janzen

Jean Janzen, who grew up in Saskatchewan and the upper Midwest, has lived most of her adult life in Fresno, California. Like many contemporary women poets, she began writing in earnest only after raising a family, but since 1980, when she began taking poetry classes at Fresno State University, her work has progressed rapidly. She has studied with Philip Levine and other well-respected poets, published poems in leading poetry magazines, and recently received a large fellowship from the National Endowment for the Arts, one of the most prestigious honors for American poets. Yet of the Mennonite poets working today, she is probably also the most comfortable within the church. A number of her hymn texts, some of them derived from medieval female mystics such as Julian of Norwich, are included in the recent Mennonite *Hymnal: A Worship Book.*.

Janzen's most obviously Mennonite poems deal with her ancestors' European experience, especially in Russia. She has been able to return to meet surviving relatives, visit villages where her parents and grandparents lived, and hear family stories. Commenting on the writing of these poems in *Mennonite Life*, she reflects on their relation to her family history:

> This moon, usually full, seemed to insist on its presence in the Russian poems. Maybe it became an unconscious emblem, a representation of borrowed light, the way these poems are borrowed essentially from the told experience of my family. The naked truth is clothed with my protected life, the sun's searing light on the other side of the world. . . . My family's stories are always mine. I see by them. (18)

Like Neufeldt, Janzen tends to see her own life as "protected," fortunate in contrast to the suffering of relatives. Yet her poems, for all their gentleness, are driven by an emotional precision and honesty that can be startling. "Chicken Guts," from *Snake in the Parsonage*, begins with a fairly conventional memory, but takes an unexpected, nervy turn:

> After the sticky steam of plums
> and the fuzz of peaches, we caught chickens
> in the yard, stewing hens for canning.
> Dad with a hatchet on the old elm stump
> and I in the cellar scraping grit out of gizzards.
> All in a sort of ritual dance: the chop,
> the boiling body-dip for defeathering, the swing
> through the singe of fire. Then, disembowel, dismember.
> All for the grand finale behind glass—a chorus line
> of chicken legs caught in the kick, like a photo.
> This is not about death, or violence to animals,
> not even about sex. It's about those intestines
> I stripped into the bucket. About how they
> could have been saved, stretched across a hollow,
> and made to sing. It's about my cousin Eugene
> who plucks and saws the gut of his cello until
> something throbs in our own. And it's about dance,
> not the scratch and kick of the chicken's life,
> but the deep stomp that awakens the bottom
> of the lake, the dance I want to do among
> the festival of wild grass and flowers back

in my hometown. I want to lean low,
to paint my face with mulberry juice
and stay up all night. I want to put my ear
against the belly of the earth to hear
it rumble, to hear it sigh. (17)

Janzen's willingness to deal this forthrightly with disturbing images
and emotions is tempered by our sense that they remain on the level of
fantasy, that she is unlikely to have actually spent many sleepless nights
with her face painted purple. I do not say this as a criticism; surely one of
the prime functions of literature is to enable us to recognize and deal
with feelings and impulses that cannot or should not be acted upon. But
another strand of Janzen's work is the celebration of feelings, bodily and
emotional, and the mysteries and ecstasies of sexual love:

You Talk With Your Hands
You talk with your hands
           as if the shapes of the alphabet
                    need tracing, move each phrase

like a character on your stage of the air.
           But when you stroke my familiar body,
                you speak without sound,

your tactile sentences searching
           for a language lost—a labyrinth we enter
                together, again and again.

We come out clutching and gasping
           for breath, so close were we
                to the original word for union.

And then we lie exhausted, your hands
           motionless now, except for a caress, light
                as the air we divide when we wave
                    goodbye. (46)

Keith Ratzlaff
In Keith Ratzlaff's work what I see as Mennonite influence takes the
form of a pervasive concern with small towns, isolation, smallness, dry-

ness; his poems face the set-apart quality of their landscapes without self-pity, but with a combination of will and whimsy that is all his own. Having grown up in Henderson, Nebraska, and lived for many years in small-town Iowa, Ratzlaff is thoroughly steeped in the spaces of the upper Midwest. His work is seldom overtly Mennonite, though often subtly religious; it is less hostile to the tradition than (I would say) somehow removed from it. There seems to be more weariness than anger, more bemusement than pain.

In a rare prose statement in *Mennonite Life*, Ratzlaff offers a figure from his boyhood, a lonely town eccentric living in the old railroad station, as his image of the poet in the community; the key situation in many of his poems is a sort of interior exile. His John Nachtigall is simultaneously present and distanced, in the middle of communal life and estranged from it. "The basic connection between artist and community isn't reciprocal or commercial or utilitarian," Ratzlaff points out; "poets aren't plumbers (and thank heaven for it). At its core the relationship is wholistic and mystical, the kind of symbiosis you get between the shape of hills and the sky you see them against, or the inseparable bond in the way a curve bends a road" (23).

Many of Ratzlaff's best poems are too long to quote here, but "Mural From the Temple of Longing," from his *Man Under a Pear Tree*, shows the clarity and resonance of his style, and its situation is typical of much of his work:

> Today, for a while, I was given
> to such a ruckus of wishing:
>
> for the jay's bubblepipe
> to be all songs. For this wind
>
> to be the only wind
> in the only tree.
>
> But two people
> across the street
>
> have pulled a blind down
> together. Such gracefulness,
>
> the sun and moon living
> in the same room. And
> now leaves and their arrows,

the evening flares of longing and
now the jay

in the wind in the tree

is not what I want. (39)

Ratzlaff's wariness about the Mennonite academic community (he graduated from Bethel College) emerges wonderfully from "Lies to Tell a Presidential Search Committee," which was triggered by an actual invitation to apply for the Bethel presidency. These sections must represent the whole:

> I have had a good trip.
> I am willing.
> I am able to effect change in a consultative environment.
> I have looked out the window into the expressions of trees
> . . . .
> I once had a cat you could walk to town on a leash.
> Once as a child I thought I saw Jesus waving to me from the
>   second story window of my church.
> I go to church.
> Once I made a large donation to this college.
> I think developing new constituencies would be fun.
> I can dress well.
>   killed a nest of rabbits with the flat side of a scoop.
> Once I thought a car's headlights were God come to find me on a
>   gravel road. The car in the layby. The girl.
> Balancing the budget would be my top priority.
> I have never voted for a successful presidential candidate.
> My vision is not too bad.
> I am coming to the point. (14)

The abrupt shifts of diction and subject here seem, at first, merely (although very) funny. As the poem continues, though, its treatment of the incongruities and suppressions of modern presentations of self—particularly, but not just, Mennonite and academic ones—deepens and turns quite serious. What is the "real" self? The well-dressed one that shows up for the interview? The one with all the right phrases about "consultative environments"? The one who remembers killing rabbits with a scoop and parking with a girl? And at what cost do we habitually suppress some of these selves in favor of others? Ratzlaff's determination to face such issues fully, if not exactly squarely, gives the poem its edge. With its nervy, precarious balances and unexpected range, his work deserves to be better known.

Jeff Gundy

Having made one extended effort to analyze my own work in print (see "Separation") I have no desire to charge at that moving target again. Here I offer only a poem, whose ambivalence I hope will be clear, and a few brief remarks.

How to Write the New Mennonite Poem

Choose two from old Bibles, humbly beautiful quilts,
Fraktur, and the *Martyr's Mirror* in Dutch.
Get the word "Mennonite" in at least
twice, once in the title, along with zwiebach,
vareniki, borscht, and the farm,
which if possible should be lost now.

Grandmothers are very good, especially
dead grandmothers, especially speaking
German in Russia. They should have
Suffered. Mothers are good and may
have Quirks, if lovable. Male ancestors
are possible but presumed to represent
the patriarchy and to have abused
"their" wives, children, farm animals;
steer clear unless you are Angry,
or can supply affidavits from
everybody who knew them.

It is important to acknowledge
the spiritual and reproductive
superiority of plain coats and
coverings, the marvelous integrity
of those uncorrupted by television
and Mennonite higher education.
Use quaintness, brisk common sense
and a dash of barnyard humor to show
that they are Just Folks Too.

Remember that while the only good Mennonite
is not a dead Mennonite, many dead
Mennonites were really good. Work in
two or three. Dirk Willems
is hot this year. Include a woman,
an African if you know any, and
a Methodist with redeeming qualities.

You, of course, are a backslidden,
overlearned, doubtridden, egodriven
quasibeliever who would be less anxious
and surer of salvation if you could
only manage to give up the car,
the CD player, and coaching soccer.
You really *want* to be like Grandma.
You believe in discipleship, granola,
and the Peace Tax Fund, but things are
Complicated. You think about them plenty.
You plan to give up something, soon.

If you're in a major city, which
you should be, say something about
the streets, how you really hate
the place but get all charged up
walking around on your days off
looking at stuff and drinking
exotic coffee. Mention that this
seems strange to you, as does
the fact that sometimes you like sex,
even when you know the people in
the next apartment can hear.
Put your wedding ring in the poem
to reassure your parents.

Use the laser printer, and send
a large, glossy, black and white
photograph, just in case. Wear
something simple and dark. Smile
but not too hard. Let your eyes

reflect the miles you have come,
the centuries, your gratitude, your guilt. (*Greatest Hits* 17-18)

I wrote this poem sometime in 1993, thinking of it mainly as a sort of joke. As somebody remarked recently in Sunday School, having written a poem like this one eliminates whole categories of others I might once have written—though of course other poets can, and will, happily continue. Except for this poem, almost everything I have written on explicitly Mennonite subjects has been in prose.

Julia Kasdorf

Julia Kasdorf's rather sudden emergence, with *Sleeping Preacher*, as one of the most prominent Mennonite poets seems in many ways to spring directly from her ambivalent, semi-nostalgic, semi-acerbic treatment of the kind of situation I have just described. At the book's center are the ironies and strangeness of her life as a modern, urban American woman only two generations removed from the Amish life of Big Valley, Pennsylvania. In the opening poem, "Green Market, New York," she encounters an Amish woman selling pies at an outdoor market, and discovers they share that heritage:

> "Towns you wouldn't know,
> around Mifflinburg, around Belleville."
> And I tell her I was born there.
> "Now who would your grandparents be?"
> "Thomas and Vesta Peachey."
> "Well, I was a Peachey," she says,
> and she grins like she sees the whole farm
> in my face . . .
> . . . .
> "Do you live in the city?" she asks, "do you like it?"
> I say no. And that was no lie, Emma Peachey.
> I don't like New York, but sometimes these streets
> hold me as hard as we're held by rich earth.
> I have not forgotten that Bible verse:
> Whoever puts his hand to the plow and looks back
> is not fit for the kingdom of God. (3)

Poems like this one have a plainness of style and syntax that Kasdorf's Amish ancestors might have appreciated. Yet below the plain style lie a whole tangled nest of ironies and complexities. Even Emma

Peachey has left the valley, after all, and made her own accommodation with changing times. Is it only a matter of degree, then? What does it mean to remain true to a heritage, to a self? Even the biblical advice Kasdorf recalls is ambiguous. The verse seems to support her move to the city, to warn against nostalgia, even while much of the poem bemoans the urban life and desk job she has found. Even as she invokes the verse, of course, she is "looking back," unwilling to forget. Is she then unfit for the kingdom after all?

In its plain way this poem confronts the postmodern world of indeterminacy and undecidability, places it not only in the streets but right there on the table with Emma Peachey's pie. And of course texts, and selves, that threaten to shake themselves to pieces with their internal contradictions are not exactly new. After all, Jesus insists that we need to be as children, and Paul says just as firmly that we need to put away childish things.

But *Sleeping Preacher* has even more immediate concerns. Consider, for example, the social implications beneath the seeming matter-of-factness of "When Our Women Go Crazy":

> When our women go crazy, they're scared there won't be
> enough meat in the house. They keep asking
> but how will we eat? Who will cook? Will there be enough?
> Mother to daughter, it's always the same
> questions. The sisters and aunts recognize symptoms:
> > she thinks there's no food, same as Mommy
> > before they sent her away to that place,
> > and she thinks if she goes, the men will eat
> > whatever they find right out of the saucepans.
> When our women are sane, they can tomatoes
> and simmer big pots of soup for the freezer.
> They are satisfied arranging spice tins
> on cupboard shelves lined with clean paper.
> They save all the leftovers under tight lids
> and only throw them away when they're rotten.
> Their refrigerators are always immaculate and full,
> which is also the case when our women are crazy. (7)

The tracing of neurosis caused by sexism and rigid gender roles here is painfully sharp, as is the women's seeming complicity with their own oppression. Yet while the social criticism here is clear, it is also understated; Kasdorf's first impulse is often toward charity, understanding, especially toward people who become victims of communal repression or cause hurt to others through unthinking acceptance of community values. The title poem treats her great grandmother, who when inspired by a traveling preacher burns all of her photographs in the cookstove, with typical gentleness: "She did not think of us, / only to save us, leaving nothing / for us to touch or see / except this stubborn will to believe" (6).

A representative recent poem, "Sixth Anniversary," turns away from explicitly Mennonite subjects, toward concerns that are perhaps more "worldly":

> What separates us from the cats
> yowling like famished newborns
> behind our old house is
> we can choose how we'll act,
> though there's no controlling
> how the bump of a near-stranger's
> elbow could light up my back
> in a room of dull cocktail chatter.
> Six years into this marriage,
> I admit that some summer nights
> I long for an air conditioner—
> anything to drown out those cats—
> I am that jealous of their
> groaning under our window,
> which seems to be the voice
> of that old, insufferable itch
> we scratched until we were raw,
> then emerged, groggy, to prowl
> the streets for dinner,
> a smarting between our legs.
>
> By now, my body must feel as familiar
> as the gold hills outside Fresno
> scattered with tufts of scrub oak,
> where for hours each day you rode
> a racing bike, its light frame
> fused with your own. You knew
> each hole and bump in the road,
> each place your weight shifted,

and pedaling up into the Sierras
you once lifted above your body,
hung there, watching your thighs
pump with each rasp of breath,
as sometimes making love, I see us,
gripped by our slow heaving,
and wonder what form of animal
we finally are, who crave
both safety and hunger. (*Eve's Striptease* 31)

Raylene Hinz-Penner

Kasdorf is not alone as a Mennonite woman whose poems explore issues related to women's identity, bodies, and sexuality. One of the most energetic emerging voices belongs to Raylene Hinz-Penner, who recently completed an M.F.A. in creative writing at Wichita State University. Her master's thesis, a collection of poems entitled "Betrayals of the Body," deals with betrayals, and bodies, of several kinds. Most centrally, it presents a woman refusing to accept the conventions and order generated by any body without careful scrutiny. "Rich Hill" describes a new colony of Old Order Mennonites and their spokesman who insists that people need to keep to "Simple things [that] keep the circle small." The speaker reacts strongly, almost violently, remembering slipping out to cars after the services of her youth:

> Moments like these can never contain my regret.
> I hate the circle and I hate the unbound thread.
>
> Sunday nights we gathered in an old white wooden church,
> *Friedensfeld, peaceful field* on an Oklahoma prairie, a huddle
> of believers singing in harmony. In the quiet of the night
>
> the hymn strains dissolved, our longing withering to whispers,
> and afterward we stayed, lingering in the darkness, lonely
> and afraid to make our way toward the sinister lights. (63)

Here the "sinister lights" are an ambiguous image: I think we are meant to connect them with the orthodox but somehow suspect spirituality of the church, and see its inadequacy to deal with the longing that leads the speaker out into the darkness. Numerous other moments in the collection deal with dangerous, even suicidal urges and impulses barely held back:

> I fear that one day I too
> will voice a curse in church,
> sitting in a third-row pew,
> or . . . suddenly throw myself
> from a high bridge
> into the long fall. (80)

The real yearning in Hinz-Penner's poems, however, is not for death but for a renewed, revived life. The final poem in *Betrayals* imagines the end of the world not as a conventional rapture, but as a calling by geese:

> Give us a cool blue dawn, awakened
> by a moon too bright to bear
> and the float of heavy bodies
> as they take the air, primordial
> guides true to some sensual knowledge. (86)

Sheri Hostetler

Sheri Hostetler is best known as the editor (with Steve Mullet) of *Mennonot*. Like Kasdorf, she has moved from a rural childhood to adult life in a big city—in her case from eastern Holmes County, Ohio to the Bay Area. Hostetler's poems are brisk and lively, with their own keen awareness of the tensions between traditions and contemporary life. In "Baptism" she wryly recalls one rite of passage:

> We dribbled in our church except
> one year when the new pastor
> held our baptisms down at the
> Doughty Valley Creek. Into the
> creamy brown waters, Pastor Harold
> dunked the heads of the almost and nearly
> pure, up to their waists in muddy water,
> legs planted firm in river silt,
> backs arched, necks stretched like
> saplings bending to the wind, like
> chickens at the chopping block.
>
> I got baptized the right way, up front
> during church one Sunday with four boys.

I had to wear a head covering, the only day
I ever did, humiliation burning a
ring where the edge of the white net
covering sat on my skull, humiliation
at being a woman and needing, thus,
to have my head covered, humiliation
at being so plain when I knew already
in my heart I was Greta Garbo sophisticated
city scorn for pathetic plain rituals. Maybe
this is why I have the desire to cut
my hair shorter and shorter. I wore the head
covering only once, it burned a ring
on my skull. Even now, 16 years later,
I will shear away my natural covering.

Along with the urge for change and discomfort with patriarchal traditions, this poem also registers certain complexities. There is no single,
permanent tradition, for one thing: a new pastor may come in and start
dunking at any time. The desire for short hair, and the urge to "shear
away my natural covering" at the end, is a reaction against being forced
to wear the covering, if only for a day. But the word "natural" in the last
line suggests a certain lack of ease with that reaction, an awareness that
while we can perhaps choose among cultures and influences, we cannot
escape them.

Juanita Brunk

Juanita Brunk has a good Mennonite name—so good that, someone suggested to me, it is not surprising that she should feel a need to
keep her distance from the Mennonite world. Like Julia Kasdorf, she has
migrated to New York, and published a number of poems in high-profile magazines. The quality of her work will be readily apparent, I think,
from even a brief sample, such as "My Father's Tongue":

My father could not say the words.
They were heavy as bricks of lumber;
they took the shape of stairways, scaffolding,
buckets of stucco or concrete.
They multiplied,
became buildings with rooms and puttied windows,
walls braced and sheathed to hold in heat

or hold a whisper out, doors
that could be slammed.
They were the clothing strangers left
in a ditch, reeking and stiff, crusty trousers
that he found and carried home in cardboard boxes,
rank woolen jackets waterlogged
with mud and soot,
heavy coats that shrank
in the washer and shed chunks
of gritty lining in our clean socks and underwear.
They were the neighbor's discarded appliances
salvaged on trash day and piled up
in our basement to be fixed:
hair dryers with melted innards, doll carriages
without wheels, lamps with frazzled cords
and dangling necks.
The things my father couldn't tell us
were cars that stuttered and broke down
by the side of the road,
nothing to do but stop
and see if you can make it right,
his hands with wrench or crowbar or hammer
battered from trying to make us hear,
one thumbnail always bruised
or growing back. (28)

This poem proceeds by piling up details while all the while insisting it is about something else: not about the father's work, the clothes and junk he brought home, his perpetually scarred hands, but about all of those things as both substitutes for and images of the words he cannot say. The poem itself, in a strange way, both evokes and participates in the tongue-tied state it ascribes to the father: seemingly fluent, it is at the same time massively reserved, giving away only the most indirect glimpses of the troubled family dynamics it circles. It is a complaint that becomes, perhaps, a complaint about its own inability to speak more plainly, to make anything come clear besides bruises. The muted discontents of this poem resonate with the general concern of many Mennonite (and other) women for resisting and changing patriarchal familial and social structures, without much overt expression of anger.

Sharon Fransen

Of the many poems and other writings by Mennonite women in the performance piece "Quietly Landed?"—which premiered at the 1995 Millersville conference on Anabaptist women's history—Sharon Fransen's "In the meadow yellow with dandelions and croaking with crickets" exemplifies a celebratory dimension often undervalued or dismissed as mere nostalgia:

> I want to spread out an old, worn quilt.
> The pink one with scraps of Grandmother's
> printed blue work dress, the one she wore
> while snipping chicks' beaks at the Hatchery.
> Red squares of Grandpa's plaid flannel shirt
> wrapped tight around baby lambs born late in the night.
> And forming the center of each log cabin
> snippets of Mother's pink Easter dress
> cut up long after the hem was let out the last time.
> I want to spread out the quilt that has been folded
> and hugged so long the fraying edges reveal
> the dirty cotton innards bunched together
> like kin for a family photo.
>
> I want to spread out my history
> and my mother's history and her mother's history,
> wrap my arms around the earth,
> cover it with this quilted life
> of newborn daughters, whooping cough, dying fathers,
> and all church picnics on Sunday afternoons in May.
> As I lie alone in the tall grass,
> the stars will beckon like a full pin cushion
> before a quilting.

In this poem, the history of women becomes a quilt, a warming and comforting presence that surrounds and consoles. The details are selected carefully and arranged artfully, like scraps for a quilt, to create a pleasing aesthetic effect. This benign vision of Fransen's personal history may seem a little easy; even whooping cough and dying fathers seem strangely comforting as she presents them, nearly as pleasant as church picnics. Yet somehow I want to believe the poem does treat her own experience, at least, authentically, remembering William Stafford's warning: "I am *most unready* to be hustled by those people around me who say that suffering is more authentic than love" (*Writing* 132).

Eric Rensberger

Eric Rensberger's poems, while not by any means always angry, also know what it is to contend with a tradition. Raised near Goshen, Rensberger has degrees in English and counseling, and works as a mental health counselor in southern Indiana. His work is various in theme, but often deals with Mennonite concerns, as is evident in "Contention Against Shunning":

> I rage with you, Menno Simons
> for the cruelty of your shunning:
> to set table at a distance from hunger
> to pull flesh from flesh
> to deny the kiss of peace
> *and* the kiss of the whole mouth
>
> From the mystery of your hiding
> you come at me implacable
> against all sense parting
> me from the world
> thrusting my pallor from you
> as though chilled
>
> "Body dismissing a member":
> you would cut me off as if
> a man should put his belly from him
> say no more will I fill you
> I will live on the fat of my pleadings
> and mouth the names of my food
>
> I warn you, such a man dies raving
> of lack at butchering time; having
> no substance wherewith to get,
> begs not to give offense
> by the compulsion he names as
> necessity's, not his own

> Menno
> corpulent man with twisted face
> I will settle this with you
> I will throw myself on you
> and wrestle you to earth with embraces (108-09)

Rensberger's Menno, fat and self-righteous and cruel, is one more image of the bad father, the overcontrolling patriarch, who haunts so much recent Mennonite history and literature. Here we are, after all these years, still wrestling. Some of us, myself included, would have to say this father is not the one we know. But who can say he does not exist?

Shari Wagner

I considered ending with that image of struggle, but it seemed too extreme to be altogether representative. Instead let us look briefly at the work of Shari Wagner, who writes (in terms familiar to those who have followed this far), "I guess there is inevitably a tension between the artist and the community regardless of the particular community. So I have a Mennonite identity but rather cautiously so . . ." (personal letter, 11/15/95). Her poems show the clarity and unaffected tone such a sense of dual audience might create. Some of her best poems manage to include the Mennonite world and the larger human one as well.

In "A Cappella," she imagines her ancestors singing in Amish barns and sixteenth-century dungeons, and feels a sense of connection across time and generations that is both intimate and sustaining:

> All of the old ones
>
> are here in the dark
> room of a house that
> stood where corn grew
>
> because God sent
> the sun. We end with
> "Praise God From Whom
>
> All Blessings Flow"—
> the version with echoing
> alleluias and amens.

We don't need the book
and no one sets the pitch.
We've sung this one

at every marriage
and funeral. Even in-laws
with eyes on the last

five minutes of a game
join in from their corner.
From every direction

there are voices within
voices, husks beneath
husks. The dead sing

in a house so haunted
we breathe
the same breath.

Coda

How to conclude an opus like this one, already too long? There are many more threads I would like to have followed, many ideas and people I wish I had paid more and better attention to. I hope others will write more thoroughly and closely about individual poets, delve deeper into the range of concerns that Mennonite poets are engaging, investigate the sociological relations between their work and the complex developments of the moment in the wider church, particularly the ongoing contention between what I suppose I must call conservative and progressive forces. I hope someone will investigate why for every serious male Mennonite poet there seem to be two or three equally accomplished women.

I see plenty of vivid, provocative, compelling writing being done by American poets with some sort of Mennonite connection. As a poet and a reader in love with poetry, I can't help but think that is good. As a mainly convicted birthright Mennonite who wants the best for my tradition but am often conflicted as to what "the best" is, I believe we will benefit from listening to our poets. I doubt that they will save us, but—as the next chapter will explain—I believe they can make us a little less lost.

CHAPTER SIX

IN PRAISE OF THE LURKERS (WHO COME OUT TO SPEAK)

From Joseph Joder to Julia Kasdorf, to be a writer among Mennonites has been a strange calling. We have little practice at how to treat them, and Mennonite writers have struggled to know what to do with Mennonites as well. I suppose little of this should surprise us. After all, many—perhaps most—writers and artists have always had some kind of borderline position in their communities. Borrowing a term from the new internet lexicon, we might call them "lurkers." Like Walt Whitman and Emily Dickinson, those prototypical lurkers, Mennonite writers are in their world—and often their religious community—but not quite of it. Controversial or beloved, tolerated or ignored, they are bound to be at least partly "other." We might, then, take that marginality as a given and explore some of what it means, for writers and for the community.

I want to look briefly at the social functions of lurkers, at their role as inner and outer travelers and the news they bring, at their relation to what I will call, loosely, "truth" and "imagination," and finally at the strangely linked topics of angels and laughter. I will briefly discuss some Mennonite writers and texts, but I will also examine some ways that writers from a much wider sphere have explored these issues. They are our concerns, but not only ours.

SOCIAL FUNCTIONS

During a recent reading of Plato's *The Republic*, I had the eerie feeling that I was overhearing two good, upstanding, traditional Mennonite men of a slightly earlier era—a preacher and a college president, say—discussing how to keep their institutions in order. Consider this part of the discussion between Glaucon and Socrates, who speaks first:

> "But if you receive the honeyed Muse [of poetry] in lyric or epic, be sure that pleasure and pain will be kings in your city, instead of law and whatever reasoned argument the community shall approve in each case to be best."
>
> "Very true," he said.
>
> "So much then," said I, "for our defense . . . we were justified before in banishing [poetry] from our city. For it was reason which led us on. And lest she condemn us as rather harsh and rough, let us tell her that there is an ancient feud between philosophy and poetry." Book X (407)

Plato refuses the poets entry because he knows they cannot be trusted to be reasonable, rational, and helpful. He accuses them, quite rightly, of saying things that are neither orthodox, nor strictly true, nor calculated to maintain the social order. The traditional Mennonite view of imaginative literature repeats Plato's caution: the most powerful poets must be kept out of the city, lest they lead the people astray with their wild, seductive images and stories. Only "the more austere and less pleasing poet and storyteller," who will limit his work to pious, edifying tales of the sort useful for the instruction of children, can be safely admitted (Book III, 196).

A long time later, Kierkegaard took up similar questions and came to similar conclusions about the utility and danger of poetry. In *The Concept of Irony* he argues—following Socrates—that poetry provides only an illusory sort of truth:

> Poetry opens up a higher actuality, expands and transfigures the imperfect into the perfect, and thereby softens and mitigates that deep pain which would darken and obscure all things. To this extent poetry is a kind of reconciliation, though not the true reconciliation. . . . Only the religious . . . is capable of effecting the true reconciliation, for it renders actuality infinite for me. (312)

As you might expect, I am not content to let either Plato or Kierkegaard have the last word. Poets have always sensed, and sometimes argued, that what they do has a social function, although one not easily defined or understood in purely rational or utilitarian terms. Here is what that prototypical lurker, poet and insurance executive Wallace Stevens had to say:

> What is [the poet's] function? Certainly it is not to lead people out of the confusion in which they find themselves. Nor is it, I think, to comfort them. . . . I think that his function is to make his imagination theirs and that he fulfills himself only as he sees his imagination become the light in the minds of others. His role, in short, is to help people live. (*The Necessary Angel*, 29)

With these rather contradictory claims in our heads, it is time to look at some real Mennonite lurkers. Of course, the purest lurkers never say anything; they are in deep cover, for reasons that range from shyness to schizophrenia to pure self-preservation. We should not need reminding these days about the human and Mennonite capacity to ostracize and persecute anyone we perceive as too different from ourselves. Despite the risks, of course, some lurkers do sneak out and speak; others, even in their silence, strike a chord in those around them.

One example of the latter is a man named John Nachtigall, whom Keith Ratzlaff remembers living in the middle of his home town of Henderson, Nebraska. In his essay "The Poet as John Nachtigall," Ratzlaff describes Nachtigall's lonely life in the old train depot, known to everyone but talking to nobody, spied on through the windows. Ratzlaff argues that Nachtigall, even in his silence, performed an important communal function:

> I've come to see John Nachtigall's role in my home town as a kind of allegory of the role of the poet in the larger world, as an answer to the question of whether art and artists matter. That Nachtigall lived in the very heart of town, not on the edge of it or on a farm by the river, forced us to think differently about ourselves. We had to include him because he lived with us and we had to account for what it meant to include him. We didn't have to like him or talk to him, but he made us think inclusively—as a community not a tribe. (23)

A lurker who *did* choose to speak, and was estranged although not quite shunned as a result, was the poet, farmer and part-time school-teacher Joseph Joder (not to be confused with another classic lurker, the J. W. Yoder who wrote *Rosanna of the Amish*). Joseph Joder's universalist beliefs and poems like "Die Frohe Botschaft" helped to trigger the Stuckey Amish schism in the 1870s in central Illinois. Well into his eighties, long after he had been excluded from communion for the dangerous idea that God loves all his children too much to torment any of them throughout eternity, Joder was still driving his buggy into the village of Carlock for the mail, stopping the children to quiz them on their German and exhort them to learn the old tongue, studying his Hebrew and Greek, hoping someday to get to the heart of the Scriptures. He was with his people, deeply engaged in their lives and their efforts to be faithful to their tradition, their God, and their destiny. Yet he was also set apart by his particular, unconventional, perhaps heretical vision.

TRAVELS, INNER AND OUTER

Joseph Joder became a lurker largely because he traveled—not physically, but intellectually—into places that his fellows were content to leave alone. This seems to me one of the most universal qualities of lurkers: they leave the valley, cross the mountains, they go on reckless physical or mental journeys and come back changed. Lurkers are always crossing cultural boundaries of one sort or another; what they return with, whether or not it has anything to do with poverty or oppression or salvation, may be powerful and even life-changing.

Lurkers find themselves outside the sanctioned channels, in the company of junkies and rock musicians and adulterers and homosexuals and assorted other Bad People. They encounter Rumi or Mirabai, Leonard Cohen or Sappho, Adrienne Rich or Allen Ginsberg or the Grateful Dead—I could name fifty other names, and we all could make our own lists—and realize that they will never again be able to live without ideas and images and words that originate in traditions and cultures wildly different from—and opposed to, in major ways—their home communities. They discover human beings who are not Mennonite or Christian or heterosexual or white or American but still seem smarter and clearer and deeper than just about anybody in Bluffton or Goshen or even Lancaster County.

It does not take much of this, if you are of the true lurker character, to destroy forever the idea that everything you will ever need is right there inside any one tidy enclave. And so lurkers live out their lives in more than one world, even if they live in places like Bluffton, Ohio; and Pella, Iowa; and Camp Hill, Pennsylvania. In those other worlds they find what Kenneth Burke called "equipment for living"—images and ideas that enable, or condemn, them to live in ways just a little, or a lot, out of the ordinary. They live in worlds of the head and the heart that make phrases like "keeping salvation ethical" or "the discipling community" or "official denominational position" sound bizarre and unreal, the way words do if you say them ten or twelve times in a row.

Lurkers come back from those other worlds the way children come back from the creek, with treasures that their parents are not sure should be in the house. Sometimes they come home in fact, sometimes in story, sometimes soon and sometimes late. Dallas Wiebe spent a good part of his life trying to get as far from his Kansas Mennonite roots as he could. In one of his *Kansas Poems* he puts it this way: "When I visit Kansas / I take the slow train out / and fly back" (34). Yet after writing one of the archetypal Mennonite kiss-it-goodbye novels, *Skyblue the Badass*, and spending many years teaching and working in Cincinnati (which might in a strange way be as much like a Mennonite city as one with only a handful of Mennonites can be), he wrote a wonderful novel about his Russian Mennonite roots. *Our Asian Journey* is both postmodernist and deeply traditional, and I think it is safe to say we would not have it if he had not spent that long period of lurking and traveling.

The central dynamic of Julia Kasdorf's *Sleeping Preacher* is the strain that develops out of her travels, physical and imaginative, between the two worlds of New York City and Big Valley, Pennsylvania. The book's first poem "Green Market, New York," describes a wonderful, strange, familiar moment when the speaker and an Amish woman who is also from Big Valley play the Mennonite game on a New York street. Her speaker knows that in some ways she can never go home again, but that in other ways, as the title of "I Carry Dead Vesta" suggests, she will always carry that ancestral home within her. And so, the poem suggests, lurkers may have their own interior lurkers, figures of memory and desire and imagination that haunt and tempt, obsess and infuriate and inspire them.

TRUTH AND IMAGINATION

I have lived for a long time under the institutional motto "The truth makes free." But I have also lived for a long time with the sense that "the truth" was much too complicated and messy to ever get my head around. William Stafford said part of it in a poem about teaching: "Well, Right has a long and intricate name / And the saying of it is a lonely thing." Wallace Stevens muses on the relation between truth and imagination in this passage:

> We have been a little insane about the truth. We have had an obsession. In its ultimate extension, the truth about which we have been insane will lead us to look beyond the truth to something in which the imagination will be the dominant complement. It is not only that the imagination adheres to reality, but, also, that reality adheres to the imagination and that the interdependence is essential. (33)

Stevens insists here that imaginative constructions have a kind of value, a kind of use, that is different from the uses of truth but equally important. His long meditation on such issues led him into speculation about a "supreme fiction," something we could believe in even though we knew we had made it up ourselves. I am not sure I accept that idea, but as a fellow lurker I share his sense that "truth"—especially in the narrow sense of adherence to common-sense "realism" or some abstract, credal version of orthodoxy—is considerably overrated. And the lurkers' function, perhaps above all, is to make their strange and sometimes dangerous visions of that complicated, inexhaustible reality available to us.

As examples of Mennonite writing that follows along these lines, I might quote almost any of Jean Janzen's poems, which cumulatively represent a deep and rich world of memory, knowledge, and desire. "Cover Me," for example, moves unobtrusively from the simplest memory to far deeper levels of meditation:

> When I offered to wash dishes after supper
> you sent me to practice the piano.
> I wonder now whether you wanted the music
> to take me to places you had never seen,
> playing Mozart and Rachmaninoff in the scents
> of my first cologne from my first boy,
> your hand waving me off into danger.

You knew that my dresses moved like water
when I walked, or was it fire, our true covering?
The way you now let your good dresses hang
unused, your skin so thin and translucent,
it wants to flare and rise. (54)

There is much here that is unsaid, or only intimated, and yet very firmly present. The poem says a great deal about the movement of a girl from innocence to experience, about music and feeling, about the knowledge that passes between mothers and daughters, with or without words. It is a poem about love, sex, and death that never uses any of those words, a poem that moves toward an imaginative apprehension far deeper and more complex than the mere surface reality of a woman and a girl in a room. There we are, lurking with her in that strange, deep new room of the imagination, where the physical details are only a blurred shadow of the human reality the poem directs us toward.

ANGELS AND LAUGHTER

The great romantic lurker, visionary, and heretic William Blake said, among many reckless things, that "Without contraries is no progression." Wallace Stevens likewise insists that reality and the imagination are necessary to each other, that "reality adheres to the imagination and that the interdependence is essential" (33). Stevens, Blake, and the great Czech writer Milan Kundera all write of angels and devils. Kundera's *Book of Laughter and Forgetting* proposes a sort of Manichean vision that associates angels with order and devils with individualism, recklessness, and artistic creativity. And he insists that both are necessary:

Angels are not partisans of Good, but of divine creation. The Devil, on the other hand, denies all rational meaning to God's world. . . . If there is too much uncontested meaning on earth (the reign of the angels), man collapses under the burden; if the world loses all its meaning (the reign of the demons), life is every bit as impossible. (61)

Kundera suggests that the laughter of angels rejoices in order and harmony, that of devils, in chaos and absurdity. They are not always easy to distinguish. Which sort of laughter comes from the lurkers? Both, I suspect. I also suspect that lurkers often feel compelled to take whichever side seems least popular. When the communal order becomes too powerful, they cry out for freedom and the individual; when order breaks down, they sing of the harmonious community. Finally, perhaps the lurkers are here to be a counterbalance, to remind us of what would otherwise be lost in consensus and conformity and majority rule, to allow and insist that we laugh as well as mourn, dance as well as sing, not forget whatever is counter and spare and strange and yet also within our circle. Let me end this chapter in that spirit by quoting the great Sufi Mennonite poet, mystic and lurker, Rumi:

> There is a community of the spirit.
> Join it, and feel the delight
> of walking in the noisy street,
> and *being* the noise.
>
> Drink *all* your passion,
> and be a disgrace.
>
> Close both eyes
> to see with the other eye. . .
>
> Why do you stay in prison
> when the door is so wide open?
>
> Move outside the tangle of fear-thinking.
> Live in silence.
>
> Flow down and down in always
> widening rings of being.(3)

To be a lurker is to walk the streets knowing at once that you are in the community, inseparable from it, and at the same moment in a world far away, one where strange voices whisper brilliant, frightening sentences and demands—the most frightening demand of all being that you listen even when you know that doing so will mean that you must change your life. It is to feel yourself a disgrace to both worlds, knowing that you really are at home in neither, and that you can never do justice to either one. To feel responsible and alien, bound and free, sinful and prophetic, at the same moment. To sense that your work in the world may be, not to find some pure, true Word and sing it once for all, but to bend the hints and glimpses and obstinate questionings that come your way into some shape that might be of some use to a few others. Not such an easy way to spend a life, but not such a bad way either.

CHAPTER SEVEN

AT THE VISION CONFERENCE

A Return to the City that I Once Called Home

I still cannot drive down Indiana Route 15, Main Street of Goshen, past the student union without singing "Goshen College, ever singing" once, out loud. Just the chorus, and once is enough, but I have to do it, a greeting ritual, a salute.

I have come back for a conference on the fifty-year anniversary of the "Anabaptist Vision," the address by Harold Bender that, according to the people who know, shaped thirty-plus years of Mennonite-hood in America more than any other single document. These days, of course, we're deep into revisionism, and most of the historians say that HSB's version of the proto-Mennonites in Switzerland as the One True Church and the carriers of the grand vision of discipleship, brotherhood and nonresistance was too simple by half. He more or less just lopped off a lot of other reformers and rebels who also called themselves Anabaptists but whose words and deeds didn't quite fit with Bender's sense of what Anabaptism ought to be. It was an experimental time, after all.

But while he's paying for it now, he's dead anyway, has been for years. His view of history may have been "mystical," as somebody put it, but it had all the virtues of simplicity; among other things, it made him not only a mainstay at Goshen but in just about every other realm of Mennonitism for years. They called him "The Pope," several people tell me, and knowing how Mennonites feel about Catholics it doesn't take advanced degrees to figure out what that meant.

On the other hand, the Anabaptist Vision's simplicity and apparent orthodoxy helped him and the college to keep the fundamentalists at bay. Those folks had closed the whole place down tight as a drum for a year in the twenties, when they thought the liberals and modernists were getting too strong, and for a long time Bender's greatest fear was that they'd do it again.

Now I've spent my whole adult life, except for four years in graduate school, either studying at or employed by Mennonite institutions of higher education. I've made a reasonable living at it, and I have mainly liked my time in those places quite well. By now I admit my church affiliation to almost anybody who asks, with only modest explanations and provisos, depending on the situation.

Still, by the morning of the second day of this conference I was sunk deep into a haze of caffeine, paranoia, overheated mental activity, and fight-or-flight anxiety that I only gradually recognized as the nearly forgotten state in which I lived for most of my college years. I'm still trying to figure out exactly where it came from.

One source was the sense of conspiratorial comradeship that comes with sitting around in small groups late at night, trying to figure out ways to outwit and thwart the powers that be, how to survive without surrendering to them. I'd almost forgotten that too, but all the Anabaptist Vision talk brought it back so clearly, the way I felt all through college that I was leaning back against some steady tug, not exactly evil, in fact more or less benevolent in many of its intentions, calm and pleasant and high-minded, yet either blind or actively hostile to most of what I thought really mattered. I half-feared I would be taken over some night like those poor souls in *Invasion of the Body Snatchers*, replaced by some nearly identical version of myself that would sit placidly through the longest sermon, serve earnestly on the most glacial of committees, and cheerfully give up all this prideful and worldly business about writing.

Nobody there ever asked me to do so in so many words, of course, but that only made my paranoia worse. I had come through the emotional hurricanes of revivalism—fading out in my area by the fifties and sixties, but still real enough—without being entirely swept away. Deep down I knew I had never had a real conversion experience, but just as deep down I wasn't sure I *wanted* to have one, not if it meant turning into one of those clean-cut, chipper young folks who seemed convinced of their own salvation and ready enough to judge mine. I stayed as far from them as I could, as I did from religion classes and professors, though I'm a little sorry now about avoiding the classes. The professors were earnest enough, but not nearly as rigid or self-righteous as the students.

So I stewed my way through the conference, muttering confusedly to anybody I could buttonhole, while the solid scholars made their variously respectful and revisionary presentations. It wasn't till near the end that a paper by Scott Holland, on the disappearance of the holy kiss, the Mennonite fear of the body, and other such underdeveloped topics, crystallized some of what I'd been trying to put into words. He talked about the idea of "the other": "[Julia Kristeva] suggests we can only learn to live at peace with strangers around us if we acknowledge and tolerate strangeness and otherness in ourselves. . . . To invite the stranger to speak—indeed, even the repressed other of our desire—threatens to subvert the power of Anabaptist super-ego, since its vision of spirituality and morality demands *Gelassenheit* and *Nachfolge* . . . ."

That's my whole fear and terror in a nutshell: the Anabaptist super-ego, the man in the plain black coat. He's smart and calm and confident, he's filled with the Spirit, or some spirit. This is it, he says, trust me, the rest is dross and chaff, just concentrate with me now, yield your self up and follow and we'll disciple each other right on into heaven.

This seems to be a pretty good program for things like Mennonite Central Committee and church-owned colleges, especially for administrators like Harold Bender whose biggest fear is being stomped into oblivion by fundamentalists and reactionaries. But it's pretty tight for anybody who dreams of being an artist, of following the wavering and contrary impulses of the creative spirit. This essay is one more piece of evidence, I suppose, that such folks are not to be trusted.

Harold Bender was long gone by the time I arrived at Goshen in 1970, and not nearly everybody there was a Benderite. I was drawn to the English department mainly because some of the people there seemed to be circling the center as suspiciously as I was. There was Nick Lindsay, imported from South Carolina to preach the gospel of beauty and poetry as he'd inherited it from his father. He was gnarly and impassioned and wonderfully unpredictable; after a five-minute oration on some subject, when he'd dazzled us into thinking he must be some kind of prophet, he'd shrug suddenly and say, "Ah, or else it isn't," and we'd go on. There was Jack Dueck, a Mennonite Brethren from Canada with a fine tenor voice and a penchant for asking us how reading this particular book would require us to change our lives. Once he burned a set of essay exams (on fire imagery) in the front of the room. J. Lawrence Burkholder was the president, a gnarly and enigmatic presence himself; from a few hints here and there, we suspected the borders of his thinking might not be as narrow as certain members of the constituency would hope. Still, I remained convinced that life among the Visionaries required a certain kind of cunning, preserving and feeding that other, hidden part of me, hiding it away, biding my time.

Oh, all right, of course I'm painting this as more lurid and grotesque than it was. I met a lot of wonderful people at Goshen, and learned about as much as I was ready to learn. I was grateful, and still am, for the idea that there is, or should be, a unifying vision around which a people can gather and work together for their common good and the greater glory of God. I still remember telling a friend, after a few months at graduate school, "Troyer, some of those people don't even believe that there *is* a true nature of the universe!" And I'm glad for the idea that it's all right to be part of a group that's at odds with the larger society.

Still, there is something chilling to me in the way that Bender vision has played itself out. On the last day, when various church and college leaders were telling stories about how HSB had sent them to this school or that school, set them up with their spouses, gotten them jobs, another feeling from my early college days came back to me. It was the feeling I got when I realized that many of my classmates were already hooked into a network that I hadn't known existed. Their parents taught at Goshen or the seminary or worked at the Mennonite Publishing House; just the way they walked around campus made it clear they expected to be doing those things themselves someday. The hands had been laid on, early; what chance did another farm boy from a small town and a smaller high school in darkest Illinois have?

That sense of unease faded too. All the chance I deserved, and maybe more, I found. The church drew me back in, not quite against my will, to teach English and eventually to do my own research and thinking and writing about some small corners of the Mennonite world. Now I am a more or less established part of the network myself. . . . I have my academic job, and tenure, and articles in this and that publication, and some sort of reputation. And what does that mean?

It means, among other things, that as I sat in that conference, these were the sorts of things I wrote down in my little red notebook. Some of it draws on what participants said, though I hope I won't be held accountable, and they certainly should not be. The other things just ran through my head, or have since, and I tackled them and wrote them down, having been an undersized but determined linebacker in high school. Old habits die hard.

WHAT I LEARNED AT THE VISION CONFERENCE— OR, HAROLD BENDER WAS NOT A CHAMPION SURFER

Harold Bender was not a corporate raider. Neither am I, but I'm here again on sacred ground, I made it past the white pickup stopped across both lanes but not abandoned, just waiting for the last stranger to pass, to leave the way clear as I saw in my mirror that it was. Some were convinced their own small band had God's truth, don't you know. In the thicket of contemporary spirituality french fries are less healthy than those potato slabs we bake in the oven, oh, do they taste good, says Rudy, almost wincing with the pleasure of memory. Rootless individuals call themselves liberals, someone sneers. Can double amputees put their best foot forward?

Brother Bender was not a torch singer, or the captain of a banana boat. Now then. Can one find salvation behind the third door, between the two toes where the athlete's foot keeps coming back? The old German scholar said in '46 that he wished he could die a Mennonite.

Don't you wish you could stop and relax? This is the apostolic life, with good blankets, with ear piercing optional, with plenty of comfortable shoes. I love the word "eschew," though less than I love the quest for the historical Jesus, less than I love the green ferns and little brass lamp by the podium, less than the great but fading churches of Europe, like the fake fronts of movie cowtowns.

Harold Bender was not an athlete. The coercive religious establishment has just about managed to convert itself to stone, a beautiful but uncomfortable process, worse than minor surgery or coaching the soccer team through seven losses in a row. Hope springs, but so does the tiger. How about "flaccid"? Do you like "flaccid"?

Our values have imploded, unimaginably. We're in danger of regressing to Christendom. Do you like "sinful spiritual triumphalism"?

Do you drink coffee so late in the day? You all remember that wonderful statement of Simon Stumpf. Read Matthew. Read Mark. What *is* the sin against the Holy Ghost? Do they ever look across the tracks? What's happened to the proto-Protestants of the Iberian Peninsula?

Nobody says that Harold Bender's nickname was "The Pope," at least from the podium. However considerable lack of ease is expressed re his driving habits, his treatment of his self-sacrificing spouse, certain rarely seen letters, his laying on of hands. What *is* culture, for service, anyway? Where were Freud and Marx and Darwin while all of this was going on?

Harold Bender bought two big jars of peanuts at the PX and ate the contents of the first one on the trip to Stuttgart. Harold Bender said history was to be an instrument for evangelism. Harold Bender told this guy to go to Princeton, that one to go to Yale. Harold Bender washed feet with the plumber down the street. Harold Bender took the late train for the sake of another piece of pie. Harold Bender was the first Goshen faculty member to use a ballpoint pen. Harold Bender was not an icon, and that's why we're all here, isn't it?

Harold Bender believed in mystical history. The hotheads and sexual deviants who didn't fit, well, they just disappeared, like the unlucky villagers who displeased the boy with the powers. Don't *you* get annoyed by all those folks that just don't get it? Don't you yearn for the power?

It's been fifty years, and just now are they shimmering back into view, sort of like Kirk and McCoy and Uhuru on the transporter. We crowd around, not sure. We ask the questions: Where have you been? Could you see anything? Are you ready now?

They're shaking off the cobwebs, rubbing at their eyes. They're not talking, though some of them seem to be trying. Some of them are beautiful. Some of them are carrying books, pitchforks, tools. Some of them are dead.

CHAPTER 8

BLACK COATS, PIG-HEADED FATHERS, AND GROWING SOULS: SOME REFLECTIONS ON THE FIGURE OF HAROLD BENDER

This chapter began as an address to the 1999 Annual Meeting of the Mennonite Historical Society at Associated Mennonite Biblical Seminary. The occasion was to recognize Al Keim for his book *Harold S. Bender 1897-1962*. I began by saying thanks: for the invitation to speak with such an august group; to Al Keim for writing a fine, readable, balanced, insightful biography of a man who is clearly at the center of Mennonite history in the middle of this century; and to Harold Bender, without whom this organization, and many of the other major Mennonite institutions of the end of this century, would surely not exist in the same form.

♣

I want to take as given all the important and lasting things Harold Bender accomplished—things I do not need to rehearse here. Assuming that my audience is mainly familiar with Bender's many accomplishments as church leader, as college and seminary administrator, as scholar, I want to do something less gracious and grateful, but perhaps more substantial, than rehearsing his achievements once more. I want to talk about the Harold Bender who troubles me, the one with whom I do not feel much harmony. I will speak boldly because my time is brief, though I am plentifully aware of all that I am leaving out. We can negotiate later if you like.

I have envisioned how to start this many times. I thought about Ezra Pound's poem, "A Pact," which he wrote to Walt Whitman:

> **A Pact**
> I make a pact with you, Walt Whitman—
> I have detested you long enough.
> I come to you as a grown child
> Who has had a pig-headed father;
> I am old enough now to make friends.
> It was you that broke the new wood
> Now is a time for carving.
> We have one sap and one root—
> Let there be commerce between us (Pound 27).

I would like to be friends with Harold Bender. I am not sure, though, whether he would want to be friends with me. And there is the rub, I think, especially for those of us Mennonite intellectuals who aspire to what we clumsily call "creative" work.

Let me offer a few selective quotes from Al Keim's biography to illustrate the sides of Bender that trouble me. Again, let me say that these are obviously not the whole story, but I do believe they represent a significant part of his story.[29]

#1: The Man Without a Private Life. "This is the biography of a public man. Despite his huge written record, Harold Bender revealed almost nothing about his private life. . . . seldom are we invited to observe or share his innermost joys, hopes, and fears" (14). Helen Alderfer's review of this book in *Christian Living* made a similar point: "This book has been valuable for me who knew Harold Bender personally but did not know him, for he divulged little of his private life."

#2: The Man Who Will Make His Way. "Harold had a pragmatic view of how to operate in the Mennonite milieu. As he explained to his friend Hartzler, 'A man can't let petty things stand in the way and compromise his whole future position and usefulness. . . . if a man starts out by being a rebel in our church, he usually ends up on the dump'" (77).

#3: The Defender of the Borders. Bender in the Goshen College *Record*: "Not everyone has the moral right to criticize. Who has the right? Only he who is a living part of the organism which he criticizes. Only he who has and keeps his life in the Church, who suffers with her, and whose spiritual fellowship with the Church is unbroken" (206).

I must pause here to say that this seems brilliant, in a political sense. It seems common-sensical, but it also allows "the Church" to define its critics as not really "living parts" and to dismiss their critique as irrelevant. Surely anyone so bold as to criticize the church on anything important *must* be no longer in "spiritual fellowship." Notice also the metaphor for church here: a single "organism" with "living parts" and, by implication, dead or former parts as well, although how those parts become that way is not examined. Am I being paranoid to expect that such a church will be especially closed to critique from those that it has driven away?

#4: The Teacher in Hiding:

> Students complained that Bender missed too many classes and that he frequently came to class unprepared. Since he too often ran out of time, his classes tended to skim the surface and sometimes failed to help students fathom the depths of the issues they ought to have been addressing. . . . Bender was not a poor teacher: what his students deplored was his failure to give them the best of which he was capable. . . .
>
> Yet even faculty overload was not the main reason for the lack of rigor. More important was the desire and need to be cautious and noncontroversial. For twenty years Bender had embraced conventional theological understandings. . . . Bender had an almost compulsive need to present himself and the seminary as safe and orthodox. (342-3)

I do not think this kind of teaching happens very often at any Mennonite college any more, and surely these comments do not represent Bender's entire career as a teacher. But I suspect that the felt need to present ourselves as "safe and orthodox" has not altogether vanished, and I cannot help but worry about what important matters may be skimmed or avoided because of that need.

#1A: The Man Without a Private Life, part 2. On Bender's letter to Melvin and Verna Gingrich when his daughter Nancy was ill, Keim writes: "The almost ritualistic quality of his words, while deeply felt, exhibit Bender's near inability to express himself in profoundly personal terms. He could not find the words to convey his anxiety and fear. Thus he turned to conventional religious language" (380).

This division between the public and the personal is really what troubles me most, and what I think should trouble anyone who believes that real learning, real teaching, and real Christianity all have a good deal to do with the inner life. Those of us who have been drawn to interior and aesthetic modes of experience and expression—despite several hundred years of prohibitions and skepticism—can hardly help feeling like interlopers in Bender's world, frivolous time-wasters if not worse. And those pursuits can hardly help but take us outside the borders that Bender feared to trespass.

Would Bender spend a whole afternoon fussing with the words of a single poem, as I have? Surely he would not take the time to learn to play the guitar, much less play a few sad, worldly love songs on it over and over as I have been known to do. Would he read Rilke and Kafka, those heterodox misfits, even if they did write in German? What about all the rest—Nietzsche, Freud, Marx, Darwin, and now Derrida and Lacand Foucault and Kristeva—who are decidedly outside the borders of the orthodox, the cautious, the non-controversial? Would Bender pay serious attention to any of the other writers and thinkers I cannot imagine going without? Would he listen seriously to Alice Walker and Toni Morrison, Julia Kasdorf and Di Brandt, Lee Snyder and Shirley Showalter?

Personally, I must say that at least since I learned to read my inner life has been far more diverse, colorful, and interesting than my outer one. Much of what I have encountered there is decidedly unorthodox and controversial, even dangerous, and partly *because* it is interior, it is also difficult to regulate. But I am convinced that it is in that realm of slow, difficult, unregulated encounter with the biggest, toughest, strongest, strangest, most beautiful and dangerous productions of the human spirit that anything meaningful I may have managed to learn and say and do myself has its birth. If I keep some space in my life for those sorts of encounters, and for playing guitar, and for walking out in God's world, then poems come to me. If I get caught up in doing things with people, they do not.

While preparing this essay, I stumbled on a quote from Kurt Vonnegut that almost stopped my breath. "The primary benefit of practicing any art, whether well or badly," he writes, "is that it enables one's soul to grow." I thought at once of the parable of the talents, and that indeed this might be what God expects of us: to grow our souls, to bring them back bigger than they were.

We can hardly do that without the arts, and I would argue that we can hardly do it in a narrow set of prohibitions and prescriptions. I have spent much of my life as a teacher and writer crossing borders that Bender seems to have been willing to keep closed, and I cannot imagine going back inside. I can imagine letting the most conservative elements of the Mennonite church define who is and is not a part of the group or what should and should not be part of the discussion, but I pray that it does not happen.

So—yes, Bender is scary to me when he represents such things. But I want to say something else about him too, something that may be slightly more generous. In an essay titled "Marilyn, H. S. Bender, and Me," Julia Kasdorf writes very acutely about Bender and Marilyn Monroe as public figures, and about the costs to Norma Jean of becoming Marilyn Monroe, the woman in the famous photo, the object of so much desire. Kasdorf only touches on one of Harold Bender's well-known gestures: early in his Goshen career he rather unwillingly put on a plain coat to reassure the Eastern conservatives of his orthodoxy (*The Body* 121-42).

Surely in doing so Bender also accepted a public persona—one rather different than Marilyn's, of course, but also one with a quite rigidly and narrowly defined set of expectations. Bender, I suspect, sacrificed a good deal of his inner life *and* changed his outward appearance for the sake of public accomplishment. He seems to have done so more or less consciously and willingly, and if he was not perfectly selfless, surely he was largely driven by a real desire to be of service. More than one person who knew him has suggested to me that he was really a closet liberal who accepted the plain coat and the task of placating the conservatives as the price of keeping Goshen College open, and that may well be true.

I mean here not to criticize Bender, but to reflect on what those choices cost him. I cannot help but wonder what would have changed had he refused to put that black coat on, had he refused to let the most conservative elements of his constituency play so large a role in defining the context of his thought and work, even when he resisted or opposed those elements as much as he thought he dared. Would Goshen have been closed down long ago, or taken over by the fundamentalists and made in their image? Or might it have thrived on the energy of a less cautious pursuit of a more expansive Anabaptist Vision?

I have no answer for these questions. But when I arrived at Goshen from the Illinois provinces in 1970 in a haze of anxious bravado, Bender was still a rather active ghost. And what I have come to call the Man in the Black Coat of narrow, dogmatic, authoritarian Mennonite orthodoxy was an even more constant presence. This figure was not Bender himself, of course, nor any actual human being, but a weird amalgam of mostly shadowy figures—wealthy constituents, board members, pastors, even students—who seemed to hold some equally obscure power as they lurked in the minds of those nominally in charge, so that everything we did had to be either made acceptable to him or carefully hidden away.

I am grateful to those who did their best to placate the Man in the Black Coat, so that the self-styled rebels like me could cause trouble and bend the rules and try out ideas that we knew would horrify him. I am even more grateful to those—teachers, administrators, students—who did what they could to resist the Man in the Black Coat and his grip on our minds, our bodies, and our souls.

But I mourn that thirty years later we still seem stuck in these old contentions, one way or another. I mourn for my own complicity and timidity in sometimes knuckling under to the darkness and fear that black coat represents. I mourn also for my own mean-spirited difficulty in recognizing the grace and truth that dwells there also. On the one hand, I want to say, as Thoreau did, that if I were to repent of anything it would be my good behavior. On the other, I have long been bound into a community where I accept my accountability to the group and have learned to try, over and over, to cherish the gifts and the views of people from all over the spectrum. Sometimes that is easy; it is most difficult, of course, when the desire for open and respectful conversation is not reciprocal.

Can we have commerce now with our pig-headed fathers, as grown men and women? It is almost easier, isn't it, if they are dead, their pig-headedness completed, and those of us still here able to judge and sort out their faults and their virtues as we will? What sort of conversations can we have with those who have already drawn a line that excludes us? Recently I visited a new web site created by a group calling for the creation of a "New Fundamentalist Evangelical Mennonite Church." "The current trend of liberal theologians, homosexuality, pro-abortion and other social sins are signs of spiritual death," I read there, and I did not know whether to weep first for the grammar or for the enormous gulf I felt between whoever wrote those words and me.

I would argue that this point of view is at least as "worldly," in drawing on corrupt and unreliable sources, as one that draws on Blake, Whitman, Dickinson and Rilke, all of them steeped in long and rigorous spiritual and aesthetic disciplines. I would argue that these people, whoever they are, have already done what Bender said deprived people of the right to critique: broken willingly from the traditional Anabaptist spiritual fellowship that I know and love. I know they would not agree, and I have no desire to set them apart. But neither do I desire to let them set me apart. What would Bender do? I wish I knew.

How *does* any tiny group such as we are define ourselves and maintain the fellowship? Must the price of that maintenance be conformity, mediocrity, and submission to self-styled authorities whose fervor and conviction are intensified by the narrow channels they run through? Do we define ourselves by drawing firm borders and enforcing them, by establishing a vital center and allowing people to set up camp as near or far from it as they choose, or in some third way we have not yet been able to imagine?

As we muddle on with all of this, we will need God's help. But we know God through human beings, and surely we will also need all the human resources we can muster. Let me claim one last time that this is, paradoxically, where the inner life might yield fruits in helping us reckon with and comprehend our human and spiritual realities more deeply. If the truth is the truth, should it be left unspoken? Should a group of old men—or any group—be allowed to set whole areas of the world off limits?

In Bender's life, I must say, he seemed to answer "Yes," and here I at least must part ways with him. "Be it life or death," Thoreau wrote, "we crave only reality." Reality and truth are often dangerous, but illusion and ignorance are even more so. And so I think we owe it to each other, and to Harold Bender, to grow our souls, to practice our arts, to speak our truths as boldly as they come to us.

(IN)VISIBLE CITIES, (F)ACTS OF POWER, (HMM)ILITY, FATHERS AND (M)OTHERS: ANABAPTISM, POSTMODERNITY, AND MENNONITE WRITING

(IN)VISIBLE CITIES

To be a Mennonite writer in a postmodern time might mean, among other things, encountering powerful, formative texts as much at odds as these two:

> Although the definitive history of Anabaptism has not yet been written, we know enough today to draw a clear line of demarcation between original evangelical and constructive Anabaptism on the one hand, which was born in the bosom of Zwinglianism in Zurich, Switzerland, in 1525, and established in the Low Countries in 1533, and the various mystical, spiritualistic, revolutionary, or even antinomian related and unrelated groups on the other hand, which came and went like the flowers of the field in those days of the great renovation. (Bender)

> [S]tructure—or rather the structurality of structure—although it has always been involved, has always been neutralized or reduced, and this by a process of giving it a center or referring it to a point

of presence, a fixed origin. The function of this center was . . .
above all to make sure that the organizing principle of the structure would limit what we might call the *freeplay* of the structure.
(Derrida, "Structure" 960)

It does not take great interpretive skills to see the tension between
these two statements. Harold Bender proposes to define an origin, establish a point of historical and theological presence, draw a clear line
between "evangelical and constructive Anabaptism" and various aberra-
tions from it. This is precisely what Derrida skeptically says Western
metaphysicians, theologians, scholars and politicians have always
sought to do: to create a center that will not only organize the structure
of society or a subset like the Mennonite church, but also limit the
"freeplay" within that structure and function as a means of control and a
way of defining boundaries. Derrida does not deny the power of such
claims about origins, but does insist that all "origins" are human constructions rather than objective Truth. For him, everything is difference;
there is no first principle, no origin, no Unmoved Mover.

I do not mean to argue that Derrida is entirely right in this matter or
Bender entirely mistaken in his efforts. The literature on both subjects is
far too voluminous and complex for my amateur status as postmodern
critic and Anabaptist historian. But the contrast between their ways of
thinking about history and meaning provides a starting point for exploring what Mennonite creative writers have been doing, consciously
or not. They have been complicating and resisting the idea that there is
one identifiable True Center of Anabaptist history and experience, and
the corollary idea that the Anabaptist community rightly belongs to
those who wish to establish a fixed set of standards from which others—
including our own "mystics, spiritualists, revolutionaries, and antino-
mians"—can and should be excluded.

Since Rudy Wiebe's *Peace Shall Destroy Many* arrived some thirty-
five years ago, a whole series of startling new imaginative texts under
some aspect of the term *Mennonite* have emerged in the United States
and Canada. Whether we like it or not, today all sorts of novelists, poets,
dramatists, and others claim some kind of allegiance or connection, current or nostalgic, to Anabaptism. They also claim the kind of imaginative freedom that historically many Anabaptists have distrusted if not
banned outright. These texts generally deal with lived experience and
often with the relation of such experience to the abstract creeds, dogmas,

and disciplines of various Mennonite communities. They do not seek to replace history and theology but to supplement them. They aim to provide other sorts of news and information, to bring a wider range of voices into our hearing.

Postmodernism tells us that Harold Bender's Anabaptist vision, whatever else we might say about it, is a linguistic construct. Its relation to historical events and verifiable reality is by definition problematic and imperfect. Of course this recognition applies to every text we produce. If anything, accepting this premise makes our work both more imperative and more problematic, because we are (or should be) always aware that we will never get anything quite right, that if our work is remembered at all it will quite surely be critiqued and corrected by others whose work will itself be in turn forgotten or abused. We are constantly driven to generate meaning which is inevitably, constantly incomplete and imperfect. To be aware of that incompletion yet press on with the work anyway I take to be one crucial element of the postmodern condition.

Consider Edgar Allen Poe's famous story "The Purloined Letter." What does this story "mean"? To trace just one series of fairly recent interpretations, Marie Bonaparte reads the story as a Freudian sexual allegory, with the letter as the clitoris—hidden as it is in "plain sight" in the letter-box just above the womb-symbol of the fireplace. Jacques Lacan's post-Freudian psychoanalytic reading finds the story structured around a series of "triads"—groups of three people around the letter, which functions as an open "signifier" whose meaning is never revealed (Lacan 32). Jacques Derrida argues that Bonaparte and Lacan both miss the essential mystery and open-endedness of the story, that in fact it embodies "an endless drifting-off-course" and a nearly infinite nesting of stories and texts one within another (Derrida, "Purloined" 971).

Who is "right"? Each of these readings offer certain insights, surely—and surely none exhausts the story or closes off further readings. Had we the time, we might make finer distinctions among them, compare them to others, judge this one to be more persuasive and that one more relevant. In that process we would continue to generate new understandings—by synthesizing, comparing and critiquing, by bringing our own critical and theoretical categories to bear, by returning to the original text with fresh or more informed perspectives.

As we work at any such process, our readings may strike others as profound or ridiculous, important or trivial, and their distribution will be subject to such responses and other factors of the literary economy. But the process remains one of constant and open-ended negotiation. Surely interpretation, literary, biblical, and otherwise, has always proceeded in this fashion. Postmodernism has only made us more aware of the process.

I do not take this endless deferral of "final" meaning to imply a mindless relativism in which, because no reading is absolute, all readings are reduced to hapless undecideability. But I will resist the temptation to take up the complicated argument about how meaning is negotiated here, because I am more interested in the production of texts than in their interpretation. My concern is to argue that the deferral of absolute certainty—the refusal to claim that as limited human beings we have access to Truth, capital T—opens a valuable and important space for discourse that has often been unavailable to Mennonites. Such discourse may seem frighteningly anarchic, even subversive, but I believe that the multiple voices and visions we are beginning to hear and see have a great deal to tell us.

This poem by Di Brandt speaks in one of those long-silenced voices:

> **nonresistance, or love Mennonite style**
> (for L. & the others)
> turn the other cheek when your brother
> hits you and your best friend tells fibs
> about you & the teacher punishes you
> unfairly if someone steals your shirt
> give him your coat to boot this will
> heap coals of fire on his head & let him
> know how greatly superior you are
> while he & his cronies dicker & bargain
> their way to hell you can hold your
> head up that is down humbly knowing
> you're bound for the better place where
> it gets tricky is when your grandfather
> tickles you too hard or your cousins
> want to play doctor & your uncle kisses
> you too long on the lips & part of you
> wants it & the other part knows it's
> wrong & you want to run away but you
> can't because he's a man like your father

& the secret place inside you feels itchy
& hot & you wonder if this is what hell
feels like & you remember the look on
your mother's face when she makes
herself obey your dad & meanwhile her
body is shouting *No! No!* & he doesn't
even notice & you wish you could stop
being angry all the time but you can't
because God is watching & he sees
everything there isn't any place to let
it out & you understand about love the
lavish sacrifice in it how it will stretch
your woman's belly & heap fire on your
head you understand how love is like
a knife & a daughter is not a son & the
only way you will be saved is by
submitting quietly in your grandfather's
house your flesh smouldering in the
darkened room as you love your enemy
deeply unwillingly & full of shame (Brandt, *Agnes* 38-39)

As I read Bender and Derrida together, let me investigate this poem using Michel Foucault's comments on the operation of post-Enlightenment social power. Foucault finds a visual image for such power in Jeremy Bentham's plan for a circular prison in which all the inmates could be observed while unable to see their observer, which he called the "panopticon."

> Hence the major effect of the Panopticon: to induce in the inmate a state of conscious and permanent visibility that assures the automatic functioning of power. So to arrange things that the surveillence is permanent in its effects even if it is discontinuous in its action; that the perfection of power should tend to render its actual exercise unnecessary . . . in short, the inmates themselves should be caught up in a power situation of which they are themselves the bearers. (Foucault 183)

In Brandt's poem something very like the system Foucault describes is clearly in operation. The subtly but radically pernicious understanding of "nonresistance" the "you" of this poem has internalized traps her into radical subordination to men who are aligned with the terrifying image of an eternally watchful masculine God that rules her claustro-phobic world. As Foucault suggests, this "you" disciplines herself; the system of power has convinced her that she has no option except utter submission.

This poem and others like it have helped me understand the dark ways terms like *humility* and *nonresistance* can function, especially when used as code words for submission to patriarchal oppression. Di Brandt unpacks the hidden senses of these terms by using elements of her personal experience, the testimony of others, and her intuitive sense of one facet of Mennonite reality to create a text that demands our attention—if not as the "whole truth," as *a* truth among the others, one seldom found in official denominational pronouncements.

Some readers may resist this poem, argue that it overdramatizes and exaggerates for effect, that most Mennonites are not so oppressed. Others may react with satisfaction—"Yes, they're all that way." Both these reactions seem to me partly valid, but "partly" is the crucial word. It is too simple and easy either to accept or to reject this poem, and other such texts, wholesale. We must learn, I think, to complicate our understandings, to open ourselves to such testimonies and take them for what they are: necessary supplements that are each incomplete but which, cumulatively, can bring us closer to knowing the world as it truly is.

One of my favorite postmodern texts is a strange, short book by Italo Calvino titled *Invisible Cities.* In that book the explorer Marco Polo describes to Kublai Khan the exotic cities he has encountered in his travels—though it is not clear whether these cities "really" exist or whether Polo is making them up to please his host and friend. And of course the cities are "really" made up by Calvino, the author. Yet in their weird specificity and quirky detail they seem *almost* the sort of places that might actually exist. They invite all sorts of intriguing speculation about the nature of life, language, and reality.

We might think of poems like Di Brandt's as making visible the invisible cities among us—those exterior and interior places of incredible variety and intensity that our fellow human beings, Mennonite and otherwise, inhabit. In reading such work I find myself drawn into lives and images that have forever changed my sense of the "real world," whether the poems and stories are "really true" or not.

I think we need such work to be as various and even contradictory as possible. Let me dwell for a moment on the question of apparent contraditions. I must confess that my own "Mennonite" book *A Community of Memory* is partly a response to texts like Di Brandt's. My own experience of family and of Mennonite community was much less brutal and repressive than the one she describes, and my book clearly reflects that.

I have been pleased and gratified by the book's reception. More than once, however, I have heard it said that my book is somehow a "correction" of the "angry" poets, that because I do not seem resentful about my childhood they should not complain about theirs, that because I wrote a book that flirts with nostalgia and dallies with sentimentality I must think all Mennonites are really pretty good.

As you know if you have read the book—and if you have not, I hope you will—I *do* think that some Mennonites are pretty good. I am not taking back anything I wrote there. But I have no desire that it become some sort of definitive image of "the Mennonites." My book, Di Brandt's books, and all the other poems and stories by Mennonites and others that we come to know must each be seen as at most a summing-up of one person's vision at what my old teacher John Oyer used to call "this point in space and time." My new work may have a quite different tone, as indeed it is much too simple to take any one of Di Brandt's poems as summing up her whole worldview. As writers continue to do their work with honesty and passion and integrity, it will be as varied in tone and substance as Mennonites are, as life itself is.

F(ACTS) OF POWER

If poems are necessary supplements, they are also unavoidably acts of power. The Palestinian-born critic Edward Said has written well on the "worldliness" of texts; he argues that they are "always enmeshed in circumstance, time, place, and society" (1024), that they have their "meaning *in the world*" (1030, emphasis in text). Said draws support from Nietzsche and Foucault for his analysis of texts as "fundamentally facts of power." One difficulty of the kind of supplementarity and interplay among texts I am promoting here is, of course, that such interplay is never just play. If Di Brandt is allowed to complicate the Mennonite master narrative with a story of nonresistance gone terribly wrong, how can that narrative be used, as Harold Bender hoped to use history, as a tool for evangelism and institutional progress? What other, even more disconcerting voices might demand to be heard, and what might happen to the church as institution if they are "allowed" to speak?

Imaginative writing has often been perceived as a threat to the elites that govern self-defined communities, though that threat is usually described as a threat to the community itself. Its stories may well question, if not undermine, the primary narrative. I have heard it suggested quite openly that control of "the" Mennonite narrative belongs with historians and theologians, who can be trusted to get the story right, at least mostly, due to their commitments to reason and certain kinds of evidence and their working within a community of mutual critique and evaluation. Poets and creative writers, this line of thinking goes, lack such self-governing mechanisms and are susceptible to willfullness, whim, individualism, and pride.

Let me quickly agree that the Mennonite church needs its historians and theologians. We have produced some extraordinary ones. But their very fidelity to fact and reason also creates limits. A historian can not (or at least should not) write lengthy narratives based on hunch, intuition, or ideology and pass them off as objective history. A theologian can not, or should not, argue a theological vision just because she is in love with the language that she finds when she muses on it. Poets and novelists, however, can and must work beyond fact and reason. This is not a task to undertake lightly, but neither is it a task that we can abandon because it makes others nervous.

I might also propose that we are stuck with the poets whether we want them or not. Something has happened akin to the process that Jonathan Schell describes in Poland during the rise of Solidarity. At the key moment, Schell writes, the opposition ceased trying to seize political power from the state and simply began to take action

> "as if" Poland were already a free country. And once those in opposition began to act that way something unexpected happened. As soon as they started to act 'as if,' the 'as if' started to melt away. . . . There a small realm of liberty was created. . . . merely by fearlessly carrying on the business of daily life it grew powerful. (Schell 61)

It seems to me that the recent outpouring of Mennonite writing similarly began when enough Mennonite writers simply began to act as if they were free to write what they chose or felt compelled to write, regardless of the consequences, and to find places to publish that work, especially outside strictly Mennonite circles. Strangely, it seems that only after their work became public "outside" Mennonite communities could it filter back in to be paid serious attention within the church.

Shifts of power and authority follow, of course. For women like Di Brandt, Jean Janzen, and Julia Kasdorf to have become almost household names among Mennonites would have been unthinkable even a generation ago, unless they were missionary martyrs. (I suspect that some days Di and Julia, at least, may think that phrase is uncomfortably relevant.) But it is clear that their poems have done cultural work among Mennonites that was not being done otherwise—and, incidentally, quite different work for each of them.

Both the production of imaginative writing by Mennonites and its reception or rejection in Mennonite communities are bound to be entangled in power relations. We have little choice but to continue what is surely an eternal negotiation about the master narrative by which we will live, how we will tell our story to our children and our friends, our enemies and our new recruits. What this story will be, and who will decide how it will be told, are questions of power. Allowing a few people to decide what this story will be and how it will be told concentrates that power in ways I think not truly Anabaptist and makes it all but inevitable that the story will be incomplete. Encouraging many voices to speak in conversation, even those that frighten or dismay us, is vital if we are to tell the whole, rich, troubling, inspiring reality of our history and experience. In a recent essay Julia Kasdorf also suggests as much:

> This is the work we all have been given to do. To live our lives and know ourselves, so that we may be present to others in the world, we must constantly construct ourselves in conversation with others. We cannot see ourselves as given or already "consummated," for then we would be static, "finalized," in Bakhtin's word. We would be dead. (Kasdorf 178)

What does it mean, in Kasdorf's phrase, to "be present to others in the world"? What is "the world" anyway? Everything outside our home church? Our local conference? Are some Mennonites of "the world," and others not? What about the Quakers and the Brethren? What about James Dobson and Pat Robertson? As she asks elsewhere in the same essay, "[would] Mennonites regard their community as the self or the other?" (Kasdorf 173).

I was quite young in the days of the Vietnam War when I began to sense (dimly) that neither "the church" nor "the world" were single, unitary entities. "The world" outside the church had many sides, and I found myself quite drawn to some that distrusted "the Establishment" at least as much as my home church distrusted "the world." The counterculture of the sixties valorized sincerity over smooth surfaces, pacifism over violent nationalism, simple living over mindless consumption, emotional honesty over hypocritical platitudes. Of course this counterculture also valorized electric guitars, "free love," casual drug use, and bell bottoms—but still its critique of American popular and civic culture overlapped in significant ways with what I learned in church. I can still remember my mother having to admit that she could not argue with the sentiments of the Beatles song "Can't Buy Me Love," though she did not have much use for the music.

On a different level, I would suggest that in some ways Mennonite communities *are* "the world" that Mennonite writers must be "in" but not entirely "of" if they are to write. The people I live among now, most of them well-educated, sophisticated, and broad-minded, have been exceedingly supportive of my writing. And yet it is still something that sets me a little apart. This is not a complaint. I want to be that way, for reasons hard to explain, as I like sitting up in the balcony where it is usually less crowded and, if I get into the front row, I can sing as loud as I like without worrying that the person in front of me will hear my shaky notes and wish I would tone it down.

Throughout this chapter—and this book—I have repeatedly used the first person plural. Yet I know how problematic such usage is. In the Mennonite world I often find myself stirring restlessly at the ways this "we" is used. The question of who "we" are, who speaks for "us," and the extent to which "we" identify with or dissociate ourselves from such communal pronouncements is a complicated and important one.

As it matters among Mennonites, it also matters in wider spheres, where similar claims of definition are often made. Consider the use of "we" in this passage from an essay on the recent novel and film *Damage*, in which a man's affair with his son's fiance leads to the son's death:

> According to a psychoanalytic cultural theory outlined by Mac-Cannell that posits a universe beyond Oedipus, in place of the oedipal, patriarchal father, we now have the brother. . . . By forbidding oedipal desire and demanding narcissistic *jouissance* . . .

the new regime promotes an infatuation with death in actual or symbolic forms that engenders what might be called Lacanian tragedy. (Mellard 396)

Essays like this one tempt me to respond, as the old Lone Ranger joke has it, with "What you mean 'we,' kemosabe?" I am, indeed, enough a part of this literary-critical world to know some of the terms, to have even seen the movie, but mostly my life, it seems to me, has very little to do with such arrangements. Yet it is all too easy to reject such analyses without paying careful attention to them. The glib dismissiveness with which some respond to anything under the sign of postmodernism can cover a rather desperate fear that seeks to avoid the new and threatening simply by mocking it.

What is said under the sign of postmodernism surely needs response and critique on any number of levels. But I think we need engaged and informed critique, not mere fearful rejection. And there may be surprises along the way, for postmodernism offers a great many possibilities. At a conference a few years ago I attended a reading by postmodern novelist Kathy Acker. She described her work as "post-secular" and "post-cynical" then read a passage describing the relationships of women in an Egyptian brothel, including extremely specific descriptions of various sexual activities.

The next day I bought one of her books—strictly as a souvenir, of course—worked up the nerve to ask her to sign it, and got into a brief but intriguing conversation. As a small-town Mennonite academic and boringly monogamous heterosexual I did not expect to find a whole lot in common with a crew-cut, tattooed, and multiply pierced West Coast bodybuilder whose work deals, among other things, with the possibilities of pornography and free sex for social change and liberation. Yet when I told her a little about my work on *Community of Memory*, she responded with what seemed genuine enthusiasm, especially about the importance of personal community and writing that grows out of such community in vital ways. There are many ways of finding connection, though I have not yet worked up the nerve to include extended descriptions of sex here or in my next book.

(Hmm)ILITY

The claim implied in using the communal "we" connects directly to questions of arrogance and humility. I have probably written too much about that last term already, much of it in an essay that some of my friends assure me will never be forgiven—although I have dared to make it chapter two of this book. In that piece I was groping toward what I would now describe as a *voluntary* humility, a yieldedness that can only be realized from a position of a certain security—a surrendering of power only possible if one has some power to give up. I would still argue that some people—especially white guys with official positions and/or tenure, like me—need very much to keep learning and practicing that kind of humility. But I have learned to distinguish such a stance more clearly from what my friends have made me realize has all too often been a phony rhetoric of humility, a tool of the powerful for enforcing sub-mission, a "yieldedness" that means mere silencing and oppression, es-pecially for women and minorities.

In a recent essay Elaine Swartzentruber describes something very like the kind of humility I had in mind:

> This Embodied Body of Christ is marked with a humble aware-ness of the limits of bodiness that neither eschews the real effects of criss-crossing lines of power, love, desire, and so forth, nor tries to dissolve the productivity of those lines into some claimed "transcendental authority." This marking would not allow any among us to claim a transcendent authority for decisions we make, for lines we draw, for people we include or exclude from our fellowship, for the lines we will not cross. (Swartzentruber 264)

Such a vision of humility, I suggest, implies that Mennonite writers might willingly accept a role as "minor" authors who might aspire to produce a "minor" but genuine literature. Gilles Deleuze and Félix Guattari, writing especially about Franz Kafka and his status as a Ger-man-speaking Jew in Prague, argue that such a position has its advan-tages. Against the dream of instituting an "official language," even in a local way (surely a dream we institutional Mennonites should recognize) Deleuze and Guattari suggest that Kafka takes an opposite approach.

> There is nothing that is major or revolutionary except the minor. To hate all languages of masters. . . . To make use of the polylin-

gualism of one's own language, to make a minor or intensive use
of it, to oppose the oppressed quality of this language to its op-
pressive quality. . . . How many styles or genres or literary movements, even very small ones, have only one single dream: to assume a major function in language, to offer themselves as a sort of
state language, an official language. . . . Create the opposite
dream: know how to create a becoming-minor. ("What Is," 171)

The dream I have is of a community of many voices, all of them free
and none of them in control, all of them listening to many voices: of the
Spirit and Scripture, of their personal and shared traditions, of each
other. Deleuze and Guattari elsewhere suggest that a good metaphor for
postmodern society is the rhizome, the sort of branching, organic, de-
centered network formed by the clumps of foxtail that keep invading my
garden. The modesty and interconnectedness of this image are appealing: "A rhizome has no beginning or end; it is always in the middle, between things, interbeing. . ." (*Thousand Plateaus*, 25).

In *Thus Spoke Zarathustra*, Nietzsche tells a suggestive story about
the writer's role in postmodern community. "Of three metamorphoses
of the spirit I tell you," Nietzsche writes, "how the spirit becomes a
camel; and the camel, a lion; and the lion, finally, a child" (137). The
camel is the "strong reverent spirit that would bear much"; "What is
most difficult, O heroes, asks the spirit . . . that I may take it upon myself and exult in my strength? Is it not humbling oneself to wound one's
haughtiness? Letting one's folly shine to mock one's wisdom?" (138).
The humble, obedient camel must give way to the rebellious lion, however, who contends with the "great dragon" of received authority.

Though the lion cannot himself create new values, he resists the
closed institutional system of the dragon, demanding the freedom of "a
sacred 'No' even to duty," and thus prepares the way for the child:

> The child is innocence and forgetting, a new beginning, a game,
> a self-propelled wheel, a first movement, a sacred "Yes." For the
> game of creation, my brothers, a sacred "Yes" is needed: the spirit
> now wills his own will, and he who had been lost to the world
> now conquers his own world. (139)

What is this sacred Yes the child utters? Jane Hirschfield says that it
is "the beginning of genuinely original creation, the moment in which
the writer can turn at last toward the work without preconception, with-

out any motive beyond knowing the taste of what is" (41). In such a metamorphosis the "camel" and the "lion" do not vanish; their commitments to reverently "bearing much" and to necessary rebellion remain somehow within the reborn child's new beginning.

To claim the freedom and innocence of the child over the burdens and responsibilities of the "adult" is no small thing, however. What might it mean to become as children again, to take a new chance at the game of creation? Hirschfield also writes suggestively on the artist's role in culture in crossing liminal boundaries:

> As a person who carries the liminal for his culture, [the artist's] role is to be undefended, to take what is given. . . . What is put into the care of such a person will be well tended. Such a person can be trusted to tell the stories she is given to tell, and to tell them with the compassion that comes when the self's deepest interest is not in the self, but in turning outward and into awareness. (Hirschfield 223)

This unselfish, outward turn of the self is not easily accomplished, nor always easy to trust, I recognize. I would not claim to have achieved it myself; yet somehow I think I know it when I encounter it. It is there, I believe, in much recent writing by Mennonites; here is just one example, from the vision that comes to Joseph Toevs near the end of Dallas Wiebe's *Our Asian Journey*:

> It is difficult to know what to write in my memoir when my time is at hand and death will soon come like a thief in the night. I could write that you can't go out and meet God by walking back and forth on the same field. I could write that you can't own a farm and be a pilgrim. I could write that if you see tongues of flame on your farm your crops are on fire. . . . When you're running from the antichrist you don't stop at a hotel. When the antichrist is on his way you don't sit on a rocker and wait for him. When you walk with the Lord your feet have to touch ground. When you've been to Samarkand, Aberdeen isn't much. . . . In America, the woman clothed with the sun is hooked to an electric wire. I could write that you won't suffer and be purified if your plagues are land, stock, machinery, money, clothes, your wife and the neighbors' dogs. I could write all that but I won't. (Wiebe 443-44)

Wiebe's narrator makes a good postmodern move at the end, claiming to cancel his own prophetic utterance while leaving it stubbornly present, ringing in our ears. In this complication, I think, is the voice of Nietzsche's child-artist, who on the one hand demands our attention and on the other claims to know nothing for sure, who insists on both the right to testify and the freedom to make things up, who like Whitman accepts his and her own internal contradictions and the multitudes inside every human being. To accept such mystery and turmoil means abandoning the dream of a neat and tidy and singular way to follow. But the dream of such simplicity, we should know by now, is only a human dream, and a dangerous one. As Auden wrote in his "Epitaph on a Tyrant," "Perfection, of a kind, is what he was after, / And the poetry he invented was easy to understand" (Auden 51).

FATHERS AND (M)OTHERS

You may have noticed how many of the quotes in this essay concern fathers. In a workshop recently, Hildi Froese Tiessen presented a quick anthology of contemporary Mennonite writers. I found myself thinking that the tone, though not the form, of much of the work she read seemed closely related to the author's relationship to his or her parents, especially the father. For those of us with churchly backgrounds, of course, family and religious issues are inevitably and almost inextricably intertwined.

My book of poems *Flatlands* ends with a poem called "Seams" and with these lines, which have always seemed strange even to me, but which I believe have something to do with these issues:

> See the red-tailed hawk
> that just found dinner in the pond. See
> the hill's curve, like a fine rump,
> too big and dark for you to hold. Feel
> the seam of earth and sky, how every moment
> you are on the border. This won't last.
> The giants will return, and pity us,
> and say we can go with them if we find
> our mothers, if we ask them first. And if
> we find them, they will say we can. (Gundy 77)

In her remarkable book *Black Sun: Depression and Melancholia*, Julia Kristeva writes of the powerful human yearning for reunion with some un-nameable, archaic, perhaps forever unavailable Other. She suggests that much of both art and religion are driven by this desire, which can yield both the greatest ecstasy and the blackest despair. The intensity and depth of our need make faith the terrible necessity that it is, because our quest for this Other is indeed beyond all certainty, its only reality the kind of interior experience that much of the Anabaptist tradition—and, surely, much of human history—teach us to regard with suspicion. Oscar Wilde writes unsettlingly, "Men die for what they *want* to be true, for what some terror in their hearts tell them is not true" (qtd. in Hanson 234). Faith, he suggests, is the yearning for reunion with what terror tells us may not be there at all. Among its other, concrete meanings the Church is avatar of this yearning, our collective gathering of it.

I do not know why I believe we have to go back and find our mothers, and our fathers. But I believe we do. We have to ask their permission to set off with the giants—whoever *they* are—but whether they say yes or no, we need to set off on the journey. On the way there will be time for hearing the stories of the giants, and asking them to listen to ours, and talking with each other until, perhaps, we reach a place where we know as we are known. The stories will nourish and sustain us on the way, but they will not be easily told nor understood. They will include a dream of "evangelical and constructive Anabaptism" within which we might all live joyfully, purely, and peacefully together, and a nightmare of "nonresistance" as unredeemed misery in which the powerful abuse and terrify the meek. They will contain mystery, pain, darkness, suffering that seems utterly undeserved and meaningless. They will also speak of love and beauty and meaningful sacrifice, and a world so lovely and full that it seems incredible that we should be born into it.

We can talk at length about how this telling might take place, as I have been doing here, but more important is the telling itself. There are many cities and more to be built, visible and invisible, beautiful and ugly, old and new, with streets of mud and of gold. Let us build them and walk their streets, alone and together. Let us speak and listen, learn and teach, worship and cry out, and in so doing perhaps discover something of what it means to be people of God, together.

CHAPTER TEN

STORY, MASTERY, *GELASSENHEIT*, IMAGINATION, EROS: WHERE DO I SURRENDER?

"But 'glory' doesn't mean 'a nice knock-down argument,'" Alice objected.

"When I use a word," Humpty Dumpty said, in rather a scornful tone, *"it means just what I choose it to mean—neither more nor less."*

"The question is," said Alice, *"whether you can make words mean so many things."*

"The question is," said Humpty Dumpty, *"which is to be master—that's all."* —Through the Looking-Glass (Carroll 198)

"Is it possible for Mennonite thought to find a way out of its own 475-year 'drift' into self-induced aesthetic masochism?" —(Stolzfus 77)

"He's been trying to surrender
to the real things but can't find
the right flag. . . ." —Jeff Gundy, ca. 1979

Controversy about Mennonite writing and artistic expression is just one part of a larger struggle to define Mennonite culture, its qualities, and its borders in a time of rapid change. As rural Mennonite communities shrink, as urban and suburban ones grow, as young Mennonites

171

go to college and into professions rather than becoming farmers and housewives, as people and churches without Swiss-German or Dutch-Russian origins transform membership rolls, North American Mennonites find themselves forced to return to questions that once seemed settled and to encounter other questions of which Pilgram Marpeck and Conrad Grebel never dreamed. Is Anabaptism a tight and clearly defined group in possession of unique truth? Is it one small strand within the fabric of Christian and human history? Is the traditional Mennonite community—if there is such a thing, in the singular—a garden or a prison, *Gemeinschaft* or *Gesellschaft*? Is there—has there ever been—some singular, constant, unchanging Anabaptist identity, or has it always been a multiple reality even if reduced to some ideal, abstract purity as defined by the empowered? Are artists to be restricted as dangerous rebels, ignored as irrelevant eccentrics, trusted as inspired messengers from God? Of what use might their products and their presence be?

Having addressed the problem of the Mennonite artist caught between individual expression and communal accountability in chapter one, I have no desire to return to that marshy ground. As Hildi Froese Tiessen demonstrates convincingly in her excellent reconception of the current situation for Mennonites writing, the usual sets of binary terms—center/margin, insider/outsider, and so forth—are neither especially accurate nor very helpful in understanding the real dynamics of influence, pressure and desire within which contemporary Mennonite writers operate. "The fixed categories of identity that Mennonites once believed they could slip into unproblematically are no longer useful," Tiessen writes, and "the place that Mennonite writers are writing from, like the place most of us occupy, is not eternally fixed but is 'somewhere in motion'" (Tiessen 20). Let us examine, then, some of the temporary places and situations, some of the possible locations, and some of the warnings, exhortations and imperatives that are emerging both from writers and from those seeking to influence, inspire, or control them.

In the absence of magisterial figures like Harold Bender who took on larger-than-life roles spanning several functions, these days theologians, historians, sociologists, church administrators, and creative writers within the Mennonite sphere all offer their visions—sometimes complementary, sometimes conflicting—of what the church is and ought to be. In a way, this contestation is a struggle for power, of course. One way to see it is as a contest about the *location* of authority. In Scripture? Written history? Oral tradition? Particular places? Institutions? The contemporary community? Theology? Leaders? Individual conscience? Lived experience? Reason? Imagination? Most would agree that each of these is problematic as the sole nexus of authority, but in practical terms it is hard to live without privileging one, or some combination.

What follows is a survey of recent efforts to address these questions from a variety of Anabaptist perspectives; perhaps it is best thought of as an engaged summary of some elements of the ongoing conversation among Mennonite intellectuals about just what kinds of texts and views they wish to encourage, tolerate, or resist. It is organized by seven terms, each of them itself contestable: story, control, imagination, *Gelassenheit*, the world, doubt, and eros. These issues and ideas resist such categories, of course, and so many matters will bleed back and forth across the lines.

Although I do not hope to make a prescriptive judgment about where authority *should* be lodged, I will say this, descriptively: there is no going back to some Golden Age of a clear, univocal, universal Anabaptist master narrative. Among many other factors, Mennonites writing have arrived in enough profusion and diversity to ensure that the Mennonite story will be, well . . . complicated.

STORY

One key area of contestation clearly concerns the narrative(s) upon which Mennonite identity has been, is, and will be constructed, and the exact uses to which such narratives can and should be put. A full analysis of these issues would be a book in itself, but there seems little doubt that among Mennonites in general there is renewed interest in telling Mennonite and Anabaptist stories. One main motive is the hope that as older markers of community become less solid, stories will provide continuity and communal memory; another, problematically related to the first, is the sense that many of the more difficult and painful Mennonite stories have been silenced, left untold if they do not seem to advance the communal cause.[30] Recent controversies about the historiography of early Anabaptism demonstrate these complexities.

At the center of the discussion is Arnold Snyder's *Anabaptist History and Theology*, the most detailed study to date of sixteenth-century Anabaptism. Snyder seeks to recognize but not be bound by the "monogenesis" narrative of the period proposed in Harold Bender's "The Anabaptist Vision" and the "polygenesis" revisionism that followed, and many other influences as well. Musing on the difficulties of this task, Snyder writes,

> In some ways, poetry would be a more powerful medium for this task than is narrative. Descriptive narrative shows its limits when it attempts to 'recreate' complex objects or events. . . . The precious old quilt is brought out from the trunk and admired. It is 'objectively' there as a fact. But it is not a matter of 'objective' science when someone describing the quilt thinks that the combination of red and blue made it particularly striking, or when someone else is convinced that the tracing effect of a particular green thread is the element that held it all together. . . . in the end, neither story nor ode (however skillfully done) is the quilt itself. (3-4).

Snyder's version of the story emphasizes that early Anabaptism was a "diffuse and varied phenomenon that developed *only over time* into rigidly defined 'separatist' or 'sectarian' forms" (7, emphasis his). This view has not been seriously challenged, but Snyder's schematic treatment of "core" issues upon which Anabaptists agreed and "secondary" issues on which they did not *has* drawn much criticism—especially since in these terms nonviolence must be placed in the second category, given the wide range of Anabaptist positions on "the sword" throughout the first half of the sixteenth century.

Snyder's most vocal critic has been J. Denny Weaver. In an initial response, Weaver wrote that as a "peace church theologian committed to nonviolence" he was

> disturbed by this new synthesis of Anabaptist history and the standpoint from which Snyder has chosen to tell the story. It is a story for the peace church, but told in a way that opens the door to the accommodation of violence rather than seeing the rejection of violence as theologically normative. (Weaver, "Reading" 42).

Having heard it argued in a Mennonite Sunday school class that the Prince of Peace *wants* us to have enough nuclear weapons to destroy our enemies and then make the rubble bounce, I sympathize with Weaver's desire to make nonviolence normative and the urgency with which he argues his case. He believes that nonviolence must be at the heart of

Mennonite theology if it is not to be lost to the pressures of contemporary culture and right-wing evangelical Christianity.

Yet some of Weaver's claims about how Anabaptist history can and should be told have unsettling implications for imaginative writers, and perhaps for historians as well:

> If one truly believes that Jesus is Lord, that Jesus is the norm for faith and practice, then the story [of sixteenth-century Anabaptism] will not be told in a way that leaves the sword an "option" for the modern church to contemplate or as secondary to the core important issues. Telling the story from a perspective which assumes that Jesus' rejection of the sword is normative will mean telling a story in which violence emerges as a failure and the "heroes" are those who advocate nonviolence or pose nonviolent alternatives to violence. (Weaver 47)[31]

Here Weaver seems to argue that because the story of Jesus leads Anabaptists to believe that "Jesus' rejection of the sword is normative," other stories such as that of early Anabaptism can only be told in certain ways—so that violence must "emerge as a failure" and only those who advocate nonviolence can be "heroes," for example. One can agree with Weaver on the principle of normative nonviolence, however, and still see problems with letting that principle control the way that history is told. This passage seems to suggest—the phrase "will mean" is the most problematic one—that fidelity to the principle is more important than fidelity to what actually happened, a rubric whose difficulties need not be labored.

At a more fundamental level, the issue here may be what use we expect to make of history. How do we tell a story that meets our desire to maintain nonviolence as normative while acknowledging that such a belief has always been contested? The idea of the sword as an option for Christians has, of course, been "available" from the start; early Anabaptist history demonstrates clearly that rigorous nonviolence was a hotly argued and risky practice in the sixteenth century, as it is today. A close look at those early Anabaptists who accepted the sword in principle or in practice provides so few (if any) examples of heroic or successful violence, however, that advocates of nonviolence might wish to encourage that study rather than worry about it. Certainly the leaders of the ill-fated "Anabaptist kingdom of Münster" of 1534-35, both lived and died by it—and no historian I know of treats the Münsterites as anything resembling heroes or their exploits as anything but spectacularly disastrous. Arnold Snyder's account hardly glorifies these misguided revolutionaries, although he asserts that Münster "sadly, belongs firmly within the history of Anabaptism" (205).

Snyder's difference with Weaver, then, may stem mainly from their differing readings of a history whose contours they largely agree on. Since nonviolence became a consensus Anabaptist belief only near the end of the sixteenth century, Snyder argues, the diversity of belief and practice rules out "casual appeals to the so-called 'normative' position of 'Anabaptist nonresistance' as given expression in Schleitheim's article 6" (220). The question, then, has less to do with "what happened" than with what it *means*. If we must recognize that the first Anabaptists did not all share a commitment to nonresistance, surely we need not ourselves abandon nonresistance as a result. In a recent e-mail conversation, Weaver clarifies and perhaps modifies the views quoted above, coming closer to the position I have been groping toward here:

> History should not be written to find worthy examples to emulate. It should be written to help us understand how we got here, and whether there were other options that could have been taken. I am quite willing to acknowledge the violent folks who were Anabaptists, and to write the story in a way that makes them part of the story. But how does one interpret the story? Is the story itself a norm, so that anything in the story then is also correct and justifiable today as well? . . . If we are Christians, the criterion is whether it can be shown to stand in the line of the story of Jesus.

Writers of imaginative or historical narratives might still raise further questions, of course. For example, must we work with only two categories, the "nonviolent" and the "violent"? Are Robert E. Lee, Abraham Lincoln, and Walt Whitman—all of whom accepted the violence of the Civil War as a tragic necessity—then morally indistinguishable from sociopathic serial killers? Can we make no distinctions among Hitler, Roosevelt, and Dietrich Bonhoeffer? I am with Weaver entirely in seeking to resist and critique the myths of necessary and redemptive violence so deeply rooted in American culture. But I still see a difference between Hans Hut, who did not accept pacifism theologically but never raised a sword in anger himself and was the most effective early Anabaptist missionary, and Jan von Leyden, who personally beheaded one of his sixteen wives in the public square of Münster when she displeased him.

Other unresolved issues exist as well. A particularly troubling one for me is this: if the original energy of Anabaptism lay in its radical departures from orthodoxy, its refusal of compromise with the institutional church, how can that energy be preserved if those very departures are now themselves an orthodoxy and the movement an institution? The early Anabaptists, empowered by the ready availability of Scripture for close study, aimed to recover what they thought of as the purity of the early church, but clearly their readings of the Bible and the new practices they devised were products of their own cultural milieu as well—they drank from the streams of both Enlightenment rationalism and contemporary spiritualism, even as they condemned "the world."

Contemporary Mennonites are similarly embedded in our own culture in ways that we can only partly and incompletely recognize, let alone extricate ourselves from. Is the effort to construct a definitive Anabaptist theology, conceived by contemporary theologians to counter the larger culture's master narratives, itself another master narrative in waiting, with its own hegemonic quality? I can only raise these questions here, but they will be explored further in the "Complications" section.

A shift from propositional rationalism to a theology based on the untidiness of story might seem to offer promise to those hoping for a more open and capacious theology. As Scott Holland points out, however, narrative theology is not necessarily more generous than other versions:

> Some expressions of narrative theology can be quite conservative, colonizing, and chauvinistic. The variety of narrative theology practiced by Karl Barth, Hans Frei, George Lindbeck, Stanley Hauerwas, and some enthusiastic Mennonite disciples unapologetically asserts that the church's story must swallow up the world's story and that the disciple's narrative must eclipse the human narrative. The true believer must practice *Gelassenheit* and submissively find her place in the plot of the faithful community's narrative. (Holland, "Response to Gordon Kaufman" 51)

Holland's use of *her* points to another key issue of recent Mennonite narratizing: the place of women within Anabaptist stories and their telling. In a ground-breaking essay titled "The Mennonite Woman in Mennonite Fiction," Katie Funk Wiebe noted that especially in texts by men, female characters have tended to be stereotypes, either "Eve Before the Fall" or "Eve After the Fall." Since Wiebe wrote this piece in the early 1980s, Mennonite women have more and more insisted on telling stories in their own voices and their own ways, often resisting and complicating the standard narratives.

One form of this resistance—found among writers and literary critics of both genders, and probably a holdover from oral traditions—insists that much of their power lies in their *resistance* to being reduced to a neat moral or a clear set of instructions. Walter Benjamin argues that "it is half the art of storytelling to keep a story free from explanation as one reproduces it" (Benjamin 89). Similarly, Julia Kasdorf's poem "Thinking of Certain Mennonite Women" celebrates stories she has heard, as well as the way that the women tell them: "honestly, without explanation / to whoever will listen" (Kasdorf, *Eve's Striptease* 79).

Such telling "without explanation" has never been more than a folk Anabaptist habit, of course—it might serve for family stories told in the kitchen, but when it came to the key church narratives, Anabaptists have always insisted that the stories they tell so compulsively *mean* something, and tried hard to control *what* they mean. Without the stories of Jesus and the martyrs told and retold over the centuries Anabaptism surely would not exist, and the distinctive emphases that set the early reformers at such odds with those around them were all rooted in the story of Jesus and the early church as they read it in Scripture.

One can be supportive of this effort to find meaning in story—indeed, one can hardly function as a writer without it—yet be wary of the ways communal narratives can become totalizing and exclusive, excluding both the world outside the story and the aspects within the communal life that do not fit comfortably within the official narrative. Di Brandt muses on these matters in terms that deserve careful attention:

> Once upon a time, I lived in a tiny Mennonite farming village in south-central Manitoba, called Reinland, the "clean land". . . . My village was located in the very heart of the Mennonite world, in the middle of southern Manitoba, in the middle of the North American continent, in the middle of the world, as we thought.

We told an elaborate but fixed story about ourselves as Mennonites in Reinland. . . . The rest of the world, for us, was *other*, but as I found out when I got there, it was not at all other in the way we had imagined, in the way we'd been told. Its otherness, I could see immediately, was not the otherness of people lounging indifferently on the road to hell, but consisted rather in a completely different set of terms, a different set of rules to live by, and I wanted very much to know what they were. (Brandt, *Dancing* 32-33)

In Brandt's village boundaries were maintained by language: Low German for home, gossip, and humor, English for school and town, High German for church. Each represented a separate paradigm, virtually a separate world, Brandt suggests. At twelve, unwilling to live with these separations, she began speaking only in English, which meant that she "started seeing the contradictions and discrepancies between these different language and thought systems" (Brandt 34). And as she describes above, when she got out into "the world," she found that the Reinland image of it as undifferentiated "people lounging indifferently on the road to hell" was simply false.

Allow me to speculate briefly on "truth" here. Stories like the one Brandt describes claim to be "the truth," but as human constructions are inevitably incomplete, at best partial truths. The world is, by its very nature, bigger and more complicated than any story, and a story that casts most of the world as simply a homogeneous, otherly backdrop to the glorious tale of the righteous few is sure, sooner or later, to be revealed as incomplete by those who escape the borders of the official story. The more such stories are proclaimed as "the truth," the greater the disillusionment when they are revealed to be at best partial truths.

Fiction, on the other hand, makes no claims to be "real" or "*the* truth" in some all-inclusive way; it is not fiction, after all, if it is literally, factually true. Yet as it claims only to represent some portion of truth about human experience through the medium of story, it can paradoxically be *more* accurate about the human condition in its recognition of incompleteness and partiality: no fiction claims to contain the whole truth, the entire master narrative.

To tell her own story, Brandt says, she found herself forced into what seemed the most guilty transgressions of the communal story: "And all the memories and feelings called up by the writing were somehow in contradiction to that [official] story, everything I wanted to say in my poems, I realized to my dismay, was forbidden in the rigid code of my Mennonite upbringing" (Brandt 34).

Brandt's early poems, in particular, challenge the tidyness of the Reinland story with their descriptions of a rigidly controlled, anti-intellectual, smugly patriarchal society. Of this work, and that of others such as Pat Friesen and Audrey Poetker who were also part of the "Winnipeg Renaissance," she writes:

> The new Mennonite writing exists as transgression, a violation of the authority of God and the Bible and the father. It begins to give a voice to the children and women silenced by the tradition. And it does this by a kind of striptease, taking off the clothes of the official story, layer by layer, stripping away the codes we have lived by to get to the stories underneath of our real, aching bodies in the world. . . . What the new Mennonite poetry does is to bring the story home, back to earth, where hurt is really hurt, and death is really death, and desire is really and truly desire. (34)

The *real* story, Brandt claims, does not simply begin with Jesus, pass through a small group of Swiss Brethren deciding that true evangelical faith means refusing the sword, and culminate gloriously in a small village south of Winnipeg. The real story must include all the uncomfortable, painful, sometimes disastrous ways that Mennonites have failed to live out our ideals as well as the complicated realities of lives in bodies that the official stories simply have not included. Surely this does not mean celebrating or glorifying those disasters, nor does it negate or make less essential the work of theologians and others who seek to understand, systematize and clarify the ideas and beliefs that the community has lived by, or tried to live by. But it does mean, for writers like Brandt, an ongoing effort to recover and to tell some portion of the many astonishly specific, personal, experiential stories in which the story of communal belief and action—still a concrete and real and important one, but not "the" whole story—is embedded.[32]

CONTROL

Calvin Redekop's *Mennonite Society* presents itself as a "comprehensive introduction to the North American Mennonite world," so it is not surprising that it includes an analysis of "Mennonite Intellect and Aesthetics." The direction his analysis takes, however, is quite surprising. Redekop begins with a rather standard discussion of mistrust of "worldliness" and the resultant "love-hate attitude toward the development of the mind and the creative instincts": "Thus, both the creative person and the consumer of arts within the community were caught in a bind. Both were attracted to certain creative aspects of life, but because creativity was seen as glorifying humankind, both needed to avoid those attractions" (118).

Redekop offers three "typologies of Mennonite intellectual life" in response to this bind. The "retreatist approach" "considers the world of contemplation and expression a sign of pride and deceit," and is found in Old Order and Hutterite groups which restrict expression and consumption of art—even quilts and sermons (Redekop, C. 119). At the other extreme lies the "integrationist" approach, which holds that "the aesthetic and intellectual spheres [are] in no way inimical to the Anabaptist-Mennonite way of life." This view may exist in Europe among the Dutch Mennonites, says Redekop, but "There is no Mennonite congregation in North America which would allow free rein to intellectual and aesthetic expression" (119).[33]

Redekop poses a "cooptative approach" as a third possibility: that "the aesthetic and intellectual life is not evil so long as it [sic] is used for the right objective. . . . Poetry could be useful for expressing faith, and fiction could make a religious point, if carefully monitored." This is the majority Mennonite position, Redekop says, but he is not enamored of it:

> The cooptation position is premised on the assumption that critique also involves commitment. Thus, the life of the intellectual cannot be given free reign, but must be tied to an ultimate foundation or faith. . . . This situation is not unlike the status of the artist intellectual under Soviet communism. To be totally free to express oneself would lead to the forsaking of or, worse still, the undermining of the tradition. (121)

The Soviet comparison here is good for a painful wince, and the difficulties of keeping together self-expression and *Gelassenheit* are apparent enough. But surely the opposition of faith and intellect is less total than he suggests here. For most of the last two millenia many artists have proceeded as if Christian faith and art belong together quite naturally.

Dante and Milton would have hooted at the idea that there was some essential opposition between being Christian and being a poet. The church has, indeed, often been hostile to innovation in the arts and sciences, but the artists and artisans who built the great cathedrals and the painters and composers of the Renaissance operated in a context in which the idea that faith could enable the highest art and craft rather than restricting them was largely taken for granted. The idea that art belongs to the fallen world and that the faithful could or even must live without it belongs to Reformation and Anabaptist iconoclasts, a part of the rebellion against churchly corruption.

Redekop is not done, however. If the integrationist approach is simply beyond the pale, and the cooptation position is inherently unstable, then his own logic and categories seem to force him to conclude that a "retreatist" position is the only tenable one. By the end of the chapter, he has argued himself into such a corner regarding the dangers of both art and intellection that one might expect him to throw down his pen and renounce his own book in mid-sentence, before it destroys the whole Mennonite enterprise.

> A central dilemma of Mennonite society . . . is that self-conscious reflection—by way of the arts and through giving free and creative rein to the intellectual impulse—eats at the very heart of the sectarian commitment. The intellectual and aesthetic impulse, nurtured both in the process of handing on the tradition *and* in the process of maintaining and defining the boundaries of a society, tends, however, to question both. . . . the freedom of aesthetic and intellectual experience that is craved by many, if not most, Mennonite may well prove to sound the death knell for the Mennonite ethos and reality. (126)

Probably most Mennonites will recognize the anxiety that underlies such analyses; setting people to learning, thinking and speaking freely indeed makes them harder to control—as the Catholic authorities found during the great uprising of independent learning and thinking in which Anabaptism originated. The more I think about such pessimism about the community's ability to survive free intellectual and aesthetic activity, however, the more it suggests a strange lack of confidence in the strength and vitality of the Anabaptist project, if not of the gospel itself.

Redekop seems to make the truth into something to fear. If the story of Jesus and their people's attempt to live in faithfulness to that story for five centuries is as close as Mennonites can come to embodying the ultimate truth of how human beings are to live in the world, should not such a truth be durable enough to survive efforts to explore the story in all its complexities and ambiguities, and re-embody it in words and artifacts with a certain degree of novelty and independence and beauty? If this little group of believers is so unstable that it can survive only by demanding that its most sensitive, creative, intelligent members do not allow themselves to be sensitive and creative and intelligent, and expecting them to go around in a half-aware daze all their lives, should Mennonites really be fighting with all their nonviolent powers to keep themselves in existence? Did Jesus really come among us in order that we might live in our sleep?

Against Redekop's vision of control, I will in the next section sketch several Mennonite views of the imagination. But I will close this section with a passage from Gordon Kaufman that may serve as a transition. In an interview, Kaufman argues that the Mennonite glorification of and nostalgia for community often hardens into idolatry:

> The other idol is the Mennonite community. Mennonites think they are the really true Christians. This is a strong impulse that I think derives from our long history of persecution. . . . Mennonites had to live in corners of the society where they would not be persecuted and even executed in the early days. So they developed a consciousness of themselves as a special group with the truth about life and death and God in a way that others didn't have, and I think most Mennonites grew up thinking that. That's just blatant idolatry in my opinion. (Kaufman 11)

IMAGINATION

Gordon Kaufman's ambitious and widely respected theology—after John Howard Yoder, he is probably the best-know Mennonite theologian in the wider world—is insistently expansive and non-credal. We must not forget, he argues, that both "God" and "Christ" as we know them are essentially *human* constructions, however fervently we hope that they point toward realities too large for us to understand fully. His books have titles like *In Face of Mystery*; in an address summarizing his recent work, he indicates just how different his approach is from those we have examined thus far:

> To acknowledge forthrightly and regularly that our theological statements and claims are simply *ours*—the product of our own human study and reflection, and of the spontaneity and creativity of our own human powers imaginatively to envision a world and our human place within it—is to free us from these all too easy moves toward authoritarianism and arrogance which have characterized so much Christian theology in the past. Simultaneously we are opened to the broad ranges of experience, life, and insight lying outside our own tradition, and we are provided with a powerful incentive to engage in serious dialogue and interchange—on equal terms—with representatives of other religious and secular points of view. (Kaufman 41)

Kaufman insists that there is no escaping our "human powers" in theology or other intellectual activity. Limits placed on imaginative construction by conservative and traditionalist approaches thus do not eliminate the role of the human imagination; they simply seek to freeze earlier constructions in place. Clearly Kaufman's theology is far more friendly to imaginative workers than some others; it provides, as Scott Holland notes, "hospitable space for artists, scientists, writers, poets, and political activists" (Holland 50). If imaginative activity is not only permissible but inevitable, then we can only seek to do it with all the vigor and rigor that we can muster.

One recent effort toward reconceiving what she terms the "Mennonite religious imagination" is Sheri Hostetler's masters thesis. Hostetler argues (making much use of Gordon Kaufman) against what she calls the "absolutizing imagination" which "needs absolute clarity and certainty" and "seeks to clearly define the world in terms of right and wrong, good and evil" (Hostetler 17). Among other difficulties, Hostetler points out, those holding this point of view tend to believe that they have not "religious imagination" but "Truth." In search of a more flexible and constructive imagination, Hostetler offers highly sympathetic readings of three texts by Rudy Wiebe; she suggests that Mennonites need a "parabolic, wholistic" religious imagination that would be more pluralistic, more socially conscious, and more aware of "the awesome Mystery that surrounds us" (Hostetler 53).

An even more critical perspective on efforts to construct limited versions of Mennonite history and identity comes from Magdalene Redekop, who writes:

> Mennonite historians sometimes remind me of an elderly bride who gazes into her mirror and says to herself, "I am the fairest of all churches." We are so busy admiring ourselves that we may not notice that the position of the husband has been usurped by an abusive tyrant. . . .
>
> To see Jesus as an abusive husband and the church as a geriatric bride is the image that results from the profound failure of the imagination among Mennonites. If the imagination is denied, all that is left to communicate religious vision is the feeble voice of reason. The best it can come up with is a ridiculous tyrant in the sky. You know the one I mean. He's the man with the white beard wagging his finger at us all. He's the man who has a *reason* for everything he does. . . . Blake called this product of reason "'Nobodaddy" and viewed it as a form of idolatry. (245)

Redekop's spirited defense of the religious imagination is (as she notes) at least as old as the source she mentions, the early nineteenth-century British poet, visionary, heretic, and favorite of other poets, William Blake. Like Kaufman, she calls attention to the human origins of all our images of God and of history, and like him she insists that in the absence of an active religious imagination the "feeble voice of reason" will inevitably fail to offer compelling religious vision.

A distinct but somewhat parallel defense of the imagination can be found in a surprising Mennonite source. Recent surveys of Mennonite literature and its theory ritualistically invoke the venerable John Ruth as the voice of communal control and of literature that would aspire to tell the Mennonite story from within the community rather than outside it. With the publication of the first significant modern treatment of *Mennonite Identity and Literary Art*, as his 1978 pamphlet is titled, as well as his long career as historian, filmmaker, and interpreter of the eastern Pennsylvania Mennonites and Amish, Ruth has established himself as both an authority and a target.[34] Having aligned myself fairly closely with his views in "Humility in Mennonite Literature" (chapter two in this volume) then tried to redefine the discussion somewhat in chapter five, "Beyond Dr. Johnson's Dog," I would now like to return to Ruth's classic statement for a closer look at the third chapter, which is titled "The Role of the Imagination."

Ruth recognizes that imagination "is as much a part of our genuine worship as it is of our temptations to do evil. . . . Further, imagination is the means by which, with the help of memory, we gain access to and are given the courage to claim our heritage—our story" (49). Noting that "The artist's version of the story is not always welcome," Ruth describes the tension with considerable sympathy for the artist: "To a conventional mind, committed to an order of this world, its apparently anarchical 'destruction of order for the sake of reordering' (Robert Penn Warren) may seem blasphemous, as Jesus' or Stephen's view of the temple did." Here, we should notice, the artist is aligned with the prophetic voice of Jesus himself, and conventional resistance with the moneylenders. While Ruth hastens to add that mere questioning of tradition does not amount to art, he seems really less concerned with framing limits for artistic expression than with encouraging the development of a specifically Mennonite imagination:

> Our imagination must be our own, and its limitations must not be blamed on external factors. . . . The question is: are we in touch, have we wrestled, with the angel of our covenant-identity? Do we know, have we felt, its soul-issues? Are our dreams, our personal memories, our impulsive confessions, our involuntary historicizing—in short, our imaginative life—organically intertwined with the dialectic of our covenant-soul? (52)

Ruth sees the work of the imagination in a somewhat surprising way: "to bring out of the heritage things old and new." "One wonders," he continues, "if a new order of crystallization of our identity is not absolutely necessary it is to speak in the changed social arena" (54). The last pages of his chapter bemoan the loss of appreciation for the "plain" vision and virtues of Ruth's Pennsylvania community amid rising secularism and assimilation. Clearly his call for artists to be engaged deeply with their communities is driven by the fear that the community is endangered and the hope that the artist might help preserve it. Ruth states directly that his call for an affirmative Mennonite literature is driven by this hope: "I have been testifying, in these lectures, to my feeling that what I can affirm about my heritage, in these days, is more interesting and more valuable, even to a general audience, than what I can discredit" (Ruth 63).

I find much that is attractive in this argument, but let me note a few caveats. First, one can applaud Ruth's general impulse yet remain uneasy about the singular and totalizing way that he refers to "our covenant-identity." I am quite sure that my memories and dreams and imaginative life are intertwined with a "covenant-soul" that is subtly but significantly different from the one Ruth imagines.

Second, one can respect Ruth's interest in affirmative imaginations on Mennonite themes—I have written some myself—without drawing some line between "affirmative" expressions and others and allowing only the former. Much recent Mennonite writing is quite clearly driven by the writer's sense that particular elements of Mennonite life are in dire need of rigorous critique.[35]

Notice that Ruth himself claims the right here to proceed on the basis of his quite personal "feeling" about what his community needs now. Even though he argues that his particular community needs defense more than critique, does he not suggest that any strong artist who is deeply engaged with a community must similarly decide on what kind of work is most important and valuable at a particular moment? In the years following Ruth's manifesto, Di Brandt, Pat Friesen, and Julia Kasdorf would publish books of poems indicating equally intense engagements with their home communities. If their imaginative engagements would lead them to much more equivocal celebrations of their home places—none of them, we should note, identical with Ruth's—still it seems undeniable that they were all wrestling hard with the soul-issues of their communities, and engaged in strongly imaginative "new crystallizations" of Mennonite identity.

Duane Friesen's recent *Artists, Citizens, Philosophers: Seeking the Peace of the City* is one of the first serious efforts by a Mennonite theologian to integrate the arts into Mennonite practice. In an extended treatment of "Artistic Imagination and the Life of the Spirit," Friesen argues that "all Christians are called to be artists"—imagine how shocking such a claim would have seemed to the general Mennonite population only a generation ago.

He also notes that "aesthetic" experience has ethical implications, as when the character Celie in Alice Walker's *The Color Purple* regains her faith through a perception of beauty that enables her to re-imagine God as more worthy of worship than an old, bearded white man: "The renewal of life by God's Spirit experienced by Celie and Shug is nothing less than the return to holiness of the Sabbath. . . . Such delight is one of the dimensions of Shalom" (Friesen 172).

Arguing that the issue "is not *whether* we will express ourselves aesthetically in material culture, but *how*," Friesen suggests that it is simply not possible to avoid aesthetic experience, and that indeed "we must open our lives to the gifts offered by the artists: poets, musicians, painters and sculptors" (Friesen 181, 192). Although he insists that artists must live in "dynamic tension between our limits and our godlike creativity," he shows much less concern about communal control than Ruth or Redekop. His primary concern is to affirm the work of artists as "an expression of gratitude for existence [that] can be received by the human community, both the church and the larger society, as one of the gifts of the Spirit" (Friesen 200, 209).

GELASSENHEIT
"With the return of Desire to theology there is less austerity, humility, morality and self-rejection and more play, poetry, story, irony, mystery, grace, carnal vitality and creative power in the blessed work of theological composition"—Scott Holland, "Theology Is," 241

Throughout a series of essays outlining what he calls "theopoetics," Church of the Brethren theologian and pastor Scott Holland has argued vigorously for the terms in the second half of the sentence above and against yielding to narrow versions of Anabaptist community. As should be clear by now, I am sympathetic with this project and have learned a great deal from Holland's work, although I quote him here partly to inquire, once more, about one of the terms he uses. As a key to Mennonite theology and practice for generations, humility and its kindred term *Gelassenheit,* or "yieldedness," have been hotly contested in recent years. I have found myself returning to these terms nearly obsessively, and arguing over their meaning and significance repeatedly, because their definitions and the use that Mennonites make of them seems so crucial.[36]

To begin, the significance of Gelassenheit varies radically depending on just what is being yielded *to.* Especially in the more closed Mennonite communities, Gelassenheit has most often meant (in practice if not in theory) yielding to communal discipline and authority, yielding "selfish" individuality to the normative claims of the group (or the group's leaders). As Di Brandt describes Reinland in *questions i asked my mother*, as Rudy Wiebe describes Wapiti in *Peace Shall Destroy Many*, this sort of authoritarian, patriarchal Gelassenheit reigns in those villages.

These versions of Gelassenheit-as-control are not the only possibilities, however. Nor do they exhaust the historic Anabaptist understanding of the term. Arnold Snyder indicates that the origins of Anabaptist Gelassenheit are "rooted in late medieval mysticism and piety, and [it] was central to the radical reformers. . . . Anabaptists believed that human beings had to respond to God's call. They had to yield inwardly to the Spirit of God, outwardly to the community and to outward discipline, and finally, in the face of a hostile world, believers might have to 'yield' by accepting a martyr's death. The necessary unity between the inner life of believers and their outer lives of discipleship and community life is here seen again" (Snyder 152).

As Snyder describes this yieldedness, even at the very start of the movement, it seems considerably more complicated and multifaceted than the relatively simple submission to authority to which it has often been reduced. The Gelassenheit he describes, if observed throughout the community, would not eliminate discipline, but surely it would make the abusive imposition of power impossible. No leader who had truly yielded inwardly to the spirit of God would find it possible to abuse those less powerful.

Gelassenheit and humility take on even wider implications in other settings. Holland writes of Julia Kristeva's work on "'strangeness' within the self":

> She suggests we can only learn to live at peace with strangers around us if we acknowledge and tolerate strangeness and otherness in ourselves, for we are indeed "strangers to ourselves." . . . To invite the stranger to speak—indeed, even the repressed other of our desire—threatens to subvert the power of Anabaptist superego, since its vision of spirituality and morality demands *Gelassenheit* (submission or yieldedness to) and *Nachfolge* (following after) the *master story* inscribed on the communally mediated celestial flesh of the body of Christ. (Holland, "Communal Hermeneutics" 107)

What, then, if Gelassenheit should be understood in a broader sense, to include a yielding to voices outside the master story and what Holland calls the "Anabaptist superego"? Holland may have picked up this term from Stephen Dintaman, who followed his influential essay on "The Spiritual Poverty of the Anabaptist Vision" with another in which he issues a pointed critique of "superego religion" in Anabaptism:

> For neo-Anabaptist theology and pedagogy there were no signifi-
> cant struggles of the soul. . . . There was only the struggle to be
> obedient. For neo-Anabaptism there was no solitary individual
> lurking inside the community member, no shadowy areas in
> which sin or sickness could hide, no spiritual depths. . . . There
> were simply the clear commands of Jesus and the contrary pull
> and power of the evils of militarism, nationalism and material-
> ism. (Dintaman 314)

The Anabaptist Vision, Dintaman argues, has unwittingly alienated Mennonites from "the deep grammar of the Christian faith," replacing the deep mysteries of the biblical story with "the merely ethical cate-gories of means and ends" (321). Like Arnold Snyder, Dintaman wants to re-draw the Anabaptist circle more widely to include the "spiritualist" stream whose most important figure was Hans Denck. As Snyder demonstrates, the spiritualists lost out in the sixteenth century to the "literalist" streams represented by the Swiss Anabaptists and by Menno Simons. For Denck, the life of "yieldedness" to Christ was crucial, and he expected the Spirit's reign within believers to be transformative, but he regarded most "outward" orders besides the love of God and neigh-bor as secondary if not positively harmful (Snyder 307).

Julia Kasdorf also considers varieties of inner and outer yieldedness in an essay significantly titled "When the Stranger is an Angel," writing of unexpected transformations that may accompany simple hospitality:

> Perhaps [the story of Jacob wrestling the angel]—like my father's
> story—means that we possess a sacred power to make angels of
> strangers when we are open to change. This can only happen
> when we leave the security of the hearth and go out to greet the
> stranger, when we sit with him and imagine his life, when we are
> able to question our own certainties and to be taught and
> changed through the encounter. (*The Body* 35).

"To question our own certainties" seems both crucial and difficult. What if we are changed so that, for example, we no longer feel compelled to obey the bishops? Or so that we find certain particular stories, Mennonite or Christian, remain necessary to our spiritual and practical lives but not entirely sufficient to provide all the nourishment that we need? In another essay, Kasdorf discusses humility, an idea she finds "both familiar and difficult to use," since traditional humility language has often "served to silence the voices of many while protecting the authority of a few." Even so, she says,

> I claim the best kind of humility Mennonite tradition has taught. . . . This kind of humility is characterized by a commitment to listening to others and to serving others. . . . It gives rise to the kind of conversation that has the potential to transform another's life, reconciling a distant individual to himself and to the community rather than angering and alienating him. It is antithetical to pride, which ultimately is the belief that individuals or communities do not need to consider the perspectives of others to understand and define themselves. (*The Body* 95)

The Gelassenheit implied here yields to open encounter with the stranger who may be an angel, to a recognition of outside perspectives and presences that may carry things of great value. Against the idea that following Christ means finding in the gathered community everything necessary for life, this wider and more capacious Gelassenheit suggests that, no matter how clear and strong our master story, we remain in need of those others within and without who, if we let them, constantly offer us unexpected and unpredictable gifts as well as, sometimes, essentials of life.

In a literary context, Gerald Bruns suggests that true poems emerge from a similarly open encounter with the world:

> Our relation to the world, to other people *as* the world, requires that we forego knowing, not in the sense of abandoning reason for something else, some alternative mental state . . . but in the sense of acknowledgment as the recognition of the otherness of other people. In the hermeneutic tradition, this is called openness, . . . a letting-be (*Gelassenheit*) of the impenetrability and ungraspability of the other, say her reserve or self-standing, her resistance to domination and control. (qtd. in Gardner 180)

Like Kasdorf and Holland and Kristeva, Bruns here seems to be groping toward the articulation of a certain humility before language and the world and others, one that would renounce the drive for "mastery," linguistic or otherwise. In his *Breaking the Fall: Religious Readings of Contemporary Fiction*, Robert Detweiler makes a parallel argument for both the religious and literary uses of this sort of Gelassenheit:

> Two German terms not easily translatable suggest what both religious and interpretive communities could strive for: *Gelassenheit* and *Geselligkeit*. *Gelassenheit*, a term already used by the fourteenth-century German mystic Meister Eckhart and developed by Heidegger, is sometimes rendered as "releasement" or "abandonment," but it also conveys relaxation, serenity and nonchalance, a condition of acceptance that is neither nihilistic nor fatalistic but the ability—and it may be a gift—to move gracefully through life's fortunes and accidents, or to wait out its calamities. (Detweiler 35)

This relinquishing of control does not come easily, of course; one might argue that Anabaptism, for all its renunciations of worldly power, is built on the dream of building a community small and self-contained enough that within its borders it might be possible to create a miniature but truly peaceable kingdom, to somehow bring *everything* under control. It is surely true that the writing impulse involves a will to power as well, as the poet creates a new, minor realm on the page. But as the poets keep reminding us, that peaceable kingdom has not yet come into existence in the physical world, and will never be created if it depends on mere enforcement of communal discipline rather than the joyful gathering of the like-minded.

Gelassenheit, then, is both central to the Mennonite tradition and, in its more generous forms, a threat to its less capacious communal versions. Mennonite artists and writers have increasingly yielded themselves to the otherness of the wider world and of their own psyches and bodies; they have challenged the long-standing Mennonite impulse to retreat rather than confront the world, and even more to control their own otherness, to put it under the discipline, even the ban. Of course, as history keeps reminding us, you cannot really escape from the world; even less can you escape from yourself without paying a great price. The kind of yielding I have been tracing here is indeed dangerous. It might lead to all sorts of unforeseen consequences—perhaps, as the ur-Mennonite joke has it, to making love standing up, then to dancing.

THE WORLD

"The 'great refusal' of the Anabaptists and Mennonites was directed against the Christian-feudal order. . . . [A] way of life patterned on gestures of resistance against a past age has produced a crisis of historical depth and increasing intensity" —Hans-Jürgen Goertz 5

As the fifth centennial of the Radical Reformation approaches, it might be well to consider the implications of Hans-Jürgen Goertz's observation that the original Anabaptists were rebelling against a Christian and feudal world order that no longer exists. Are Mennonites still trying to fight battles that were over centuries ago, preparing for the wrong war, like the French fortifying the Maginot Line, quickly skirted by Hitler's armies, whose useless towers can still be seen not far from some of my ancestral villages in Alsace?

While the influence of the Christian right in American politics is a worry for some Mennonites and a reason to celebrate for others, both the Inquisition and medieval Christendom are long past, and from a historic Anabaptist perspective it is hard to mourn either one of them. "The world" as contemporary North American Mennonites experience it is, I would suggest, both more benign and more dangerous than the one our forebears faced in the sixteenth century.

To examine those changes in detail would take me far beyond the borders of this study. But as one example, consider the changes John Ruth notes in one way "the world" began to enter his community:

My parents' generation began life thinking in German idiom. English came, for them, along with smoothness, in the era that produced Glenn Miller band music, Bing Crosby and Perry Como, hair cream and wall-to-wall carpeting. Part of my struggle of perception is to get past that wall of smoothness to the presmooth idiom of my people's mind. (Ruth 255)

I find these observations fascinating because *my* generation, which also includes John Ruth's children, rebelled in its own way against that very smoothness. Those of us who came of age in the 1960s found our lives complicated by the presence of many counter-cultures: the anti-war and civil-rights movements, the youth movement, and so on. With people of all sorts questioning materialism, violence, racism, and civil religion, it seemed natural enough to me to combine Mennonite social criticism with the newer and more colorful varieties. If I remember correctly, even John Howard Yoder's *Politics of Jesus*, just off the presses when I was assigned to read it in college, struck me more as confirmation of what I already thought than a blinding new insight. Of *course* Christians ought to be political; of course Jesus was on the side of the poor and the oppressed. I'd learned that from Bob Dylan and Peter, Paul, and Mary, and from singing old spirituals and new protest songs in my back bedroom as I tried to make chords on the cheap guitar my parents bought me for Christmas when I was thirteen or fourteen.

Through my own dabbling in the counterculture (I was always too uncomfortable in crowds to be a very good activist), I learned a lesson similar to the one Di Brandt described earlier: that "the world" was not a single thing, that in fact it was a very complicated place where very different forces and values were in constant contention, and where many "worldly" people and groups distrusted "the world" of conventional American authority figures at least as thoroughly as the Mennonites I knew did.

The music of Bob Dylan, to take just one example, spoke against militarism and conformity, for authenticity and solidarity with the poor and oppressed. In contrast, the "smooth" music of Frank Sinatra and the others Ruth mentions valorizes "love" in the most conventional and individualistic American sense. Sinatra boasted that he did it his way, while Dylan counseled us all that the times were changing, and that we must pay attention to the lessons about life, war, justice and peace that were blowing in the wind.

Obviously the world has not grown simpler in the decades since I left my farm community for college. We have gone even farther from the comparatively stable Christian/feudal society against which the Anabaptists rebelled. It is one thing to rail against "the world" when its avatars rule both church and society, but quite another when "the world" also includes such a rich, bewildering diversity of groups and causes. As I sit in my thoroughly wired office and type these words into my computer, email keeps me in constant touch with friends, relatives, colleagues, and advertisers across the country. I listen to folk music placed on the Internet by a radio station out of range of old-fashioned broadcast reception. With a few keystrokes I can search the Bluffton library and many others. If I type "Julia Kasdorf" or "Di Brandt" or "Jeff Gundy" into a search engine I get dozens of hits—books by all three of us can be ordered on Amazon.com, or through the Mennolink bookstore.

We have indeed come a long way since the Swiss Brethren in the Jura were forced into the highest mountain valleys and allowed to live only above a certain line of elevation. There is no question, really, of returning to such isolation, nor even for most of us any question of returning to the lesser separation that many maintained even a generation or two ago. We *are* in the world; where else would we be?

At the end of Italo Calvino's *Invisible Cities* is a passage that I used as an epigraph for my first book of poems, *Inquiries*. As Calvino tells it, Marco Polo and Kublai Khan are speaking of cities: of "promised lands visited in thought but not yet discovered or founded: New Atlantis, Utopia, the City of the Sun, Oceana, Tamoé, New Harmony, New Lanark, Icaria. . . . of the cities that menace in nightmares and maledictions: Enoch, Babylon, Yahooland, Butua, Brave New World." Finally, all the stories told, Khan muses:

> "It is all useless, if the last landing place can only be the infernal city, and it is there that, in ever-narrowing circles, the current is drawing us."
>
> And Polo said: "The inferno of the living is not something that will be; if there is one, it is what is already here, the inferno where we live every day, that we form by being together. There are two ways to escape suffering it. The first is easy for many: accept the inferno and become such a part of it that you can no longer see it. The second is risky and demands constant vigilance and apprehension: seek and learn to recognize who and what, amid the inferno, are not inferno, then make them endure, give them space." (Calvino 164-65)

Not to accept the world as inferno, sink into it, join it: but to live riskily and carefully in the welter, to constantly pay the closest attention to its doings and to seek its good. Surely this is the work that writers are doing, and surely it is the work we are called to do.

DOUBT

Dallas Wiebe's brilliant essay "Can a Mennonite Be an Atheist?" offers a searching, rambling, reckless exploration of his experience as a writer and professor who grew up on a Mennonite farm in Kansas but lived apart from the church much of his life, ambivalent about faith but still conscious of much good within the Mennonite heritage. The piece is at once autobiographical and theoretical, funny and quite serious. Wiebe examines at length the place of doubt within a belief system, and concludes that it creates disturbances that are troubling but necessary:

> Mennonites must be ready to address any question, including the most disturbing ones. We must be ready to articulate the enigmas of belief and to look at them honestly and carefully no matter the consequences. It's an old notion that faith without testing is bound to decay. It's obvious that belief without doubt is fantasy. (Wiebe, *"Can a Mennonite?"* 126)

Wiebe offers a strong defense of humanism as an attempt to free learning from religious control, and notes the connection of humanism with the Reformation. "Humanism never was anti-religious. In its formative years it wasn't even agnostic. It was always associated with religion and religious belief. Religious belief and the study of belief are at the center of humanism because religion is central to the mind of man" (Wiebe 126). In this context, Mennonite opposition to the arts and the intellect come to seem an attempt to freeze the revolution that was Anabaptism at some more or less arbitrary point, to forbid further thought and exploration of the precise sort that began the movement. Sattler and Menno and Marpeck and the rest hardly were content to accept the master narrative of their time as final.

Praising humanism for its "doubt, humor, and democracy," Wiebe argues that such values "undermine totalitarian control" as they "vitiate authority" (Wiebe 129). Like John Ruth, Wiebe concludes that Mennonites have impoverished themselves by neglecting the life of the mind, but he goes farther than Ruth, insisting that now "Mennonites must make room for the life of the mind or their church is dead." His comments on the "Mennonite writer," however, foresee considerable difficulties for those who take up such a role:

> Finally, there is the dilemma of the Mennonite writer. I think there is such a thing as a "Mennonite" writer. If such a person

doesn't exist, one can take on the persona or play the role. . . . As Mennonites enter the literary world and write poetry and fiction, the existential forces become ever stronger. My friend Skyblue says that "To be a writer you must know everything and believe nothing." . . . when a writer is creating a narrative he must suspend belief. His religious beliefs must be put aside to create his narrative. Narratives deal with moral incertitude, with moral dilemmas. To be a successful writer, a writer must enter that world where all belief is suspect. He must enter a world where religion is absent. He must learn to take on sympathetically and seriously the personae of evil. . . . If Mennonites are to accomplish something of importance as writers of poetry and fiction, they will have to enter that world of the imagination where there is no moral certitude, no matter what the writer's personal beliefs might be. It is not a comfortable place. (Wiebe, *"Can a Mennonite?"* 131)

We have come a long way here: against the argument that stories must only be told in ways that serve the master narrative, Wiebe claims equally forcefully that successful writers must put aside religious belief and moral certitude and enter the uncomfortable place where "all belief is suspect." Not all writers would agree with Wiebe—one famous recent dissenter would be Flannery O'Connor, whose work (no matter how lurid its subject matter) is drenched and suffused with Christian belief.

I doubt that an easy resolution of this division between commitment and skepticism is possible, or desirable. Personally, I find myself oscillating between attraction to both of these poles and several positions between. Surely Wiebe is right about the writer's need to confront the whole range of human experience, belief, and behavior. Yet I am not quite convinced that doing so requires casting aside one's beliefs and commitments entirely—in fact, I am not convinced that putting aside one's beliefs in any thorough way is even possible.

In thinking my way through this knotty question—and many others—I find myself once again drawn to the work of pacifist poet William Stafford. Near the end of his life Stafford reviewed an anthology edited by well-known poet and political activist Carolyn Forché. Titled *Against Forgetting: Twentieth-Century Poetry of Witness*, the anthology takes the shape of "a poetic memorial to those who suffered and resisted" the many wars and large-scale repressions of the twentieth century. It is, in fact, a sort of modern, secular *Martyrs' Mirror*, a record of the horrific violence of the twentieth century and those who struggled to survive it.

Stafford seems to consider Forché's intentions admirable but does not entirely trust the results, and his reservations are worth a close look. Just as Wiebe insists that writers must examine all belief carefully, Stafford questions the thesis-driven nature of the editing, noting how hard it is to attain the "shiver of the unexpected" that poetry requires given such a pervasive thesis. Even more troubling, Stafford suggests, is the cumulative effect of so many accounts of victimization: "And how vividly do you have to suffer to qualify? And how many generalizations can you allow yourself as you attempt both speed of communication and the qualifiers that life's many particulars demand?" He objects, finally, to the "speed of assessment" that Forché's thesis requires, saying that it "put a torque on me, snagged my attention, kept me wary of living on the emotional high of atrocity hunger" (Stafford 77).

Stafford concludes not that we should ignore or repress what we know of the terrors and disasters of history, but that we should recognize our own complicity in them:

> A poet, a person, a fallible human being, has to step carefully through a puzzling world. We have to remember our own surges of anger, how we sometimes choose a country or a people and load our hatred on them, how we go to war—and then how later we come to our senses and perceive that ills are not to be so simply projected on an alien group.
> Remember?
> That is what I don't want to forget. (Stafford 80)

Clearly Stafford is recalling his own experiences with modern wars—especially perhaps World War II, when he was a conscientious objector, and Vietnam, when he was active in the antiwar movement. What seems essential here is his reminder of the human tendency to project our flaws outward, to maintain in-group purity by demonizing an out-group or casting out scapegoats from within.

Mennonites have rarely gone to literal war in this fashion. Surely, however, they have a long history of casting their imperfections out into the world (or onto one member of the group) and then congratulating themselves—even against all evidence—on their righteousness. What Stafford suggests as an alternative, as I discuss in detail in Chapter 4, is a way of writing that is not value-free, if that were possible, but in which personal values and beliefs are kept in creative tension with the necessary freedom of art.

EROS

"Much later in life I came to realize how powerfully God had spoken to me through beauty, especially music. But the strangest part was this: I always returned from my most dramatic encounters with beauty fully resolved to live a moral life, a life of complete goodness and service. I have never been able to account for that feeling. . . " —John Oyer 189

The experience of beauty makes for good? Such is the testimony of John Oyer, recently deceased Mennonite historian and Goshen College professor, a man more noted for his gently rigorous scholarship than for his unorthodoxy. The connection he suggests between the experience of beauty and the realm of ethics and action has long been an especially troubling one for Mennonites. Just as the Second Amendment notes that a "well-regulated militia" is necessary for the state, Mennonites have long acted to regulate their desires and their attractions to the various forms of beauty. Icon-breaking and ordinances against worldly entertainments; temperance and plain dress; Harold Bender's "Anabaptist Vision," with its dismissal of the "mystical, spiritualistic, revolutionary, or even antinomian related and unrelated groups" as outside the pale of "evangelical and constructive Anabaptism" (Bender)—the distrust of the human desire for beauty and pleasure, and the effort to narrow the sphere of permissible pleasures, has been pervasive.

These strictures have fallen hardest on the least powerful, especially women and children, and the most innovative and restless, including artists. It is not surprising, then, that Mennonite women writers have been in the forefront of those calling us to pay more careful attention to these matters. Di Brandt's recent collection of essays, already discussed here, is titled *Dancing Naked*, and Julia Kasdorf's is called *The Body and the Book*; even these titles begin to indicate just how important issues of embodiment are to two of the most significant Mennonite poets.[37]

Di Brandt describes how she became aware of such issues while teaching poetry in Manitoba high schools. At first puzzled by the conventional, distant language of the love poems she saw, especially those by female students, she came to realize their language was a cover for a great deal of disappointment and anger, as well as denial of those emotions:

> each of the young women was holding on, desperately, to a code of love that she knew to be false. . . . These young women, on the cusp of adulthood, didn't want to acknowledge the betrayal of the world, of boyfriends and fathers, and of men in general, so they wouldn't have to acknowledge self-hatred, deep down, so they wouldn't feel worthless, abandoned, discriminated against, threatened, because they were women. (16)

Concreteness, writing the body as well as the heart into love poems, is threatening but crucial, Brandt believes: "The erotic is dangerous to this culture, not because it's destructive, but because it locates us in our bodies and in our real lives. In this racist, misogynist, violent culture, it is also tragic, because the spirit suffers so. It is, finally, transformative, in a way that makes people scared, and excited, and very alive" (Brandt 17).

For Brandt "the erotic" is a category including a breadth of experience that is often kept silenced and shadowed, by larger North American culture as well as by Mennonites. To speak more fully about our real lives is, indeed, dangerous, often painful, but possibly transformative.

Kasdorf's essays use feminist theory and categories more flexibly than Brandt's, but are equally conscious of wounds inflicted by patriarchal rigidities. In an essay drawing on the work of George Lakoff and Mark Johnson, Kasdorf reflects deeply on "Bodies and Boundaries":

> As human beings who experience our physical bodies as distinct entities possessing insides and outsides, it naturally follows that we would experience a group, metaphorically figured as a body, as a being that is distinct and manifest through its physical boundaries. . . . It may even be that the primary property of such a metaphoric body is its boundaries, and the only imaginable ways of being in relation to such a body are either inside or outside its bounds. Inside is good, pure, true; outside is bad. (Kasdorf, *The Body* 80-81)

Such a view leads not just Mennonites but many groups to a range of behaviors that "violat[e] the interests of others to protect . . . a collective self." Against such an emphasis on boundary maintenance, Kasdorf asks "what would happen if communities were regarded, not primarily as bounded entities, but as bodies capable and always in need of relationship—as individuals are?" (81)

If boundaries can be seen as limits that give form to all living, changing organisms, then we will honor them because they give aesthetic shape to our lives and the lives of the communities we inhabit. . . . The group would be seen, not as opposed to "the world," but as engaged in loving, form-giving dialogue with it. Outsiders or those who inhabit the margins of the community would be valued for their ability to offer consummating images of the Body in relation to its context, images that are sometimes painful and that are impossible to grasp from an interior perspective. Those in the community who challenge its norms would be valued—more than any writer of policy or theology—as the ones best able to initiate conversations that help to determine the Body's shape. (95)

I have referred to Scott Holland's work several times already; of contemporary Anabaptist theologians, he has perhaps been the most committed to bringing desire and the body back into communal Anabaptist discourse. Such ideas, not surprisingly, have found a mixed reception in Mennonite circles, and much of his work has found publication outside those circles, including "Communal Hermeneutics as Body Politics or Disembodied Theology," which was delivered at the same conference on Harold Bender at Goshen College that provoked my chapter seven. Published in *Brethren Life and Thought*, the essay argues against a communal hermeneutics that "effectively shield[s] us from the ambiguity of our own embodiment and from the mystery of the world as God's body. . . . Desire is eclipsed by discipleship; eros toward the world is swallowed up by a churchly ethics of perfection, and the strong singer's voice is lost in the four-part harmony of the collective body" (Holland 94).

Against the influential division of agape and eros by Anders Nygren, which Holland says "pries apart agape and eros like a cherrystone clam and calls the faithful Christian to flee eros and embrace agape" (100), Holland follows Paul Tillich's understanding of eros as the source of a spirituality which includes poetry and mysticism. "Anabaptism is an incarnational mode of being in the world," he insists, and theorists who reduce it to a disembodied "Anabaptist Vision"

have been too attached to virgin martyrs, crucifixions of the flesh, and murdered prophets. Thanatos eclipses Eros. While the faithful Anabaptist must always preach with the prophets, an embodied hermeneutics calls him or her to also muse with mystics;

dance with strangers; and break bread and drink wine with our artists, poets, and creative writers. Unless we eat the flesh and drink the blood of the son of man we have no life. Only communion with the body can save us, for as Michel Foucault reminds us, "the soul is the prison of the body, not the other way around!" (Holland, "Communal" 105, 106)

CONCLUSION

At any number of points in this exploration I have been tempted to say "Hallelujah, Amen!" and turn to other matters. There would be worse ways to end, I think, than with Holland's sermonic call to enter more fully into the embodied life. Let me close, however, with a slight variation on the theme of talking to strangers, so suspect in the paranoid modern world. This passage comes from Naomi Shihab Nye, a friend and admirer of William Stafford, and speaks eloquently of what I have more and more come to think of as the true and necessary Gelassenheit:

> On one of those Idaho back roads, I contemplated deeply the sweet emblem of a stranger's hand raised in passing. . . . I wanted to tell my friends back home who were teaching their children not to talk to strangers that they had it all wrong. *Do* talk to strangers. Raise your hands to them in strange places, on back roads where leaning fields of tasseled grass have more identity than you do. Ask strangers anything you want. Maybe they'll have an answer. Don't go home with them, don't take off your pants with them, but talk, talk, talk. . . . I remember thinking, that night, that talking to strangers has been the most important thing I do in my life. (Nye 11-12)

The welling up of Mennonites writing comes from this urge to "talk to strangers" both within and without. It emerges, I think, from the same springs that Dintaman tapped in his now-famous (among Mennonites) essay on the "spiritual poverty" of the Anabaptist Vision. Mennonite writers have shared, in a variety of ways, Dintaman's sense that the vision of Mennonites as a people whose life and history could be summed up by discipleship, peace and community was not so much mistaken as too constricted, although the alternatives they have envisioned are not adequately contained in the term "spiritual." Harold Bender's effort to make a usable past for Mennonites, brilliantly successful on several levels, simply left too much out, put too much of the past and the present outside the pale. It excluded too much history, too many strangers within and without, left too little room for the life of the mind and the body and, yes, the spirit. It included too much of what Robert Bly, in another context, called "slander of the world," too much fascination with martyrdom, too much emphasis on merely behaving well.

The nourishment it offered was, perhaps, sufficient for life, as the body can live for a long time on bread and wine, or even on bread and water. But like the body, the soul craves many foods. To grow to its full potential it craves not only stories with a clear moral import but those whose meaning seems puzzling or contrary, those that contest and compete and conflict with the official narrative. It craves red meat and vegetables, apples and oranges, chocolate and curry and coffee. And all of these things, we should remember, are also a part of God's good world.

CHAPTER ELEVEN

ENIGMAS OF EMBODIMENT IN FOUR
BOOKS OF POEMS

Jean Janzen, Keith Ratzlaff, and Julia Kasdorf, all of them my friends, conversation partners, and teachers, were introduced in chapter five and have been discussed throughout this book. They have also each published a recent book of poems, and those texts, along with my own, are the subject of this chapter. Ratzlaff's *Man Under a Pear Tree*, Janzen's *Tasting the Dust*, Kasdorf's *Eve's Striptease*, and my *Rhapsody with Dark Matter* are all "worldly" books—they all reflect on lives in bodies in the physical world, in towns and cities and the natural world. All are set in modern America, in places where buggies and bonnets and other tangible markers no longer provide communal borders. They are sparse with explicit Mennonite markers yet pervaded by the themes and tensions of contemporary Mennonite life. These are books about sex and hunger and men and women, desire and restraint, fulfillment and yearning. They take up issues that for generations were not often put down on paper by Mennonites, certainly not with such willingness to dwell with mystery, uncertainty and doubt, such effort at being accurate about experience first of all.

In a passage that has become a touchstone for poets, the young John Keats mused on what it might take to become a great poet:

I had not a dispute but a disquisition with Dilke, on various subjects; several things dovetailed in my mind, & at once it struck me, what quality went to form a Man of Achievement especially in Literature & which Shakespeare possessed so enormously—I mean *Negative Capability,* that is when man is capable of being in uncertainties, Mysteries, doubts, without any irritable reaching after fact & reason—Coleridge, for instance, would let go by a fine isolated verisimilitude caught from the Penetralium of mystery, from being incapable of remaining content with half knowledge. This pursued through Volumes would perhaps take us no further than this, that with a great poet the sense of Beauty overcomes every other consideration, or rather obliterates all considerations. (Keats 1209)

This way of working must seem strange to academics, whose training is entirely toward "reaching after fact and reason," and to those Christians oriented toward doctrine and dogma. Yet Keats's insistence that "The sense of Beauty obliterates all considerations"—at least within the poem—allows poets a space to work in which those "other considerations" may be, if not obliterated forever, at least deferred. What may enter, then, are types of information that tend to be washed out or covered up by our usual ways of thinking, driven as they are by instrumental rationality and conventionality.

In particular, these four books all address issues of gender, desire, location and vocation, and strive to push past the usual ideological treatments of those crucial issues. They talk about sex and death and love, about transgression and healing, about faith and doubt, without any prior obligations but to get down what seems true. They resist leaving these issues to the pornographers of sex and violence on the one hand and the stuffy defenders of an imaginary golden age on the other. With their unique attention to meaning embodied in poetic language, poets are better equipped than most to explore the living experience of embodied human beings, to provide the insights into that experience that may ultimately help us find the wisdom to cope with it in responsible Christian ways.

Keith Ratzlaff's *Man Under a Pear Tree* is, among other things, very much a book about longing, art, and place, and about human bodies circulating in the world in all their fragile, stubborn needs and abandonments. The first poem ("Rough-Cut Head") notes, in a line I once foolishly tried to convince Ratzlaff to remove, "We are alterable." "Winterreise" draws its title from Schubert's song of yearning, which is also the title of a self-portrait by Paul Klee that shows the artist at his mother's grave. In Ratzlaff's poem, the speaker remembers his own losses: "I've driven by the same woman's house / for 20 years remembering she kissed me" (Ratzlaff 7).[38] He offers more fragile, precious bodies in "Gladiolus," about a photo of a skeleton in the newspaper, in "Blue-Bird-Pumpkin," in which a doctor muses on reading mammograms, in "The Body Pledges Its Allegiance."

"Mural from the Temple of Longing," "The Pathos of Fertility," "The Embrace"—even listing the titles makes the pattern evident, though the poems should not be hurried through as I am doing here. The title poem begins with the speaker suddenly seeing in a new way: "August and pears falling. / It's as if I've gone / blind, as if my life has been." He hears a radio and a boy singing along, some song of almost wordless desire: "'Oh,' they sing, the boy and the radio,":

> "oh and oh baby." It's as if
> pears were breasts
> if breasts were like that,
> like rain on a day I remember
> when the everywhere nature
> of rain was on my face, in the trees,
> in my hands outstretched.
> As if I had
> climbed the pear tree
> with one part of my body and
> shaken the limbs
> for the delight of the rest of me.
> One fall I climbed the ridge,
> acorns dropping
> in the oak leaves like gunfire—
> but this is not like that.
> Pears fall,
> and what green is left
> leaches quietly into the air
> just before
> they hit the ground.
> Then yellow, then blush pulled
> into the earth
> like multiple lovers—if pears
> and the everywhere nature

of seed and fruit
can be imagined that way.
As if blindness were a cure
and delight
for the eyes; as if
the blind man hit
by lightning
in his own back yard
had his sight restored
as a curse.
I am not in danger. (Ratzlaff 19-20)

Where does the danger come from? We feel the speaker starting, then relaxing, knowing nothing is "really" happening except his sudden realization of the awe-full fertility of the earth and its circularity, the place of death within it. Would we feel desire if we did not die? "Death is the mother of beauty, mystical," wrote Wallace Stevens.

Part two is also full of bodies in all their fragility, tenderness, foolishness and lust. "Gospel" remembers the speaker's time in a religious singing group and the girl who was his real reason for being there:

—I'm singing
like the day I fell out the car window,
the first day my body discovered
its real predicament
and sent my voice out for help;
and she's singing like the day
she found Jesus
which was the trouble.
I was perfectly, shamelessly
in love and lying and doing my best.
But nothing I hoped for happened.
Either there in the church
or with her, later.
All that misdirection
and shame. Not even half
of what I've ever wanted
has risen up singing
like an impudent animal. (29-30)

The poet gets neither the girl nor the belief that he hopes for; his body remains in its "predicament," while his voice, still, goes out for help. No easy grace here, no more lying. But the problem—one the book returns to almost obsessively—is what to do with unreturned desire: "once, behind a metal shed / at the edge of town I saw them / parking, and didn't look in, / although I could have, / then spun away on the gravel / and drove for half an hour / with my lights off" ("Midmorning Glare," 40).

Part two ends with the half-sarcastic, half-visionary "My Students Against the Cemetery Pines." Assigned to write poems about death and resurrections, the students get absurdly detailed instructions from their poet-teacher: "there must be water, there must be light / of some kind, there must be a bird in the poem." Suddenly, the teacher has his own vision:

> And when suddenly the literal dead do rise up,
> my students' backs are turned. They are looking
> at the water, inventing dark birds and nuns
> married to Christ. And the dead rise up
> with no dirt in their mouths, with clean shoes
> and crystal voices singing "This is it! This is it!"
> And I tell my students to stay focused,
> to wait for it. Stop. Don't turn around.
> Say no it isn't, I tell them. No, No, No, No.
> The first line of stanza three is "No, it isn't." (50)

What is the refusal here? Is this the Anabaptist superego evading the miraculous once again, demanding that we all remain on task, continue doing our work, Apocalypse or not? Notice here a kind of miraculous transformation parallel to those I once traced in Ratzlaff's earlier work, one of those half-serious, half-fictional apocalypses that seem both yearned for and feared.[39]

The final section is full of angels and bodies, with many references to Klee paintings. "Fitful Angel" describes dreams of singing; again, as in several of the last poems, it contains upraised arms and emphasizes the body as separate:

>   but of course
> my throat has other business. Mostly my body is completely
> on its own. Somewhere, in a hollow I used to have, is a little
> scar of pines and unstable grass. I miss the crisis of sparrows

and the slump of water in useless pools. Oh God, who once
was behind the door, this is a terrible room to wake in as if
it were everywhere. (57)

For a self-professed doubter, Ratzlaff writes a great deal about God,
turning the conundrums of faith and doubt over and over. "God is a
chair / to sit in / and the act of sitting // it makes all the difference,"
claims "Forgetful Angel" (59). "I once thought holiness was a big dog /
that would follow me like a halo," says the "Surgeon (peeling an orange)" (60). This sense of belief that is more remembered than present is
accompanied by more on the body: "For years you can cut / and cut it on
the table . . . and you still won't save it. The body is not divisible like
that" (60).

The book ends with the luminous "Woman Flying," which muses
even more deeply on the possibility of God intervening directly in a
mundane life. The female protagonist is described

> Wishing then that God would simply lift her out
> And thinking, this self at any one moment,
>   the man who survived being hit by lightning
>   seven times, who then committed suicide
> And the glaze on the road going home
> The picture her daughter drew of a house
>   some clouds, two ankles, two shoes
>   disappearing off the top of the page
> It's a woman flying above our house, the girl had said
> And thinking of the abstraction, the new stage
>   it signaled in her daughter's development
> The five simple lines around the shoes that mean motion
>   and up and trailing away
> And wishing it might be her, the woman flying
>   blessed for no reason with a great invisible gift. (69-70)

A good Jungian might suggest that this beautiful concluding image
is Ratzlaff's anima sailing away to glory, blessed with the great gift that
has been withheld throughout the whole book. Here again the dream of
transformation, of flying away, recurs, and it does not seem accidental
that it is associated with women—where else do men, especially those
ridden by doubt, look for relief from their daily lives, for intimations of
holiness? Ratzlaff makes no claim to be telling the whole story, but only
that of a "self at any one moment," transfixed by memory and love, pain

and yearning, and the constant possibility that the "great invisible gift" is just about to arrive.

"How can she not be furious?" Julia Kasdorf wrote once in a tribute to Jean Janzen, noting her long years of raising children before she earned her M.F.A., her place in the still-retrograde Mennonite Brethren church, the violent dislocations of her Russian Mennonite family (Kasdorf, "Thank You" 15). Janzen's *Tasting the Dust* uses Vermeer's paintings as Ratzlaff uses Klee's, for both imagery and context. Each section of Janzen's book begins with a poem on a Vermeer painting of a woman, and the women are often in postures of service, scenes which many poets would describe furiously. But if open anger is not Janzen's style, neither is she resigned to acquiescence or second-class status. This book describes many things that a woman's body can do besides pouring itself out in forced service.

In the first, the young girl is "held in uncertainty," "suspended in the air / of spring which has filled / the room, ready to loosen / whatever is bound" (Janzen 3). The second describes a "Maidservant Pouring Milk" who must spend her lifetime "confined / to bread, table, wool," to serving others, reduced nearly to that single gesture: "all of it held / in a pale morning light, / her whole body pouring" (Janzen 17).

The images of perfection Janzen is drawn to are set against, not within, the Anabaptist dream of a perfectly ordered community; "Getting It Right" juxtaposes three vultures, described as "the bent elders, judging," with the grace of a song played and sung beautifully:

> "O Divine Redeemer" my sister sang
> over and over, trying to get
> everything right—tone, attack,
> breath control, and I pressed
> the piano keys, Gounod's melody
> straining. What have we in us
> to want perfection, to think
> we can get it right? . . .
>   These vultures see
> that my heart is still beating.
> They'll soon stretch their awful necks
> and flap away, easily reaching
> those clear highways where they
> will circle like winged hearses

ENIGMAS OF EMBODIMENT / 211

and wait, then float back down
to wade in the spilled bodies,
tearing and feasting.
My sister and I will make careful
choices, but at the end nothing
will be perfect. Pardon, we'll cry,
trying to get it right. (Janzen 30)

Trying to be perfect is glorious, the poem suggests, but judgment is odious. Who are these elder/vultures anyway, presuming the right to wade in and tear the flesh of the dead?

In the third section, beginning with a poem based on "Woman in Blue Reading a Letter," the letter's message—from a husband, it seems—becomes tangible, not only a voice but a mountain range, fields, valleys, until "he is present in her face." (35) This sense of being overwhelmed, overtaken by another presence, runs through the next poems, several of which deal with Holland and Anabaptists who were martyred there. In "The Language of Light" it is again the written word that eventually dominates:

The pages burn in Haarlem,
1557, ashes lift off

the scorched skull of the bookseller;
men toss words into the fire
and others run off, arms full.

The hunger to know, and the stooped
figure writing. The inked letters
unraveling out of the first

illuminated "I," the beginning of this world. (38-39)

In "Triptych: After Ghent" the speaker feels a strong connection with the martyred Mayke when she holds the withered remnant of a pear that Mayke offered to her son just before being tied to the stake. In the next poem, however, the speaker doubts her connection: "We dip hummus and swallow, / talk easily as evening folds. / Sliced bamboo driven under fingernails. / The jeering. The betrayal of dawn. / I never said I could do it" ("After the Martyrs Exhibit," 41).

The relation of art to orthodox religion is, it seems, constantly on Janzen's mind. When pushed, she is, like Keats, more likely to trust the former; in "Isaiah Fifty-Three," she begins, "Van Gogh stopped painting / the black Bible"—symbolic, it would seem, of the same sort of religious convention the vulture/elders represent. "Instead he took / black apart, color // by color, and let / its strands pulse // and moan in chairs / and stars, in trees // and ears of wheat." This is no mere selfish artistic egotism, though, as Janzen renders it: "He did it for us / so we could look // if we dared, taste / the ache, let it sizzle // under our own skin. / So we could be healed" (43).

The last section meditates on how we are *placed* in the world, on exile and home, and on the final displacement of death. A suite of poems attend the death of Janzen's mother; she is "an empty house" (63), "earth itself" (65), an elemental, still mysterious figure:

> Not the rush
> and glance of your hands,
>
> but what lay hidden and waiting
> in you. All those years a gathering
> of streams for such a place
>
> as this, where you hold me
> and let me go.
> Where I will find you again. (65)

The final, title poem takes up dust and gardens through the poet's husband, who brings the taste of dust into her domestic space, and along with it "an origin so deep and dense" that it draws her into a meditation on the garden and how it rewards artful labor, becomes generative and connective through both place and time. Death and loss, "tumble and breakage," are necessary, even integral to this vision, and the poem shows no dismay that the garden is "his" place rather than hers; "Sometimes I join him," the poet says, and surely in the visionary final lines his work as gardener and hers as poet are drawn together, movingly fused:

> it rose
> like fire to make the mountain,
>
> a narrative of tumble
> and breakage from its sides,
> the wet roar of ages
>
> under the slow beat of the sun.

The mountain offering itself
in mud, sticks and stones

for his spade, his touch
to make of it a shape and fragrance,
to taste the center of this earth. (66-67)

Among the many poems on Amish and Mennonite subjects in Julia Kasdorf's first book *Sleeping Preacher*, the brief "The Interesting Thing" is something of an anomaly. It describes "a girl" who endures being tied to a tree by her brother and being molested by an "old neighbor" and (this is "the interesting thing") would afterwards walk home, spitting out the taste of his tongue, "and tell no one" (Kasdorf, *Sleeping Preacher* 30). The silence that the poem ponders and begins to break is, it seems, the point at which Kasdorf's second collection, *Eve's Striptease*, begins. It is as though the whole of the book is in recompense for the first poem not having been adequately heard. Far more than an account of abuse, though, *Eve's Striptease* is a book about desire in many forms, both within and without, about gestures of resistance and joyful joining with others as well as pain and submission.

The book forms not a smooth narrative but a mainly chronological series in which a girl grows into a woman and confronts the complex world of sex, desire, and power. From the first Kasdorf muses on how "Our thoughts get laced / with strange aches." In "First Gestures" "a girl makes love for the first time," then weeps in her lover's arms. The speaker of "Freight" also remembers her sexual awakening: "That whole brutal summer / I pulled weeds in my father's garden, / my body stunned by its great momentum / and a halting restraint like bad brakes" (Kasdorf, *Eve's Striptease* 5). In "The Sun Lover" sunbathing through a Sunday afternoon is the context:

At sixteen
she is a virgin. While her parents sleep
in the quiet house, she knows
the sun is teaching her about love,
how it comes over your body
making every muscle go soft
in its pitiless gaze,

how it penetrates everything,

changing you into something dark
and radiant. She craves it,
knows it is everywhere like God's love,
but difficult to find. . . .

Every hour, she turns over but prefers
to face the sun. All her life
she'll measure loves against this
gentle ravishing. . . . (7)

"What other sin gets such attention?" as sex, Kasdorf wonders in "Sinning." But not only sin is attached: there is, again, the old neighbor with his invitations: "he tracked my height / on a cellar door frame, a dated line for each time / he backed me against it, driving his tongue // into my mouth" ("Flu," 10-11). "Ghosts" tells of the feelings of dissociation and disembodiment that abuse trauma brings, of late night urban fear and anger as "the ghost foresees it all from above, / and I rage against the vulnerable socket / I cannot gouge out of this body" (12).

These moments are poignant and deeply imagined; the great strength of this book, however, is in Kasdorf's unwillingness to remain in a simple ideology of victimhood. "Of course it sets me back" Kasdorf muses of yet another man's groping hand, yet she also recognizes her own power to attract and refuse:

as the girl grows, the bones

of her cheeks and pelvis jut
like blades beneath her skin,

gorgeous weapons of revenge.
At last, the lusts of *those*

who trespass against us bear
some resemblance to our own:

shame and rage, heavy as coins
sewn in the lining of an exile's coat.

When an immigrant ship went down
in Lake Erie, passengers who refused

> to shed their heavy garments
> drowned, yards from shore. (14-15)

This recognition of mutual desire and even transgression is deeply Christian in theory, of course, but in these poems it leads to startling recognitions. Along similar lines, "Bulbs" puts one man's rumored abuses in the context of his near-starvation during the German occupation of Holland: "There is no pure use for history. Years later / when I hear the rumors and accusations, / I will refuse to slap his famished hand, / even when it reaches for a breast, / round and succulent as a bulb" (17).

"Eve's Striptease" reflects on her mother's advice about sex, that "it keeps getting better and better," and on what Kasdorf has had to "learn for [her]self": "all the desires / a body can hold, how they grow stronger / and wilder with age, tugging in every direction / until it feels my sternum might split / like Adam's when Eve stepped out, / sloughing off ribs" (21-22).

The second half of the book is titled "Map of the Known World," and its effort seems indeed to be a kind of mapping of what can be known in this world. The poems in *Sleeping Preacher* pose Big Valley as the beloved but lost homeland, but these have left that landscape behind; it is Brooklyn that the poet loves and must leave here, the place which she calls "my Babylon, my Jerusalem" in a poem commemorating her leaving for yet another new place. The focus shifts to adult and relationships defined less dramatically by sex, although grief for the damages the world does to women is still a main theme. There are many tears and a lot of pain in these poems, often recognized by the poet with an uneasy identification. A Tang Dynasty concubine rues her abandonment in "The Use of Allusion," a mother and daughter are both burned in the same spot on their thighs in "Map of the Known World." "Ladies' Night at the Turkish and Russian Baths" ends with the speaker on the roof of the building:

> We stretch out there on cots, and beside me
> tears slide like sweat into the turban
> of a stunning young woman. Whatever
> the reason, I feel bound to her weeping,
> eyes locked on our city's sky
> aglow with all that lies beneath it. (54)

This openness to the pain of others is, perhaps, one of Eve's most equivocal blessings. Like her mother the traveling nurse, Kasdorf visits the sick and troubled, searches for meaning in their cancers and children born with birth defects. If desire is innately dangerous, so is life itself, as "Flammable Skirts Recalled" recognizes; wondering whether she and her friend should return their skirts or keep them, even if they risk going up in a sudden burst of flame, she asks "Haven't we—like at least / a quarter million others—always been living like this?" (58)

The dozen or so poems at the end of *Eve's Striptease* are about taking up life, risking those connections of friendship and desire and love that Kasdorf knows are so dangerous and so precious. The "passive transformations" found in Ratzlaff and other Mennonite poets are nowhere to be seen here. Instead, these poems are about a self-conscious and deliberate sort of transformation. They offer glimpses of a constructed self and a chosen community quite different from the small, ethnically and geographically closed one of Big Valley. This other community is based on work and human commitment, not religion or blood, even though it may mean turning away from one's earlier community. As "Eve's Curse" tells a student, "This work / will drive you away from us; it will make / you strange in the end . . . your curse will be to ache as you've never imagined: / your limbs will long for the scent of this ridge / as Eve's curse was to crave for her husband" (77).

This new community includes both men and women, Mennonites and others, artists and preachers and novelists, some famous and some obscure. They are celebrated for their independence and persistence, qualities Kasdorf clearly craves for herself as well. In "Thinking of Certain Mennonite Women" her admired friends tell stories of their small, solitary transgressions: climbing the windmill, jumping off the swing set, dancing naked in the flower beds. "Boustrophedon" elegizes painter Warren Rohrer, who like Kasdorf left his Mennonite community for a career as an artist: "No / one back home sees or knows that he makes." "First Bird," written for Shirley Showalter's inauguration as the first woman president of Goshen College, celebrates a lone bird that "sings for all birds, even / when she stands for nothing / but herself." The image of violation, so pervasive, is here as well: "We know nothing can be whole / that hasn't been torn. // There is no holy thing / that hasn't been betrayed, // the way notes, once forced / into her tiny throat, // come out this dawn as song" (Kasdorf, *Eve's Striptease* 82).

In the first poem of *Sleeping Preacher* Kasdorf remembered a Bible verse: "Whoever puts his hand to the plow and looks back / is not fit for the kingdom of God" (3). The injunction has always seemed a bit odd to me, since when I learned to plow, with a narrow old three-bottom plow and an Allis Chalmers D-15, I soon discovered that if I didn't look back frequently the plow would jam with cornstalks that clogged up until they lifted the plowshares right out of the ground, meaning both that no plowing was getting done and that I had to get off and kick the jam free, far from an easy task.

I *had* to look behind, and despite her own injunction so does Kasdorf. This need becomes clear in "Flying Lesson," the final poem of *Eve's Striptease*, which concerns Kasdorf's decision to leave Goshen College for New York City midway through her undergraduate years. As she talks with the college president about her plans, he tells the story of flying his little plane out into the Atlantic, a little further each time, until he had barely enough fuel to get back. Despite Benjamin's advice and Kasdorf's own admiration for those stories told "without explanation," she ends this poem with an explicit one: "his advice comes so clear: fling yourself / farther, and a bit farther each time, / but darling, don't drop" (83).

Thus the book ends at the beginning of a journey, yet on a cautionary note and with an implied desire to return, at least eventually. The speaker wants to fly over the uncharted sea but not to run out of fuel and crash; she knows, as the image implies, that "the world" may be an ocean with no place to put down. How far can she, or any of us, go?

At least as important as this question, though, is the blessing from the father-figure. The credits dedicate the poem to J. Lawrence Burkholder, former president of Goshen College and a leading Mennonite intellectual for half a century. It seems crucial that in the poem the president sits and listens but does not forbid her to go. Instead of asserting his authority to control her, he tells a story of his own testing of boundaries that is an indirect warning but also an implied validation of her need to set off on her own journey. His benevolence and concern are felt deeply enough that, remembering, she gives him the word "darling." He gives her permission to set out over the oceans of desire and danger, to fly her own plane, to go solo rather than sticking to the group. You are the beloved daughter, he says, and because we love you we will let you go; we will trust you to come back.

Every artist who feels connected to a community seeks this sort of permission, I suspect, though getting it from one person, even a powerful person, does not guarantee that the rest will agree. This is the old man as gentle guide and mentor, not violator; his presence does not cancel out the other old man, but lessens his terror and his hold on the imagination. Work and hope in the presence of love, Kasdorf suggests here, may at least console if not suffice. Listening to the inner voice that tells us we need more to live than the narrow community may make us strange, the way poetry makes the familiar strange, but it need not mean that we must live forever in exile.[40]

Rhapsody with Dark Matter begins with "Rain," a poem written long after a passing glimpse of a beautiful woman. It took twenty years to make from that scene a poem that seemed more than one more hackneyed celebration of an objectified female body. In a way, I think the drive behind much of *Rhapsody* is the inverse of Kasdorf's fierce contention with the "vulnerable socket" she cannot rid herself of; equally unable to rid myself of my gender, I live with my role as potential abuser as she lives with hers as once and possible victim. I have wondered whether it is even possible to be a white male in turn-of-the-century America without doing terrible things to people. Is it possible to write poems as a man, to write about beauty and desire and women with some degree of honesty and emotional accuracy, to reckon my own complicity in the darkness and suffering of the world without merely wallowing in guilt?

For a while I was calling the manuscript "The Sadness of Water and Women." That title soon came to seem too blunt, but as I worked on the poems I kept thinking about how much stubborn, ineluctable melancholy there was in the lives of the women I knew best, a sadness with many sources but no easy cure, something that seemed to be as much a condition of their lives as air or gravity.

Poets have known of this sadness for a long time, of course, and made much of it, for better or worse. Consider Poe's famous dictum that the most "poetical" subject possible is the death of a beautiful woman. During this time I also saw an exhibition of pre-Raphaelite art in the National Gallery in Washington and was overwhelmed by the profusion of sad and lovely women there—Rossetti's Beatrix, Millais' Ophelia, Hunt's and Waterhouse's very different versions of the Lady of Shalott. Fascinated by Frederic Lord Leighton's "Flaming June," a portrait of a beautiful sleeping woman in a thin orange nightgown, I considered that image for the cover. In a poem called "On the Bus" I tried to disentangle some of the varieties of desire and what might be done with them:

> Desire
> has no end, no bottom, no use. It's not the way you think,
>
> I'm just a little greedy, I want her and all that beauty
> to be holy and be mine and still her own, like a mountain
>
> we leave off the maps, a lake we talk about only in whispers.
> I want her to tell me I'm the one, forever. I want her
>
> to break me, heart and health. I want to wear her down
> to powder. I want to yearn forty years and die splendidly.
>
> I want never to see her again. (9-10)

As many readers have noticed, the book is also full of road poems and driving poems; several years ago I bought a little tape recorder to take on long drives alone to readings and conferences, when there is time to let thoughts and images accumulate and spin out. The longest of those pieces, "Many Strong Rivers: Thoughts on the Way Home," is something between an essay and a prose poem. Begun on the way home from a poetry workshop in Arkansas, it reflects on desire and dailyness in ways I doubt I can improve on now:

> Here's an idea, a hope: that living an everyday, frazzled, even frantic life like mine can also be a kind of spiritual discipline, a way of searching for the sacred and recognizing or seizing upon or opening yourself to it when it finds you amid it all. And that in fact the sacred will find you amid that life, if you can somehow manage the right stance toward it.
>
> Well. I'm brooding on desire, on what chance there is of living in both the spirit and the flesh, and also brooding about whether I should rotate my tires.
>
> Is it possible to recognize that your desire will never be satisfied, and come to terms with that, without becoming merely bitter or merely resigned? . . .
>
> Trying to learn the gods. Trying to learn what it means to worship. What else is worth doing?
>
> Why did the troubadours write about women that they barely touched, or never touched? Maybe that was the only safe

way. Maybe they knew that to touch, to take, to give yourself to the beloved is always to start down a road, and that all roads lead somewhere. Maybe they knew that not to touch meant never to take the road, only to look down it, and that looking down the road it does not seem to end.

What gets put into your shadow when you don't act on your desires? What gets put into your shadow when you do? . . .

6.

What do desire and the will have to do with each other? In five minutes I go from sunshine to a downpour, not because of anything I wanted, except to go along this road.

My people have always thought, always hoped, that if you wanted to bad enough, and had Jesus to help, it would be possible to be good, possible to make your desire flow within the banks if not to dam it up forever. And there's no denying that for some of them it's worked, or almost worked. And there's no saying what's been lost, or how much. Where do we get the idea that we are in control of anything? This may be the year, Thoreau says, that the water will rise within us, and drown all our muskrats. . . .

7.

These are the Kentucky hills, so beautiful. How little I see of them even when I remember to look, how fast they go by, how much I miss. This is the body of the world. This is the trace, the dwelling of God, of the gods. Desire is the woven body of the world, there in every tree, every blade of grass, every wildflower and crushed armadillo. Here is the world, and here we are in it like pebbles so small we blow in the wind, like shards of cooking pots broken centuries ago. And here we are going around, going around, thinking, dreaming, calling out, demanding to know about desire.

It's yearning that's eternal. Consummation is mortal.

I'm tired enough, I crave the bitterness enough, that this coffee tastes good even when it's almost cold, almost gone. (32-33)

What do we *do* with all this desire? That's the question. Do we organize and calibrate and separate our desires, claim that some are holy and others profane, pluck some like weeds in the garden and spray some with Roundup and pour plant food on others? Might we have been too hasty with some of them? What does it mean that our strongest desires—all right, at least *my* strongest desires—attach to women and to God?

Later in the book, among many poems of religious praise and yearning, are several that are more "Mennonite" than many I have written. They include my own poem for J. Lawrence Burkholder; as you'll see, the tone is quite different from Kasdorf's.

The Black Father
Not my real father still known as Whitey for his hair
for his open grin for his way of rubbing his head between
his work-thick hands when tired or embarrassed
but the father with secrets the black-haired father

the big smart father who learned to fly
who journeyed west & came home sad & triumphant
& filled with mysteries the black father agreed
to be the chosen one and he learned to speak in two voices

one used the old words few and strong the Bible the vision
the stern & narrow way the other voice he kept
in his dark suit in an inside pocket held between chest
& arm too tight to slip out I guessed we guessed

at what wild secrets that voice knew we argued & proposed
but the suit stayed on the arm stayed down
the first voice kept talking it talked well
it had stories dramatic & perplexing

the last refugees pushed off the plane
the engines roaring to lift the groaning exiles
above the trees the father trembling at the stick
& we hushed & trembled & pondered what did that mean

while the father slipped away to answer one more
hard narrow letter about what some young fool
said on a weary Tuesday what some young body
did Saturday night on the gym floor

the black father didn't have it easy he gave
a lot up he learned to choose his moments
& his fights & kept whole reams of careful argument
in his secret drawer for centuries

well years anyway in my last year the black father
had the class over & I stood near him & tried to say
that he had taught me something I was twenty
& from the country & I faltered & for a second

he seemed ready to speak but then just looked
down & turned away it was not his fault
I was shy & young bold only at the wrong moments
& maybe he was shy too but oh black father

I want to know what it was you almost said
what that inside pocket held & why you turned away (57-8)

For me—at least as I reconstruct all this years later—Burkholder remained an enigmatic figure, as sympathetic as his official role would
allow him to be, but with all his secrets hidden away, neither of us able to
make the right gesture that would reveal what was in our inside pockets.
Why? Was I just a boy from the prairies to him, not well enough connected to bother with? That idea seems paranoid to me now. More likely
I remember him this way, as I remember the scene described at the end
after twenty-five years, because the moment fit well with the myth of
myself as outsider and rebel that I *wanted* to believe in those days, that
could only be true if I did not get too much praise—or the attention that
is better than praise—from the powers that were.

I think most writers know this bind—however much we crave
recognition and praise, we also fundamentally mistrust it, knowing how
often it is given too lightly or for the wrong reasons. This issue is further
complicated for Mennonites by the humility tradition; we learn that we
ought to avoid attention and shun thinking too much of ourselves, although we may also learn these days that we need generous measures of
"self-worth" to function. Is there some precarious point at which we
have just enough ego strength to do our work without slipping into the
swamps of pride? There are many ways of surviving as an artist, and
maybe just as many ways of failing.

The last of the "Mennonite" poems was written at a conference on the family at Goshen College in 1999. As I listened to learned papers and discussions, I kept thinking of a story I had heard just before the conference, of a man entering a room with a plate and announcing "Here are my sad cookies." I found myself writing all sorts of variations on that theme, including bits and pieces of the discourse swirling around me. The result was "The Cookie Poem," which culminates in a perhaps grandiose, partly tongue-in-cheek vision of that elusive unity we imagine on our best days:

> Single cookies, queer cookies, cookies of color,
> homeless cookie families sleeping in the car,
> obsolete cookies broken down on the information
> highway. Sad cookies, silent cookies,
> loud cookies, loved cookies, your cookies
> my cookies our cookies, all cookies
> God's cookies, strange sweet hapless cookies
> marked each one by the Imago Dei,
> oh the Father the Son the Mother the Daughter
> and the Holy Ghost all love cookies,
> love all cookies, God's mouth is full
> of cookies, God chews and swallows and flings
> hands wide in joy, the crumbs fly
> everywhere, oh God loves us all. (53)

For all its yearning and restlessness, the book ends not with the awaking into some new awareness or pleasure or holiness that is the ultimate dream of desire, but with something perhaps more modest and reciprocal. Against all that desire and the arrogance of it, however subtly camouflaged or rationalized, after all that travel and all those new people, alluring and inviting, the last poems turn back toward home, to places and people so familiar they often seem ordinary to me, as if anything in this world is ordinary.

Landscape with Daily Life
"God is not big, he is right."
—*William Stafford*

Thistle. Milkweed. Grasses
already seeding. Rapid wings.
Geese on the island, geese in

the water. At the edge, the grass
climbs six feet or more. What would
change if I knew the true name
of anything I see? Brushing past
I loosen the seeds, carry them
with me. I don't mind all this
listening and looking, even when
it's only the world. I can breathe
deep or shallow, I can leave
when I choose. I'm not milkweed
or thistle or three-leaf ivy
though like them I live my other,
daily life. Now here we are.
The thistles don't care. The grass
tries one way, then another,
then just stays. I can't help
it, I love this place. I leave.
Tonight we will sleep in the old
new world, in the daily bed,
trees breathing near the window,
the two of us inside, steady
in the tall, sweet grass. (86)

It is not so easy, after all, to escape either the body or the mind. Yet most of us, I suspect, feel at least intermittently the yearning to believe that this world and our particular bodies might be more than the habitations of the Devil, that it might be possible to live joyfully in our bodies in this world here and now, without forgetting just how far from perfection this world and all of us are. Perhaps such a life is truly available only to the saints, but in the new space of poems we can at least point toward what such a life might be like—perhaps nothing so wildly dramatic or strange, something as common as sleeping beside our beloved, the "tall, sweet grass" somehow having found its way into our familiar bed.

CHAPTER TWELVE

IF THE EARTH IS THE LORD'S, DO WE HAVE TO HATE THE WORLD?

MUSINGS ON MENNONITE PEOPLE, PLACES, AND COMPLEXES
One of the more intriguing people I got to know in my first weeks at
Goshen College was a curly haired young woman from somewhere in
Pennsylvania (for years I had only the vaguest sense of the geography of
the place, and assumed that Scottdale and Akron and Lancaster were all
pretty much next to each other). Dawn seemed kind of shy and giggled
a lot, but she also had a hard-to-define air about her—not exactly so-
phistication, but a seeming ease with the academic world that I envied.

Her father John Ruth, I soon learned, was a big name Mennonite.
He had a Ph.D. from Harvard but still wore a plain coat. He was a
preacher, but he still wrote books and made movies. When he talked,
people listened, and if I had not heard of him, that was just one more in-
dication of how far out of things I was.

Now I had grown up among farmers; the most educated people in
my home community were preachers and school teachers and a few doctors. There were plenty of intelligent people, but few that I would call
intellectuals. My own father was a farmer—not especially shy in person,
but with a great aversion to public speaking. He would not even get up
in church to make an announcement, if there was any way out of it. So
when I started to imagine myself as a writer, a professor, an intellectual,

John Ruth became an exemplar to me, if not exactly a mentor (we would not meet in the flesh for another twenty years). He was someone who had managed to live the life of the mind, without leaving the church.

When I began trying to write about Mennonite literature, his short book *Mennonite Identity and Literary Art*, previously discussed in chapters two, five, and ten, was the fullest and most thoughtful statement on the subject around. When a few American Mennonites, mostly of the generation after Ruth's, finally began to write creatively in earnest, he was there as a kind of father figure, mostly benevolent but a bit daunting in his enigmatic presence, his massive knowledge, his charismatic storytelling, and his insistence that writing ought to serve the community rather than attack it.

While people like me went off to college and did not return to our home communities, Ruth not only went back but has dedicated his life to uncovering and preserving the history of eastern Pennsylvania Mennonites. While I wrote poems, essays, and books that I sought to publish in literary journals and university presses, Ruth wrote congregational and conference histories and documentaries about Amish and Hutterites. While he wondered why no one had made "full-throated song" celebrating and grappling with the enclosed Mennonite enclaves he knew best, I tried to capture something of the less enclosed, less massive, and less colorfully plain communities that my own ancestors had created on the Illinois prairie. Eventually I realized that while we both worried over the conundrums of community, separation, and worldliness, even those terms—like the word *Mennonite*—seemed subtly but significantly different, depending on one's personal history and associations.

We have met in person only a few times, and rarely if ever corresponded. Yet by now, John Ruth has become one of those rich, complicated figures whose work and person dwell more or less permanently in my imagination—as a mentor and example, but also as a distant partner in various more or less one-sided conversations, disquisitions, even (gentle) quarrels. I am grateful to him in many ways; perhaps especially for staking out positions and ideas that at one point or another I found difficult enough to require some kind of response of my own—and for doing all his work in such lucid, humane, faithful, and generous ways. What follows will I hope be read as I mean it, as a meditation on some issues that his latest work raises for me—not a quarrel but an inquiry into some long-running conundrums of Mennonite thinking and practice.

HOW MUCH SCHOOL DOES A MAN NEED?

The publication of John Ruth's magnum opus *The Earth Is the Lord's: A Narrative History of the Lancaster Mennonite Conference* is an event among Mennonites for several reasons: for its subject matter, for its encyclopedic detail and graceful style, for its long gestation period, for John Ruth's own stature as cultural figure, preacher, impresario, interpreter of plain culture, historian, and so on. At nearly 1400 pages with back matter—the index is thirty pages long!—it may be the longest book by a single author that I own.

TEITL provides a fascinating and nearly obsessively detailed look at one of the oldest and strongest Mennonite communities in North America—one with many vital connections to Mennonites elsewhere. It also, incidentally, helps make clear why those of us at other points on the Mennonite map have often found those from eastern Pennsylvania to be something of a breed apart.

Most congregational and conference histories are more or less celebratory, for obvious reasons, but this one seems particularly thick with superlatives regarding numbers—of congregations, congregants, farms, and wealth. To emphasize the strength and influence of Lancaster Conference in the Mennonite world is simply to recognize the facts, of course, and it would not do to accuse Ruth nor the Lancaster Mennonites of anything unbecoming to the long and deep Anabaptist humility tradition, which this book documents in many of its expressions, including some of the quirkier ones. But the community's satisfaction concerning its long history and prosperity is quite evident, as is a certain assumption that this group is not merely significant but *central*—for several centuries an easier assumption for this particular Anabaptist group than for many others.

As Ruth tells it, the Lancaster story is also one of perpetual suspicion of the world and resistance to particular elements of it. Especially of interest are attitudes and practices related to education, intellectual speculation, and imagination. Among Lancaster Mennonites, the broad pattern seems to have been that advances in technology, transportation, and the like—those that aided in making money and getting about—

were adopted with little fuss, while those that might threaten communal control encountered much greater resistance. Thus even conservative Lancaster Mennonites began quite quickly to drive cars and use tractors, but getting an advanced education remained suspect—at least until the economic advantages of education began to overwhelm the fears of it.

The costs of this suspicion, Ruth suggests repeatedly, were substantial. In the late nineteenth century, he comments,

> In Lancaster County itself, no Mennonite mind was trained in the wisdom of the world so that it could speak eloquently in the world's language to share its spiritual heritage. . . . They interpreted their lack of interest in what might be called the life of the mind as a godly humility. But . . . we also sense an unwelcome result of this attitude: the frustration of an intelligence that might have made better sense of the heritage if its story had been accessible. (631, 633).

Some of Ruth's ambivalence about this suspicion of education is apparent here. A less generous observer might put it this way: For centuries Lancaster Mennonites presented their best minds with a choice: sacrifice whatever intellectual ambitions they might have to the established order, or go into some sort of exile. During the long period when the congregations continued to grow in numbers and influence, this policy seems to have been little questioned, at least by those who remained.

Ruth describes and analyzes this syndrome and its eventual effects more thoroughly than anyone has before. Its origins, he believes, can be traced back to Europe: "The centuries-old distrust of *die Gelehrten,* the educated ones, so deeply imbibed when the main culture of Switzerland and South Germany had persecuted the withdrawing Anabaptists, was still playing a powerful role in rural Mennonite pockets of industrializing America. Most of Pennsylvania's Mennonites had never known any other way to do Christianity than to keep themselves 'little and low,' culturally speaking" (806).

Other Mennonites shared this suspicion, of course, but to varying degrees; by the beginning of the last century, many progressive Mennonites further west were thinking quite differently about the world. Historian C. Henry Smith, a key figure in the history of both Goshen College and Bluffton College, visited Lancaster in 1906. Ruth notes his bemused reaction: "With his more liberal orientation, it seemed strange to [C. Henry] Smith that Lancaster would drag its feet so stubbornly regarding education. . . . the conference was so fearful of the worldly effects of schooling that it would tarry another thirty years before it was able to make an educational move of its own."

It seems clear, as Ruth notes, that the Lancaster communities were formed mainly by immigrants who left Europe with the memory of persecutions and martyrdoms still fresh, and carried the wounds of those events with them even through centuries of general tolerance and prosperity in Pennsylvania. Later immigrants, both Amish and Mennonite, certainly had their own mistrust of the world, but in many cases their conservatism had been tempered by a less brutal European experience and by increased toleration and cooperation with their worldly neighbors. They would mainly settle farther west in the new country, and develop their own ways of sorting the essential from the optional.

One result was that the first Mennonite colleges formed in those more progressive western communities, placing the Lancaster Mennonites in a curious position. Ruth writes of Hesston: "The freer atmosphere in the Kansas community closer to the frontier eventually produced a strange historical relationship: the richer home community in Lancaster would send students and teachers all the way west to Kansas, where at Hesston an old Mennonite school was organized." (630). His commentary on Goshen College is equally rueful: "Thus would arise an ironic situation in which the older, eastern Mennonite communities, having the most potential students, were forced to send them over great distances to study in communities having far more limited economic resources and Mennonite population—if they wanted their youths to attend Mennonite colleges" (631).

These observations, and their emphasis on the material and demographic wealth of Lancaster, imply a certain frustration that its prosperity did not lead to the formation of academic institutions there to nurture leaders—perhaps ones more to the community's liking. I suspect that Ruth has envisioned a quite different history—and as a fan of speculative fiction I love to ask "what if" questions myself, even if they have no clear answers. What if, for example, there had been an early move to found a Mennonite college in Pennsylvania? If Lancaster College was now entering its second century alongside Goshen, Hesston, Eastern Mennonite, Bluffton, and Bethel—or perhaps instead of one of them— how might the intellectual landscape of American Mennonites be different? Would such an institution resemble today's Goshen, or Eastern Mennonite, or Bluffton—each of them significantly different but all about the same size? Might it be more like Messiah College, much larger for having tapped into wider streams of evangelical students and contributors? Might it be the Mennonite equivalent of Wheaton or Calvin, more conservative than any current Mennonite college but at least as academically rigorous? And, if such a college had existed for the last century, what would it have meant for generations of Lancaster Conference Mennonites to have lived with its resources near at hand?

On Tables, Pulpits, and the Death of the Universe

Shortly after *TEITL* came out, before I had read or even seen it, I had a long conversation with my friend Gerald Biesecker-Mast, who had just read the book. Gerald is often excited about Mennonite topics, and this was no exception. He regaled me with stories and anecdotes, including the one about the great Smoketown pulpit/table controversy. A considerable scandal resulted when two brothers and their sister snuck into the nearly completed meeting house in 1889, ripped out the just-installed pulpit, and replaced it with a preachers' table they had built themselves. (Strangely, the main suspect in the case was a Martin M. Zimmerman, while the real perpetrator was named Martin W. Zimmerman. But perhaps not so strange for Lancaster County, where a few names seem to repeat over and over—Ruth describes how he became almost mesmerized by the many men named John Landis who kept emerging from his research.)

Over the same break I had been reading several science fiction epics that I had picked up at a used bookstore. Those books, though not as massive as John's, were bulky enough in their own right to engross me for several evenings each in their hundreds of pages of fine print. They found their scope not by accumulating intensive details about a small group of people in a small corner of Pennsylvania, but by taking the widest and longest of views. Most ranged over billions of miles of interstellar space, at least one over millions of years as well. All assumed that the conditions of human life and even basic physical laws would change radically in the future; one envisioned the extinction of the entire universe that we know, and ended with a plucky band of humans trying to make their way into an alternate universe to survive.

I drove home slowly that night, pondering again my half-guilty, half-grateful, perhaps arrogant sense of distance from the kind of carefully bounded community that John Ruth writes of so lovingly (and not without his own ambivalence, of course). A largely oral, tightly restricted community can maintain itself and even thrive for centuries, as the Lancaster example shows. It can try to resist change, or to control change when it becomes inevitable. It can oppose education beyond a certain level, fearing the effect of too much knowledge among its impressionable young people.

Such communities naturally have little use for novels, whether of the realistic sort that portray all varieties of grim human difficulties or the fantastic type that operate on such vast scales as to make their readers reflect on other matters of scale. I was experiencing this dissonance firsthand as I tried to get my space operas and Gerald's story of the pulpit to cohabit comfortably in my mind. It was impossible not to wonder, I found: Is the God who made the enormous and ancient universe really heavily invested in the problem of whether a few dozen people in a modest building on an obscure planet in the Milky Way should hear their preaching done from behind a table or a pulpit?

This is the point at which, depending on your tradition, the bishop notes rather heavily that some questions are mistaken in their very asking—or the robot begins to flail its arms and whoop, "Danger, danger, alien approaching." If I had not read such wild tales, would I ever have thought to ask such a question? Now that I have, how can I help but ask such questions? Will I ever again be of any use to a community that defines itself in terms of such issues?

Pondering this took me once again into the tangled concerns around those much-abused words *community* and *the world*. How much openness and how much control do self-conscious communities need to endure and to thrive? What *kinds* of each? What stances toward the world, what blends of engagement and distance and celebration and criticism, are both right and practicable?

LIVING IN ANOTHER WORLD

[E]very living and healthy religion has a marked idiosyncrasy. Its power consists in its special and surprising message and in the bias which that revelation gives to life. The vistas it opens and the mysteries it propounds

are another world to live in; and another world to live in—whether we expect ever to pass wholly over into it or no—is what we mean by having a religion. —George Santayana, *Reason in Religion*

Another world to live in. Lancaster Conference has surely been one of the most successful long-term Anabaptist experiments at creating and preserving a distinct small culture which is at least once removed from the regular world. It seems clear that the origins of Anabaptism contain this impulse to create another world to live in, as Santayana suggests, and seldom has any Anabaptist group better managed to concentrate their energies to create and control even a small corner of the world than in eastern Pennsylvania. The familiar rhetoric of opposition to the world is memorably stated in the Schleitheim Confession of 1527:

> Everything which is not united with our God and Christ cannot be other than an abomination which we should shun and flee from. By this is meant all Catholic and Protestant works and church services, meetings and church attendance, drinking houses, civic affairs, the oaths sworn in unbelief and other things of that kind, which are highly regarded by the world and yet are carried on in flat contradiction to the command of God, in accordance with all the unrighteousness which is in the world. (*The Schleitheim Confession* 2)

One way of thinking about Anabaptist history is as a long and often agonized argument about the terms outlined here. The radical dismissal of "everything which is not united with our God and Christ" has been the basis for much of our thought, if not always our practice. But as even other sections of the Schleitheim Confession acknowledge, large elements of the human world are bound to disagree with this view. Most Protestants and Catholics, not to mentions Jews and Muslims and Buddhists and Hindus and agnostics and atheists, still persist in thinking that they are not entirely abominable, whatever their sins. What is to be done with them? Must we understand them as fundamentally deluded, deprived of the truth revealed only to us? Can the gathered community only relate to "the world" on such rigidly dualistic terms?

By the early twentieth century, Ruth shows, the Lancaster answer was mainly twofold: on the one hand, strengthening visible marks of separation, especially dress codes; on the other, increasingly aggressive mission programs. While the Lancaster Mennonites were strengthening their dress codes, other American Mennonites were approaching the question of how to maintain identity in the face of assimilation quite differently. Some sought to live within the world without visible markers of separation, to maintain their communities with somewhat more porous boundaries.

There is no room here for a detailed historical analysis of all this, but let me offer one suggestive anecdote. Bluffton College was founded in 1899 by representatives of the General Conference Mennonite Church. Early in its history, Bluffton became a "mixed" institution, with a majority of non-Mennonite students and a looser connection to the church hierarchy than the Mennonite Church colleges. When I joined the faculty in 1984, roughly half of the faculty and less than twenty percent of the students were Mennonite. In some quarters the opinion that Bluffton was not "really" a Mennonite college was commonplace. (I was somewhat reassured when a senior colleague at Hesston, upon learning that I had accepted the job at Bluffton, assured me that Elmer Neufeld, the president, was "a true Mennonite.")

At my first faculty retreat, Margaret Weaver, a much-beloved Latin teacher at the local high school and the wife of a senior faculty member, was the guest speaker. She described listening to Garrison Keillor's radio show—itself something that at one time would have been forbidden as worldly. (As many readers know, Keillor often sings hymns with his "Hopeful Gospel Quartet" and tells stories about Minnesota Lutherans and a small sect he calls the "Sanctified Brethren," which sounds a good deal like some stray band of Anabaptists.)

Weaver described Keillor musing on the Shakespeare sonnet which begins "That time of year thou may'st in me behold" and ends with the couplet "This thou believ'st, which makes thy love more strong: / To love that well which thou must leave ere long." The phrase she repeated and reflected upon has stuck with me all this time: "Learning to love the world," she said—that's what education is all about. Learning to love the world and its creatures in their beauty, their confusion, their pain and heartache and their kindness and solidarity—each of them, we are told, made in the image of God.

How do we square this idea with that other idea of "the world" as an abomination that we must shun and flee? Not easily. Personally, I have to say that proclaiming the whole human world outside the tiny Anabaptist enclaves to be some kind of undifferentiated abomination seems absurdly, almost comically arrogant—though I would quickly add that distinguishing what is good from what is evil in the world seems crucial indeed.

Still, after living for almost twenty years in a situation where Mennonites form a significant but not numerically dominant part of a mainly functional community, I have become convinced that among the others, the English, the worldly, whatever we wish to call them, are many in whom the light of the Spirit shines bright, and that it is important to say so. If there were to be another Amish division today, I would stand with those who believe that the Truehearted may indeed be saved, whether they keep the Ordnung or not.

Isn't it an easy target anyway, this "world"? I saw this on a billboard recently: "TV, Sports, Movies. The friend of the world is the enemy of God." There was a number to call for a complete explanation, but I did not have time to write it down, and I suppose that I would just get into an argument if I called, anyway.

There are plenty of things in the world which are worth resisting, including much of what is associated with television, sports, and movies. And I realize that a billboard is hardly the place for nuanced analysis of media culture. But such proclamations seem terribly blunt instruments once one has spent enough time in the open world to find that, along with all the trash and evil, there is much that is beautiful and true and good there.

Many others in this generation of Mennonites have made a similar journey, which is not very accurately described by the standard term "assimilation." Artists and writers, among many others, have gone out into the world to study and learn, perhaps less compelled than earlier peers to make an either-or choice between their home community or complete assimilation. Often, Mennonite artists went off to find (as Di Brandt says) that what they had been told about the world was simply not true.

> The rest of the world, for us, was *other*, but as I found out when I got there, it was not at all other in the way we had imagined, in the way we'd been told. Its otherness, I could see immediately, was not the otherness of people lounging indifferently on the road to hell, but consisted rather in a completely different set of terms, a different set of rules to live by. (Brandt 32-33)

With the partial breakdown of the separation between Mennonite communities and the rest of the world it has become easier for some artists to negotiate passage between, or to define their own places to exist. For example, Julia Kasdorf formally joined the Episcopalian church at nearly the same time as her book entitled *The Body and the Book: Writing from a Mennonite Life* appeared. The essays form a sometimes agonized and sometimes appreciative response to Mennonite culture—as one with roots in Big Valley, Pennsylvania, and a family tree full of Spichers and Peacheys, Kasdorf knows well the issues of boundaries and transgression that I have been tracing here.

I suspect, though, that the dualism of Anabaptist or "other" has always been exaggerated, that the choices have often been less simple than they may seem. Consider J. W. Yoder, the author of *Rosanna of the Amish* and a Big Valley native like Kasdorf.[41] He got a good education, traveled widely, led singing schools, worked as a college administrator and recruiter, published both defenses of Amish ways and strong critiques of certain practices. Was he then "inside" or "outside" the Amish community? Both, and neither, surely. John Ruth himself, with his Harvard Ph.D. and his return to the ancestral homestead in Lower Salford Township, with his career in film and video and his many books, has lived both a deeply traditional and a startlingly unconventional life. The same could be said, in one way or another, of Conrad Grebel and Menno Simons—in their efforts to be faithful to their tradition, they broke radically with some aspects of it. Even Jesus, surely, did so, both fulfilling the law and revolutionizing its meaning for generations and millennia to come.

Many Mennonites today find that in the postmodern world "community" can and must be multiple, spread widely over space, maintained through various means of communication and travel. Since the advent of email I keep in much closer touch with many of my scattered friends, fellow poets, and family members than we did ten years ago—it is convenient and more or less free to hit reply, compose a few lines or whole paragraphs, perhaps throw in a poem or two if there is something new. It is much easier to send photos of the new cousins, as well, as my mother remarked when she forwarded the latest ones.

I have an Amish friend, a poet, whose email address was given me by the editor of a magazine we both had published in. When I contacted him that way, he somewhat sheepishly replied that it was mainly for communicating with editors and that he expected to close the account soon. We are back to writing old-fashioned letters. It is fine. But I keep finding his letter, at the bottom of a stack of things, months after I meant to reply.

Traditionalists can talk at length of the costs of change, and this is no blanket celebration of whatever happens to be new. I would not surrender the community of memory that has sustained my own life, nor relinquish the dream and the charge of remaking the world in the image of God, which is surely our most important work. But I would insist that our current state of transformation is not necessarily cause for despair, and that indeed even to bemoan our departures from "tradition" requires choosing one particular set of traditions from a very diverse and complicated history. From the start there have been different versions of what it meant to be Anabaptist; there has never been a single practice to which everyone conformed. People have been doing it many ways since the beginning, and will continue.

FURTHER ADVENTURES IN THE WORLD

Recently I found myself driving up Route 23 in my bright blue little car, listening to Van Morrison on my CD player. I was on my way to read my poems at a conference to a bunch of people who may or may not know who Mennonites are. Two of my friends who teach at another Mennonite institution were on their way as well—with not a plain coat or a covering among us.

As I drove north toward Ann Arbor it was like driving under an enormous roof as the clouds lowered and darkened. I watched it coming, then suddenly the big drops began whapping on the windshield and the brake lights came on in front of me as drivers slowed to deal with this sudden loosening of the heavens. And I drove on, past the U-haul trailers, past the yellow buses from Bedford Public Schools plodding slowly in the right lane. To the west the clouds were lighter and higher—this would not last too long—but while it was here there was no escaping it. It was the world.

And we drove on, slower now, trailing behind us skirts of water pulled up by our tires, streamers that hung in the air like the tails of comets, like the clouds of glory that Wordsworth claimed we enter this life trailing. And the gray mini-van and the brown Trans Am and the black SUV and my bright blue Neon all pressed on toward the north, each vehicle bearing its human cargo toward some particular place, though I knew where none were going except myself, and had only instructions on a piece of paper describing my own destination.

I have been talking of "the world" in terms of *people* who are other, English, not Anabaptist. It seems just as important to consider the physical world, and the mistrust and worse with which Mennonites (and other Christians) have often treated it. A naturalist told me recently of standing by an Amish farmer's mailbox chatting with the man when the two of them spotted a nest with some baby birds in the hedge nearby. Reaching for the birds, the farmer said something like "Now there's something that doesn't need to be," and crushed them with his bare hand.

I do not mean to slander either Amish or farmers by making too much of this incident. But is this what it means to be in the world but not of it? Who is closer to *Nachfolge*, do you think, that farmer or the speaker of this poem by Todd Davis?

> *Evensong*
> Near the gravel pit just below
> the crest of Norman Hill, two
> fox sprawl, end of day warmth
>
> rising from earth. Across the road,
> hay turned into windrows rings
> William's field, gold against green
>
> against gold. To the west, sun
> lowers itself down the ladder
> of the sky, as heavy clouds break
>
> to reveal burnished red of ash
> leaves, a fox's tail disappearing
> into the undergrowth. At this hour,
>
> what isn't prayer?

I suspect the final question here is not one that many of those John Landises or those other Lancaster people whose names I cannot keep straight would have asked. They might have not been surprised by the idea that faith is somehow incarnate in one's life, in the physical world, but they might have been more inclined to connect it with well-painted barns and straight rows of soybeans than with the apprehensions of beauty the poem offers.

The natural world also offers some intriguing analogies for social organization. There is the community of the corn field—uniform, pragmatic, organized for maximum productivity and immediate yield. It will generate a lot of a useful product, if the weather is right. But it requires care from the outside to maintain its purity; by itself, the corn cannot crowd out all the weeds. It must be plowed, planted, fertilized, cultivated or treated with weedkillers. It is unstable on its own—it would not last a month, let alone a year, without attention and manipulation.

There is also the community of the climax forest. It is organized for stability through diversity. It incorporates a wide range of species, plant and animal. It yields many products which sustain its members' lives in both obvious and subtle ways. It changes constantly with the weather, the seasons, the relative success or failure of one species or another. But it is self-regulating, with feedback systems that restore balance and harmony when disruptions occur, and self-sustaining. Both cooperation and competition are part of the daily round of things.

My point here may seem embarrassingly obvious, but I will state it anyway. The climax forest, like most other natural ecosystems, tolerates and indeed requires diversity of many kinds. Unnatural systems like the corn field simplify and industrialize natural systems for the sake of efficiency and production, they resist diversity and enforce conformity and uniformity. This may or may not be a good strategy for food production, but as a model for social organization its problems need not be labored.

WHERE ELSE WILL WE LIVE?

Donald Barthelme has it right, I think, when he writes, "Art thinks ever of the world, cannot not think of the world, could not turn its back on the world even if it wished to" (Barthelme 181). Even the most extravagant science fiction and fantasy novels, no matter how strange or distant their settings and characters, cannot not think of the world, just as the most rigorous Anabaptist cannot really live anywhere else, cannot avoid eating and breathing and drinking the stuff of the universe, cannot abandon the body except in death. Going one step further, Robert Bly suggests that making art, far from being a dangerous aberration, is a necessary function for a human being who aspires to a spiritual life: "What did Blake say?—'No person who is not an artist can be a Christian.' He means that a person who refuses to approach his own life actively, using language, music, sculpture, painting, or drawing is a caterpillar dressed in Christian clothes, not a human being" (Bly 43).

What if we have been crippling ourselves and our children all these years, in the name of safety and necessity and *Nachfolge*? What if the activities of art are indeed not only not antithetical to following Jesus, but essential? Those functions will not be denied, of course—if some of their modes are denied they come out in others: singing, quilting, gardening, *Fraktur*, even in farming and in conversation. But they can certainly be hindered, even crippled, and many who cannot bear to see that happen will flee the community that tries, leaving it without their leavening presences.

Imagine if, for three hundred years, we had refused to allow our children to run. Walking is good enough, we told them—you'll get there eventually. Running is dangerous, you'll fall down and hurt yourself. If you can't get there walking, it's just too far away. Anyway, the rest of the world is just like it is around here, only more dangerous.

What happens, after three centuries of no running? Do those muscles atrophy? Does the desire for it disappear, and the knack for it as well? Do a few runners slip away through the fences and find others who run cheerfully and gaily? Where do they go? Will they come back and tell us of their travels? Could it be that, even now, we could follow them out beyond the gates? Could we open the gates and go just a little way down the path we see, faint but distinct? It follows the floor of the valley and then disappears into the trees.

A long time ago I wrote a poem, one of those that I never quite came to understand myself. As I worked on this essay, trying to understand why the dream of another world seems so powerful and so ambiguous, it came back to me.

Dream of the New Room

We have only this large, dull room, like a small-town hall
meant for 4-H clubs and oversized reunions, more space than

we'll ever need but barren, echoing, flat. There is no way outside. Who knows how we got here? Is anyone watching? No
sign.

Yet we plot escapes. We decide to hide a map in our genes. If
we can leave a sign, our children may find what else they need.

And then, through some magic or will we open a door. Too
excited to breathe, we take our first steps into the new room, not
sure it will hold air, not sure it will even be real. Quiet paces into
the darkness. *It seems to be here,* someone says.

I walk toward what may be a window, say the word *home* in
wonder, so dim I do not know the direction my yearning should
take, taking comfort from this new room, that I can walk out
into it, that it seems to be here.

I think now that we must seek out these new rooms, whether they
appear in dreams or in visions or in the hills and valleys of the earth on
which we have been given to live. We must not fear to walk out into
them, placing our feet carefully, listening and watching and sniffing the
air, talking to each other about what we think we have found. We must
not try to keep these new spaces to ourselves, but must welcome all who
wish to gather there with us. We must keep telling and retelling the old
stories, and inventing new ones as well. We must remember that all of
our stories, even the oldest, were once not stories at all—that they are
memorials to the acts and dreams and wishes of living, breathing, flawed
and contentious human beings who entered the world as did each of us,
naked and wet and helpless, to be held and comforted and fed, tended
and taught until they could take their own places in the only world we
have, the world where we have been told that God is everywhere.

CHAPTER THIRTEEN

"WHAT IS IT I KNOW?"
NOTES TOWARD AN EMBODIED GNOSIS

That is what the highest criticism really is, the record of one's own soul. It is more fascinating than history, as it is concerned simply with oneself. It is more delightful than philosophy, as its subject is concrete not abstract, real and not vague. It is the only civilized form of autobiography, as it deals not with the events, but with the thoughts of one's life; not with life's physical accidents of deed or circumstance, but with the spiritual moods and imaginative passions of the mind. . . . —Oscar Wilde, The Critic as Artist *(Wilde 139-40)*

(77) Jesus said, "It is I who am the light which is above them all. It is I who am the all. From me did the all come forth, and unto me did the all extend. Split a piece of wood, and I am there. Lift up the stone, and you will find me there." —The Gospel of Thomas *(Robinson 126)*

Although this essay was first presented at a conference on Anabaptists and ritual, I am only a casual student of such matters, and will have little to say about public ritual.[42] My starting point is the subjective experience of public event, the cohesion or tension between what is ceremoniously prescribed and enacted and what goes on within those who take part. Along the way I mean to explore tradition and experience, doctrine and intuition, orthodoxy and heterodoxy, the many parts of our beings;

241

I mean to speak for a way of knowing that is very old but ever renewed. But let me begin with something quite accessible, Andrew Hudgins' poem "Sit Still":

> The preacher said, "We know God's Word is true."
> *Amen*, somebody called. "How do we know?
> We know because the Bible says it's true."
> He waved the fraying book. "God says it's true.
> And, brother, that's good enough for me." *Amen!*
> My father's eyes were calm, my mother's face
> composed. I craned around, but everyone
> seemed rapt as Brother Vernon spun
> tight circles of illogic. A change
> that I could not resist swept through,
> and I resisted it. I tried again
> to sing the word behind the word we sang.
> I prayed. Then I gave up and picked a scab
> till Daddy popped my thigh and hissed, "Sit still."
> Up front, the preacher waved his thick black book.
> He fanned the pages, smacked it with his palm,
> And I sincerely wished that I were stupid. (Hudgins 50)

I would call the scene of this poem a low-church ritual—the script may not be written out, but both Brother Vernon's "tight circles of il- logic" and the congregation's response are clearly codified and familiar to all, even the young Hudgins, who tries desperately to feel the appro- priate response but cannot quite manage it. The last line offers a mar- velous sting of recognition, surely, but perhaps even more intriguing are the mysterious little interior events in the middle of the poem: the "change" the boy feels sweeping through him, and his effort "to sing the word behind the word we sang." Clearly he *is* changed by this experi- ence, for all his resistance—but how? His wish to be stupid is not granted, nor does he forget; years later, he is still re-enacting the scene in the space of the poem.

Some readers may resonate as I do with young Andrew's discomfort. Whatever the particulars, we restless children, too smart for our own good, seem doomed to struggle with our local Brother Vernons, and with other authority figures who, like Andrew's father, demand that we shut up and sit still. When young we have only a few choices—sullen in- terior opposition, feigned enthusiasm, flights of fantasy, effortful compliance. Eventually, of course, we become more able to choose among the communities and rituals and ways of knowing and being that we seek out or flee. Still, as my poem "Knowing the Father" also indicates, the tones and textures of our youthful religious experience often remain indelibly with us, to be recollected years later:

> It's a good day for sweat to find and coat
> my glasses in big smeary salty drops that
> I puzzle how to remove without leaving a film
> sticky and implacable as the religion
> of my childhood, the prayers that demanded
> a surrender so ultimate that even as I tried
> I could never quite grasp it as possible,
> or connect to the way the eggs still had
> to be gathered the next day, the yellow
> plastic-coated wire basket to be filled
> gingerly as I went from coop to coop, shooing
> the stupid hens aside, batting at the ones
> who'd peck if you didn't slap them away.
>
> I thought I should feel different, the day after,
> but if I did it was only in my testing
> how it felt, my puzzling: Is this right?
> Am I saved? What is it shuffling in
> the cobs with me, breathing chicken dirt?
> I already knew, somehow: I wanted
> a dark, bold sign. I didn't deserve it.
> I would have to keep looking.
>
> When the eggs were in the cooler
> and supper done I could sometimes
> wheedle my father into playing catch.
> His glove was dark and old, his fingers
> thick from the fields. He threw hard
> and left handed. People in town
> still talked about how good he'd been,
> how he started as a freshman.
> Now he was thirty, and that was over.
> The ball went back and forth until
> we lost it in the dusk, then
> he gathered me under his hard left arm,
> and we found the door together. (Gundy, *Flatlands* 9)

While Hudgins' poem grapples with the inability to experience church ritual properly, this one addresses what happens after even truly immersive moments. Another restless and obstinate child, I also found myself as an adult trying to register those complicated young feelings: something close to but not exactly guilt, more like an awareness of inadequacy, a sense that I was not getting it right, and would need a further, selfish testing of what was supposed to be once for all. The link between the yearning for a "dark, bold sign" from God and the more tangible human connection at the end came to me associatively, through a quick narrative jump—strangely, the glove in the last stanza is itself dark and old. My father here plays a different role than Andrew's, not disciplinarian but companion, an equivocal substitute for the Big Father who remains hidden. That difference, perhaps, is the key to the tonal difference with which the poems end.

This poem found its way into the reader for the First Year Seminar course at Bluffton College. I am always a bit nervous about talking about it with my class, afraid that someone will accuse me (no doubt rightly) of being less secure about my salvation than a good Mennonite professor should be. Usually they do not push me too hard; and some seem grateful for the poem's very insecurities and its shift from "official" religious experience to a reassurance that is more experiential than theological, and a small ritual is familial rather than public.

I was not thinking about this poem at all early this summer, when I found myself reading in and about Gnosticism. Especially in the first and second centuries before and after Christ, a wide variety of groups and individuals around the ancient world came to be known as Gnostics; the Christian Gnostics were named heretics as the scattered Christian movement became an organized and hierarchical structure. Eventually the Gnostic groups, never very unified, splintered and nearly disappeared, and many of their texts were lost for centuries. The Gnostics were remembered mainly through the writings of their opponents, especially early church fathers such as Irenaeus and Tertullian. In 1945, however, a clay jar containing a large group of ancient Gnostic texts was found buried in a clay jar near Nag Hammadi in Egypt; the translation and publication of those texts greatly increased the available information and sparked a considerable resurgence of interest.

Some Gnostic beliefs and practices differed strikingly from what Christians have considered "orthodox" for nearly two millennia. The

Gnostic groups were widely divergent, but one key tenet was an emphasis on "gnosis" or "knowing" rather than "belief." The Gnostic Christians thought that the true way was a process of spiritual education, its goal to achieve awareness of the "divine spark" or *pneuma* that was a part of God within the self, and a kind of resurrection through communion of this divine spark with God. In the Gospel of Thomas, the best-known of the Nag Hammadi texts, Jesus more often presents himself as guide to the truth than the Truth himself. "I am not your master," he says, "Because you have drunk, you have become intoxicated from the bubbling spring which I have measured out" (Robinson 119). Throughout Thomas, familiar stories and parables from the canonical gospels are interspersed with enigmatic sayings that promise salvation through spiritual understanding: "Jesus said, 'If you bring forth what is within you, what you bring forth will save you. If you do not bring forth what is within you, what you do not bring forth will destroy you" (Robinson 126).

In general, the Gospel of Thomas offers a subjective and subtle approach to faith, with few of the ethical teachings of Matthew, Mark ,and Luke and little of John's emphasis on belief in Jesus as "the Way, the Truth, and the Life." As Elaine Pagels, the leading contemporary interpreter of Gnosticism, writes, "Thomas's gospel encourages the hearer not so much to *believe in Jesus,* as the Gospel of John requires, as to *seek to know God* through one's own, divinely given capacity, since all are created in the image of God" (Pagels, *Beyond Belief* 34). The Gnostics lost out in the power struggles of the second and third century, Pagels thinks, largely because what became orthodox Christianity offered a version that was simpler, more supportive of authority, and more conducive to the development of hierarchical structures. "From the bishop's viewpoint, of course, the gnostic position was outrageous," Pagels writes. "These heretics challenged his right to define what he considered to be his own church; they had the audacity to debate whether or not catholic Christians participated; and they claimed that their own group formed the essential nucleus, the 'spiritual church.'"

Orthodox leaders wanted a church that would be universal, Pagels argues, in a way that the spiritual elitism of the Gnostics would make much more difficult. The bishops welcomed all members "who would submit to their system of organization. [They] drew the line against those who challenged any of the three elements of this system: doctrine, ritual, and clerical hierarchy—and the gnostics challenged them all (Pagels, *The Gnostic Gospels* 117–18).

Pagels thinks Irenaeus, the most prominent early critic of Gnosticism, finds the Gnostics so threatening because their "second baptism" into *gnosis* "threatened Christian solidarity" by dividing the select few who experience it from the rest (Pagels, *Beyond Belief* 136). She agrees that it *was* a threat: "Those who wrote and treasured innovative [Gnostic] works . . . were implicitly criticizing, intentionally or not, the faith of most believers. So, as we noted, Valentinus contrasts those who picture God as 'petty, jealous, and angry' with those who receive 'the grace of knowing him' as a loving and compassionate Father" (Pagels, *Beyond Belief* 138).

The Gnostic creation myths are particularly unorthodox. They present the creator of the physical universe as merely an inferior, anthropomorphic emanation of the original Godhead. This Demiurge (who is given various names) more or less botches the whole business of Creation, boasts ignorantly of his supremacy, and punishes Adam and Eve for their quite natural pursuit of knowledge. Pagels reads this story in parabolic terms, noting that it affirms the" latent capacity within our hearts and minds that links us to the divine" and opposes those (including most Christians) who feel an "animosity toward spiritual awareness, and also toward those who speak for its presence in human experience. The story of the creator's hostility to epinoia ["creative" consciousness], then, is a parable, both comic and painful, of conflict between those who seek spiritual intuition and those who suppress it." (Pagels, *Beyond Belief* 164-65)

I have not converted to this cosmology, but I do find its account of hostility to unconventional spiritual exploration intriguing, as is the call to a quest for knowledge which takes belief as a starting point, not an arrival. Such exploration, which is neither simply "interior" nor "exterior" in the usual sense of those terms, is at the heart of my efforts at writing poems. And surely the gnostics' encouragement of creative expression and exploration is refreshing after the centuries-old Mennonite suspicions of both the intellect and the imagination.

There is more space for imaginative and intellectual work today than for a long time among Mennonites, and for that I am grateful. The skepticism and anxiety that remain surely come from the same sources that fueled both the early church fathers' attacks on the Gnostics and the persecution of the sixteenth century reformers. Pagels convincingly argues for the difficulty of integrating gnosticism within institutional structures; Harold Bloom goes further, arguing that it stands in a fundamentally competitive, indeed antagonistic, relation to other forms of religious knowledge. As I worked on this essay I discovered that Gnosticism still creates strong feeling. When I discussed my research with friends and colleagues, I was surprised by their alarmed reactions; I was told that Gnostics hate the world and the body, that they lose themselves in trackless, arid mysticism, and that they are on a slippery slope to fascism—an especially odd worry, it seemed to me, about a movement so conspicuously unable to sustain any sort of organization.

If Gnostic heterodoxy is not the most pressing of contemporary social issues, it is still only right to recognize the wildness that Gnostic freedom claims, especially as represented by modern interpreters such as Harold Bloom. "If religion is a binding, then Gnosticism is an unbinding," Bloom writes; "Gnostic freedom is a freedom for knowledge, knowledge of what in the self, *not* in the psyche or soul, is Godlike, and knowledge of God beyond the cosmos" (Bloom, *Agon* 4). While most varieties of Christian belief have an irrational component, Bloom emphasizes the particular a-rationality of Gnostic knowing: "There can of course be a kind of religious knowledge on a rational basis, but Gnosis is more than or other than rational . . . . in Gnosis the knowledge is neither of eternity nor of this world seen with more spiritual intensity. The knowledge is of oneself." This knowledge is simultaneously "uncanny" or (in the Freudian sense) *unheimlich*, and yet "pragmatic and particular," because it is a revelation of "what is oldest in oneself" (Bloom, *Agon* 12-13).

I find this hazy outline—of an interior, independent, transformative knowledge which is paradoxically performative but not temporal—fascinating and attractive partly because, like Bloom, I have fallen under the spell of poetry and the glimpses of uncanny knowledge it offers. Perhaps my fascination is also traceable to those youthful moments when I sensed myself in the presence of a mystery that I could not grasp, but that seemed to require a kind of total investment—of mind, body, spirit, and parts of our beings that are not well named by any of these terms. Even before I knew what poetry was I hungered for this sort of knowledge, though it has taken me many years to articulate that hunger.

Mennonites deserve much credit, surely, for not stopping at "only believe," for insisting that faith must have consequences in the human world. Our ancestors rejected high-church ritual and iconography for community and nonresistance and believers' baptism, insisting that the fruits of the Spirit ought to be visible in daily life. When they harkened back to the early church for inspiration and example, however, they seem to have accepted the early fathers' dismissal of the Gnostics as heretics without question. What if they had known what we know? If they had read the Gospel of Thomas and other texts offering a spiritual gnosis as exacting as the discipline they required of each other in doctrine and action, might those early radical reformers have integrated such teachings into a different and perhaps richer sort of Anabaptism? After all, there are intriguing social and structural parallels between Gnostics and Anabaptists—both small, scattered sects who were persecuted as heretics for their resistance to church hierarchy and their insistence that a small, independent, committed group might be granted the secrets of true Christianity.

As some of my students repeatedly, impatiently inform me, such unanswerable what-if questions are quite futile in one sense; the world is the way it is. Yet it is hardly news among reflective Mennonites that in our concentration on what we ought to be *doing* in the world, much else has escaped us. The recent surge of interest in various forms of spirituality, ritual, and iconography are clear indications of a hunger for kinds of religious experience that we have long done without. The heat of evangelical emotionalism (I am speaking in very broad terms here) might not tempt us so much if we had other resources for spiritual exploration, for discovering what it might mean to follow Jesus and seek God with our hearts and our minds and our strength. Historically precedents for interest in spirituality and the "inner life" can be found in some early Anabaptists, most notably Hans Denck among the South Germans and David Joris among the Dutch. Pilgram Marpeck also wrote some important letters seeking a balance between the inner and outer lives. As Arnold Snyder writes, however, even in the sixteenth century "Anabaptism increasingly moved away from the spiritual, experiential, inner side of the Christian life and increasingly emphasized the outer, legislated marks of the 'true church.' The emphasis came to fall less and less on repentance, faith, and regeneration, and more and more on the 'obedience of faith'" (Snyder 302).

As Snyder notes, both "literalists" like Grebel, Sattler, and Menno Simons and spiritualists like Denck accepted the dualism of "inner" spirituality and "outer" obedience and agreed that "the 'spiritual' world is the higher one; the physical world shares nothing essential with it" (Snyder 309). Yet it seems to me time to ask whether this ancient dichotomy is not itself impoverished and misleading. Somewhat less a dualist than the others, Marpeck opposed the strict use of the ban practiced by the Swiss Brethren, but he was equally opposed to individualistic spiritualism. In the late "Concerning the Humanity of Christ," Marpeck insisted that "We must simply in all of our actions stand idle ourselves, as dead in ourselves, if Christ is to live in us, which life and work alone are pleasing to the Father. For human wisdom can disguise itself as an angel of light, especially the human wisdom of the scribal kind" (Klassen 510).

Noting that many who attempt to do good are in fact deceived, he suggests that "Luther, Zwingli, M. Hoffman, C. Schwenckfeld, S. Frank, and others have been only servants who did not know what their lord would do" (Klassen 512). Surely no Gnostic, Marpeck for a moment flirts with a quasi-Gnostic language of "knowing":

> I write all this in order that each one may well perceive for himself, what drives him, from what source it flows, from what source his drive stems. This the servants do not know. The friends and children however know what their Lord does and why the compulsion of the Holy Spirit is in them. (Klassen 512).

Snyder applauds Marpeck for his balancing of "inner" and "outer" concerns, remarking that his

> insights are significant because they re-vision the Christian life as a process of spiritual growth into Christlikeness. . . . Thus the Christian life for Marpeck was not the desperate defense of a perfect state, but rather a growing continually into the divine nature by means of individual and communal spiritual disciplines. (Snyder 335-36).

This "middle" position seems pleasing and sensible enough, although Marpeck's synthesis remains largely untested, since his vision of the Christian life has had little direct influence on Mennonite practice. However intriguing Marpeck's ideas may be, I want here to suggest my own synthesis: one that is more confident about the imagination and human creativity as a gift of God and a means of knowledge. I would also place the work of the imagination not in some interior, subjective realm but very much within the physical world. The productions of the imagination must entangle and incorporate the physical world if they are to engage others, after all, and they must be brought into the material world in some physical form—words, sounds, images—if others are to share them. The knowledge that the imagination seeks may include answers to ultimate questions as well as stories and images about the things and people of this world, of course. The products of the imagination may be couched sometimes in abstractions and otherworldly images, but even those abstractions and images still exist, finally and irrevocably, in the world of human life and perceptions. The products of the imagination may be self-indulgent or vague, implausible or simply wrong, but that does not mean that it is their nature to be so, any more than a poorly built wall means that it is the nature of walls to fall down.

When Marpeck calls for integration of spiritual growth with lives of regenerate love, he is not so distant from some teachings of the rebel Gnostics. The Gospel of Truth, attributed to the Gnostic leader Valentinus, offers this set of practical imperatives:

> Speak concerning the truth to those who seek it and of knowledge to those who, in their error, have committed sin. Make sure-footed those who stumble and stretch forth your hands to the sick. Nourish the hungry and set at ease those who are troubled. Foster men who love. Raise up and awaken those who sleep. (Robinson 44)

Often *gnosis* through the ages is connected with images of waking, as it is here. I have often pondered Thoreau's cryptic observation: "I have never yet met a man who was quite awake. How could I have looked him in the face?" (Thoreau 90). The language of reunion and of family is also common. Bloom's comment on a parable by Valentinus might also be a distant gloss on my "Knowing the Father": "Out of this homely parable there comes forth the terrible vision of our nightmare, to be cured only by our waking up. That awakening *is* resurrection . . . through a rhetoric of a widening circle of awareness, a renewal of knowing the estranged father" (Bloom, *Omens* 192).

As must be clear by now, I believe that such a renewal of knowledge might be part of a quest to live a renewed life in this world, an aid to right action rather than mere distraction. But enough abstraction; let me turn to a poem that attempts to enact spiritual exploration both outer and inner. It was born out of a late-evening poetry hike, one I began with the skepticism I bring to most group endeavors. But in the process of it I found myself thoroughly enmeshed, almost spellbound. I found myself writing as fast as I could in my little notebook, overtaken by a sense that I was surrounded by information streaming from some unaccountable source, one that was very much of the world but not exactly in it.

Instructions for the Night Walk
—for Terry Hermsen

Cup your hands behind your ears and you'll hear
the water moving way below. Think deer, think bats.

Nothing paler and more poised than the young poison ivy.
Nothing deeper than the circle of the last pool left in the ravine.

Daisies in the half light, the clink of stones, sighs.
Somebody who speaks as the heron launches. Suppose

your father was a stony river, or some words
chanted in the half light while other letters traced

themselves in your head, insistent, out of nowhere.
Whatever comes next you won't expect it, won't deny it,

plain and eccentric as the buckled floor of the world,
your soul-bird settling to float easily downstream.

Suppose anything you need, and pay as much attention
as you have. Don't say anything. Every leaf is singular.

There are voices that speak only once. Touch
your right temple, where something might have landed.

Find nothing. Feel nothing and suppose you might rise
earlier than anyone ever has, selfish and complete,

listen to the brilliance of the gibbous moon, throw most
of yourself away and let what's left condense, go heavy,

spiral inward until it bursts into flame and wings away.
Don't wait. Don't falter. Don't say anything to anybody, yet.

Winds you cannot feel or imagine pass through every second,
tides of secret intelligence surge and ebb. There is honey

and red wine, hard bread and cheese on a plate. There are
empty boxes, cans without labels, the final storms.

If anyone asks say how empty you feel, and how full.
When they say choose a stone, choose a stone. When they say

put it down, don't say anything. But keep it in your hand. (225-26)

Some of the images and ideas in this poem have been somewhere in
my head for a long time. But I would never have written this specific
poem except for that one particular evening at that one particular, unfa-
miliar place where I walked among a group of particular people, most of
them new acquaintances. My friend Terry read Pattiann Rogers' lovely,
strange poem that begins "Suppose your father is a redbird," and when a
woman I barely knew whispered to me "Are you going to put your rock
down?" I found myself whispering back, "I don't think so—what about
you?" Those experiences were shifted and altered in the making of the
poem—it is hardly a literal, "realistic" rendering—but the language of
the poem is utterly enmeshed in the specific, bodily circumstances of its
making.

I knew almost nothing about Gnosticism when I wrote this poem,
yet it seems to me that it may enact a kind of small-g gnosis—and, I hasten to add, one that is very much embodied and communal. What is the
poem saying, exactly? What knowledge does it offer or suggest? Is it mere
self-indulgent aestheticism, or something else? In response to such questions, I can only agree with Wallace Stevens, who wrote that "the poem
must resist the intelligence almost successfully." Like most poets, Stevens
found that language can mean in ways other than the rational and the
logical, can communicate important information that resists paraphrase
and explanation.

Harold Bloom takes this argument even further, claiming that the
strength of poems is in what he calls "evasion," however exasperating or
even frightening such resistance to ordinary discourse may be. Bloom

claims that artists may even fear their own work when it embodies true knowledge:

> A Gnostic aesthetic would say that works of artists become objects of fear, even to those artists, because the statues or poems are works of true knowledge. Yeats remarked, at the end of his life, that man could embody the truth, but could not know it, which is an inverted Gnostic formulation. . . . The Adamic "greater sounds" that frighten the angels are necessarily poems. To ask how poems can be the Gnosis is to ask what is it that poems know, which in turn is to ask what is it that we can come to know when we read poems? . . . "Poetic knowledge" may be an oxymoron, but it has more in common with Gnosis than it does with philosophy. Both are modes of *antithetical* knowledge, which means of knowledge both negative and evasive, or knowledge not acceptable as such to epistemologists of any school. (Bloom, *Agon* 56)

Does my poem have to do with what Bloom calls "antithetical" and "evasive" knowledge, in its repeated "Don't say anything" imperatives and in the closing refusal to put down the stone when instructed? The small gesture of evading the official, the public, the formulaic, and pilfering one small stone from a national park is only a gesture, of course, and I make no grand claims. It was nearly a year later that I read the exhortation that the Gospel of Thomas ascribes to Jesus: "Split a piece of wood, and I am there. Lift up the stone, and you will find me there."

What place might such poems and the peculiar work they do have in community, in the social life, especially in communities as relentlessly pragmatic as most Anabaptist ones? This poem came into being in a transient, temporary community of people who came together for a week and then parted. Ronald Grimes writes of a similar experience in *Deeply into the Bone*, describing an immersive ritual in a Haitian waterfall and then worrying about its unattached quality:

> My Afro-Caribbean-Polish "baptism" lodged itself in the bone but left me stranded. Though sensuous and meaningful, it led into no enduring community, since the community was temporary, ending when the project finished. In this respect my experience is typical of others who experiment with ritual. I know of many people initiated on weekend retreats who end up beached like whales unable to flop back into the deep waters. (Grimes 124)

I have brooded myself on the role that such temporary communities play, as I write more and more poems at poetry workshops and retreats. Am I simply stuck on the beach Grimes describes most of the time, my daily life too filled with habits and demands? Or do new places and people and breaks from routine make it easier to summon the kind of fresh, careful attentiveness to the world and to the deeper layers of the self out of which both spiritual renewal and poems come?

One response to Grimes's worry is that writing is one way of retaining at least some trace of such unique experiences, of bringing something back into the wider community, but the nature of such experiences still deserves a deeper look. In Ralph Waldo Emerson's *Nature* the first great American poet and prophet of Gnosis bemoans the poverty of living in a "retrospective" age, bound to see only through the eyes of our ancestors, and envisions a more immediate relation to the world:

> Our age is retrospective. It builds the sepulchres of the fathers. It writes biographies, histories, and criticism. The foregoing generations beheld God and nature face to face; we, through their eyes. Why should we not also enjoy an original relation to the universe? Why should not we have a poetry and philosophy of insight and not of tradition, and a religion by revelation to us, and not the history of theirs? (Emerson 21)

I have my doubts about Emerson's social history, since without history and human community we would have no culture, nor the language to communicate our revelations to each other. Still, his question surely remains relevant for those of us in whose rituals the only true poetry was crafted thousands of years ago, and in which the contemporary language often seems to have been consciously made as bland and drab as possible. Usually that is not true, but for a long time our religious language has been almost entirely entrusted to people whose training in religion, though often meager, far exceeded their schooling in the resources of language. The marvelous, almost Shakespearean rhythms and images of the King James Bible were part of my awakening into poetry; why should we treasure those poems but not seek to create our own new versions and visions?

Emerson's question has implications for Mennonite poets and writers that I can only touch on here. His call for an "original relation to the universe" cuts quite against the usual imperative to celebrate (or at least, in John Ruth's term, "wrestle through") our traditions, our history, our ethos. Mennonite writers have often been judged on their contentions with the tradition, rather than their innovations. But are we so much in the debt of our forefathers (and, more sparsely remembered, our foremothers) that we must always see everything through their eyes? Is it mere pride to think we might, even for a moment, become transparent eyeballs on our own, part and parcel of God? Are our rituals only retrospective, or do they speak to our new, living beings as well, and lead us toward a deeper engagement with God and the universe?

I do not mean to underestimate the risks of such endeavors. Marpeck was not the first nor the last to warn against the lonely lures of the imagination. Believers through the ages have critiqued the various gnosticisms and mysticisms of their day as too interiorized, too intellectual, too removed from the world and the community and the body—as well as too "creative," too independent, too innovative. We can see glimmers of this syndrome in Emerson's own famous image of the transparent eyeball:

> Standing on the bare ground,—my head bathed by the blithe air and uplifted into infinite space,—all mean egotism vanishes. I become a transparent eyeball; I am nothing; I see all; the currents of the Universal Being circulate through me; I am part or parcel of God. The name of the nearest friend sounds then foreign and accidental: to be brothers, to be acquaintances, master or servant, is then a trifle and a disturbance. I am the lover of uncontained and immortal beauty. (Emerson 24)

Bloom acutely notes the depopulated quality of this vision. "Emersonian transparency is such a stretching, a Sublime crossing of the gulf of solipsism," he says, "but not into a communion with others. . . . The farther shore has no persons upon it, because Emerson's farther shore or beyond is no part of nature, and has no room therefore for created beings." Yet Bloom also insists an early Gnostic would have "understood Emerson's 'I am nothing; I see all'" as the mode of negation through which the knower again could stand in the Abyss, the place of original fullness, before the Creation (Bloom, *Agon* 158).

This Abyss, so distant from the ordinary human realm, may be the same territory that "Instructions for the Night Walk" explores at the end. Certainly I grew up learning that to love and follow Jesus was something quite different than being the lover of "an uncontained and immortal beauty." Yet I would argue now that to explore such a vast, unmarked, lonely plain in the language of poetry may also be the work of the tribe. Even in Emerson's ecstatic description the distant echoes of the human remain, an anchor that draws him and his words back into the human world. Even more crucially, writing a poem or an essay or a story is a communal act even when it is done alone, and no less so when its argument runs against communal wisdom. The most solitary romantic cannot exist without at least an imagined reader. No matter how "foreign and accidental" its concerns may seem, the poet's work is never truly disengaged from the community; the drive to somehow bringing the vision back is fundamental to every poet and every poem.

Against Bloom's contention that "poetry as such is always a counter-theology," we might consult a nearer authority who was more optimistic about the possibility, even the necessity, of original spiritual experience within religious community. George Fox issued this famous challenge to his Quaker followers:

> The Scriptures were the prophets' words, and Christ's and the apostles' words, and what, as they spoke, they enjoyed and possessed, and had it from the Lord: . . . Then what had any to do with the Scriptures, but as they came to the Spirit that gave them forth? You will say, "Christ saith this, and the apostles say this;" but what canst thou say? Art thou a child of the Light, and hast thou walked in the Light, and what thou speakest, is it inwardly from God? (Fell)

The Quakers, like the Mennonites, like the Gnostics, have often been at odds with the dominant churches and social structures of their day. Whatever our particular issues, I would suggest, we should find that role more or less natural by now. Like the young Andrew Hudgins, we may wish we were stupid enough to accept the errors and illogic that stream around us. But must we settle for being stupid, or for accepting what we are told? I think we must seek to walk in the Light, to listen to the Spirit, to wake up. To devalue or even ridicule the personal, subjective, interior element of this search is surely to deprive the community of essential resources that are found only through the subjective.

I understand such work not to be undertaken *instead of* what Mennonites have traditionally done, but as another resource for following Jesus and serving humanity, another way of growing into a full and worthy life. The Gospel of Phillip offers a beautiful addition to Paul's trinity of faith, hope, and love, in an image that my farm-boy heart cannot help but love as well:

> Farming in the world requires the cooperation of four essential elements. A harvest is gathered into the barn only as a result of the natural action of water, earth, wind and light. God's farming likewise has four elements—faith, hope, love, and knowledge. Faith is our earth, that in which we take root. And hope is the water through which we are nourished. Love is the wind through which we grow. Knowledge, then, is the light through which we ripen. (Robinson 147)

William Carlos Williams, perhaps the most materialist gnostic poet of the last century, famously claimed that "It is difficult / to get the news from poems / yet men die miserably every day / for lack / of what is found there." I think some of the "news" poems have to offer is well thought of as a kind of gnosis, knowledge that is not simply intellectual nor spiritual nor sensual but all of these (and more) at once. Such knowledge might emerge out of communal ritual, or more private ritual, but it enriches our entire communities as well.

I felt the power and the lure of this kind of knowledge in my youth, in the stately cadences of the King James versions of the Psalms, in certain hymns, in ritual prayers like the magically repetitive benediction we often prayed at Waldo Mennonite: "The Lord bless you and keep you. The Lord make his face to shine upon you, and be gracious unto you. The Lord lift up his countenance upon you, and give you peace." Like all real poetry, this can be translated into simple prose only at the cost of its power and strength. It is a treasured corporate expression, but it comes to us as the gift of a single human being in communion with something larger than himself. That we have for so long relinquished even the possibility that more such gifts await us if we seek them out for ourselves seems to me a scandalous impoverishment.

If much in the long, convoluted history of Gnosticism and gnosis strikes us as problematic and even dangerous, so be it. Here as in everything else we must sort the genuine from the false, the sweet from the bitter. We need no more accept their every doubtful claim or extravagant myth than we need embrace the violent apocalypticism of Münster or the strange soteriology of Menno Simons to be Anabaptists. But a gnostic openness to mystery, its insistence that faith is only the first step, its willingness to tolerate difference and encouragement of the creative encounter with the mysteries of life and God and the world all seem to me to have something to teach us.

In search of a way to end this murky treatise, I found myself looking through my work for a gnostic, small g, poem. The search reassured me that I am no Gnostic, in the early and heretical sense. My inner life and my writing is too deeply embedded in both human and natural communities; I love what is true and beautiful in those realms too much, in all their tangible, frustrating, otherly beauty, in all their danger, terror, and joy, to think it all just a colossal blunder. While I am moved by much in the Gospel of Thomas and other early texts, and by the "Gnostic Sermon" Harold Bloom offers at the end of his *Omens of Millenium* as well, I find myself neither moved nor engaged by the arcane symbology of ogdoads and archons. I do not plan to become a "gnostic poet," small or large g; it is a mistake for a poet to try to be anything but a poet, I am convinced, and the best "gnostic" writing has mostly been done by those with no intention of producing such a thing.

But I will continue to be a poet in search of gnosis, of those elusive glimpses of a truth that is larger, deeper, older and stranger than we will ever reckon fully, a truth that is strangely but surely entangled with intimations of divine presence. After my brief time with the Gnostics I am more convinced than ever that we need an *embodied* gnosis, one that never forgets either in its theory or its textuality that we know God in and of and through the world, through the voices and gestures and bodies of our brothers and sisters and the ten thousand things.

Let me end with two more poems that may enact moments of that search. Curiously, both are writers' conference poems. The first was written near the end of a week of talking constantly about memoir, poetry, and all sorts of other things in a small Ohio town, when I snuck away to the woods for an hour. The epigraph was spoken by my friend Julia Levine amid an impassioned discourse about writing poems. It is itself, I think, a marvelous burst of unstudied gnostic wisdom.

Meditation in Glen Helen
*"Who knows what you know that you don't
know you know . . . you know?"*

So I went to the Yellow Spring, cupped the cold water
flowing from the red rock and tasted a little,

chill and metal-hard. So the park closes at dusk, and
I've been so much with people that for a while

I disremember how to be alone. So the summer trees unfold
around me, careful, steady, and two guys and a girl
peel their jeans and frolic in the pool below.
Oh, the water will splash. I have my questions.

I will stand together with the others lost and lame
when the time comes, cool at the edge of the river,
mudding my toes in the brown coarse sand,
crying with all the children: what is it I know,

how can the iron-clean water have so little to say?
The forest makes it easy to hide anything, an eyelash,
a brown long-limbed spider, the bones of the first man
to put a hand into the spring and say cold, say good.

Even the last ridge can hold the trees only so high.
Some of the paths are closed for reconstruction.
Some of the paths are broad and clear. Some days
I walk around and around my little town, fussing

at the tv haze, stumbling over the brick sidewalks
quietly being swallowed by the grass. Some days
I believe that everything can be stomped or outrun.
Some days only the highest bridges stand a chance

of surviving the floods. Some walnut trees
are lonely mothers, last year's crop all swept off
by the squirrels who broke the bony sheaths open
and chewed themselves fat on the oily, convoluted hearts.
　　　　　　　　　　　　　—for J. L.

What place might poetry and the search for gnosis have in the rituals and routines of our days? I can only say that I cannot not do this
work, regardless of its utility. Surely the old rituals and stories, ways of
learning and doing that have endured for millenia, have their place.
Surely the drive to make something new, to evade the traditions and the
histories and seek to encounter the world and all within it freshly is just

as old and just as necessary. The Gospels of Matthew and Thomas agree on this much: if we seek, we shall find, and if we knock the door will be opened.

In this final poem I found myself moving through a series of images of an indwelling, upholding presence in the world, toward intimations of an ultimate homecoming:

Small Night Song from Oneonta

It's good that the world has more beauty
than it needs. It's good to walk into
the smooth Catskill night and discover

that the night has no edges, no sympathy,
no grievance against me, that any place I step
will hold me firm, not like a lover,

not like a child. It's good to be a child,
and then for years to be something else,
and then something else. It's a hard world

but the rain is persistent, the deer
are quiet and discreet, and for ages now
the trees have known how to dream their way up.

A man with a pack on his shoulder
saunters down the path below me, knowing
the lights he sees ahead are burning for him. (31)

AFTERWORD:
HERESY AND THE INDIVIDUAL TALENT

*How vigilant we are! determined not to live by faith if we can avoid it,
all the day long on the alert, at night we unwillingly say our prayers and
commit ourselves to uncertainties. . . . This is the only way, we say; but
there are as many ways as there can be drawn radii from one center. All
change is a miracle to contemplate, but it is a miracle which is taking
place every instant.* —Henry David Thoreau, *Walden*

The Christ Child was not obedient to his parents. —Robert Bly,
"Turning Away from Lies"

*Tradition. . . . cannot be inherited, and if you want it you must obtain it
by great labor. . the poet must develop or procure the consciousness of the
past . . . What happens is a continual surrender of himself as he is at the
moment to something which is more valuable.* —T. S. Eliot, "Tradition
and the Individual Talent"

These curiously Anabaptist words from the Anglican poet-critic T. S.
Eliot seem both strangely relevant and subtly wrong today. Eliot was
surely right that the poet must learn the tradition, or some tradition, or
some set of traditions, but in avuncular pronouncements like this one it
seems to me that he understates the complexities and the necessary
quirkiness of that task, and misstates the role of the personal in it as well.
It is more accurate to say that poets must discover, if not invent, a web of
traditions that will shape and sustain their own work. Much of Eliot's
own brilliance as a poet stems from the odd and unexpected sources

from which he learns, borrows, and sometimes steals.

Mennonites have long believed themselves deeply traditional while paying more lip service than close attention to our actual, tangible heritage. When John Ruth sought to write the history of Lancaster Conference, he found that for generations the deep suspicion of education and intellectualism of those Mennonites had prevented them from maintaining close contact with many of the particulars of their own history. He returns to this irony over and over again

> The Mennonites themselves had not taken the trouble to keep even a modest written account of their spiritual heritage. They interpreted their lack of interest in what might be called the life of the mind as a godly humility. But in the urgent claims of an upwardly mobile descendant such as Edwin K. Martin, we also sense an unwelcome result of this attitude: the frustration of an intelligence that might have made better sense of the heritage if its story had been accessible. (Ruth 633)

Ruth's writing of *The Earth Is the Lord's* is clearly at once an act of recovery and homage and a transgression of his own tradition: with his Harvard Ph.D. and his lifelong dedication to recovering and telling the history of Pennsylvania Mennonites, he is both a blessed preserver of the tradition and in violation of some of its most powerful taboos, including those which have militated against the full preservation of the tradition.

I mean here to celebrate such violations of the received order in pursuit of the truth, to testify for a personal tradition strangely filled with contrarians, loyal rebels, and iconoclasts, one that I will argue is only appropriate for writers in the Anabaptist tradition. Like the Anabaptist martyrs who sang as their flesh burned, the most earnest and rigorous seekers after truth have often been branded as heretics by the mediocre and the corrupt who continue to rule our world and our institutions. The true voices may be hard to hear among the many false prophets, but if we wish to sing the blessed presence of God in the world we must seek out those who continue in that great tradition of energetic, rigorous, communally engaged pursuit of an ever more intricate and accurate naming of the world and our place in it. For ourselves and our world, the risks of that pursuit are less than the dangers of abandoning it.

Heresy for the writer thus becomes not a matter of falling into or out of step with some unitary orthodoxy but the challenge of cobbling together something liveable out of the heterodoxy within which we move and breathe.[43] We live in a time when official pronouncements are ostentatiously heretical, blasphemous, or both (consider the hastily re-named "Operation Infinite Justice," and the announced and ongoing quest of the American government to somehow exterminate evil in the world, in the best Ahabesque fashion). Seeking out the less militaristic and arrogant heresies of our forefathers and mothers and offering up our own, in the hope that they might prove less pernicious than what passes for truth, today seems not just a right but a duty. I can do very little of that actual work here, but let me make a few more remarks about contemporary conditions and then offer a very brief and exploratory effort of my own.

Surely fear and trembling are in order as we proceed. Just because most of our heroes were denounced as heretics does not mean, of course, that all heresies are either lawful or edifying. We are surrounded by what seem to me the most rank and dangerous heresies propounded by those who most loudly proclaim themselves faithful, while the meek and the holy are ridiculed, derided, and accused of all manner of perniciousness for failing to kneel at the duly swathed altar of Justice from whence our officials issue their pronouncements.

A brief list of currently popular ideas that seem like heresies to me might include these:

• that God has a special love for Americans and the United States of America;

• that God wants and indeed helps Americans to kill their enemies;

• that God hates fags;

• that ultimate truth may be rendered satisfactorily in abstract propositions couched in human language and arbitrated by institutions;

• that the soul is a precious invisible object contained in the treacherous husk of the body.

Then there are the anabaptist variations already flourishing, some of which must by the elementary rules of logic and fair play be heretical in small or large ways, although I mean to imply no judgment in listing them here:

Fundamentalist Anabaptism, I'm OK and You're Not Bad Anabaptism, Evangelical Anabaptism, Television Anabaptism, Patriotic Anabaptism, God Hates Americans Anabaptism, Love the Sin Hate the Sinner Anabaptism, God Hates Me and I Deserve It Anabaptism, Episcopalian and Neo-Orthodox and Benedictine Anabaptism, GLBTI and Promise Keeper and Married Monastic Anabaptism, Charismatic and Universalist Anabaptism, Capitalist and Anti-Racist Anabaptism, Post-modern/Premodern/Antiquarian Anabaptism, Ford Crown Victoria and Beemer and SUV and Minivan Anabaptism, White Wine and Prozac and Granola and How-Long-Were-You-Overseas Anabaptism, and so forth.

Now perhaps I am wrong about some of these. No, certainly I am wrong about some of these, and probably about most other things as well. No doubt I have fallen unwitting prey to other heresies, even more dangerous than the ones I proclaim openly. I may speak lightly, but I know that I deal in grave matters. If I invite your laughter I pray that it be the true and holy laughter of recognition and delight and terror, not the bitter cackle of cynicism and defeat. We have little choice but to press on. Do we? The spirit persists. We've only got, as Kate Wolf sings, these times we're living in.

I meant here to multiply examples, pile illustrations and analysis high and deep. But space is precious, and how can I approach the topic of heresy and not offer what might be one of my own? I do not much trust manifestos, but I have often taken a curious pleasure in reading them. Writing one, I thought, might be a salutary exercise in imagining the better world to come, or at least provide a cautionary example for those who follow. So in lieu of all else I offer this,

THE MANIFESTO OF ANABAPTIST SURREALISM, OR, SURREALIST ANABAPTISM

Preface

In 1525 Blaurock, Manz, Grebel and the rest gathered in that up-stairs room in Zurich, talked and prayed, poured water on each other's heads, took the big chance. Four hundred years later another group gathered in the same city, in another time of war and crisis, and also de-termined to rebel, to transform themselves and their relations to society if they could not transform the state itself. So the practitioners of Dada gathered in the Cabaret Voltaire, issued their manifestoes, made their grand gestures of resistance and imagination, in ways that, once again, struck the honest citizens about them as a shock and an abomination.

Pride is the star that yawns and penetrates through the eyes and the mouth, she insists, strikes deep, on her breast is inscribed: you will die. This is her only remedy. Who still believes in doctors? I prefer the poet who is a fart in a steam-engine—he's gentle but he doesn't cry—polite and semi-homosexual, he floats." (Tristan Tzara, *Dada Manifesto on Feeble and Bitter Love,* Rothenberg and Joris 300)

Now this could be the manifesto of Dada Anabaptism but is not, because I am in charge, and all this about farts and semi-homosexuals is catchy but seems unlikely to take us where we need to go. At any rate, Dada (as we all should know) quickly gave way to surrealism, and it is this movement, with its iconoclasm, its rebellion against the orderly, rational, disastrous European civilization that led to the calamities of the First World War, its nearly superstitious faith in chance and autonomous processes, its effort to transform or transcend prior categories and structures, that I propose now to fuse with the preternatually clear, closely reasoned, wretchedly pragmatic spiritual efficiencies of Anabaptism as I know it. The result can only be something tentative, temporary, contingent, unwieldy, impractical, inefficient, and dangerously unstable, but perhaps useful for something: at the least, a brief spectacle, a cautionary diversion, a source of amusement if not edification hereby submitted to the community for further discernment.

Doctrinal Sources

As Borges noted that Kafka, and every writer, creates his own precursors (Borges 202), Anabaptist Surrealism accepts arbitrarily chosen fragments not only of the Schleitheim and Dordrecht Confessions but also of the "First Manifesto of Surrealism" by Andre Breton, to wit: "Surrealism . . . asserts our complete *nonconformism* clearly enough so that there can be no question of translating it, at the trial of the real world, as evidence for the defense" (*PFTM* 470).

Surrealist Anabaptism recognizes and insists upon its own ignorance, inadequacy, and incompetence above all, and is committed to progressive revelation, seeing through a glass darkly, *Demut, Gelassenheit,* fear and trembling, communal interpretation, and so forth, even while it ignores all these to say anything at all. It would prefer to remain entirely silent and simply point this way and that. Still, certain proposals and postulates must be made.

Propositions

1. The Union of Surrealist Anabaptists proclaims the fusion of dream and reality into a surreality that contains both dream and reality, chaos and order, faith and doubt, past and future, culminating in the instantiation, reification, obfuscation, and final transcendence of all binary dualisms everywhere, hallelujah, amen.

2. All human beings, and all interested animals, plants and other creatures, are immediately declared both members in good standing of the Union of Anabaptist Surrealists and perpetually and simultaneously under its ban, as both eternally innocent and originally sinful. It is hoped that this dual and non-negotiable status for all will make schisms and internal turmoil more difficult if not impossible.

3. These harbingers, forerunners, and seminal texts among many others are noted with gratitude:

• The Schleitheim Brotherly Union, surreal in its claim that the sword is the instrument of God outside the perfection of Christ.

• Jan van Leyden for his surreal nude race over the cobbles of Münster, for his surreal ascension to the throne of the city, for his twelve wives and his surreal and personal beheading of she who displeased him right there on the cobbles of the Dom Platz.

• Dirk Phillips and Menno Simons in their struggle to explain that the whole sordid mess was a combination of surreal mistakes and surreal misunderstandings, and that further surreal hoisting of corpses in cages to the top of the church tower would not be necessary.

• Those authorities who, unconvinced, surreally disinterred the body of David Joris well after his death and burned it to ashes, along with his books and documents.

• The Dordrecht Confession, surreal in its praise of the civil order and its silence on the sword and its surreal instructions to the faithful: Run away. Be a victim. Give up your goods if anybody wants them. Promise to be good if they'll just forget to notice you.

• Menno Simons, surely worth mentioning twice, for his surreal Christology.

• The Flemish House Buyers and Contra House Buyers for their surreal contentions.

• The great poet, soldier, and casualty of war Guillaume Apollinaire for his invention of the term surrealism and his praise of the beauty of the shells bursting over the trenches like flowers, like breasts.

• Harold S. Bender for his surreal anabaptist life of autocratic servanthood.

• Robert S. Kreider for his surreal anabaptist refusal to go where Harold Bender told him to go.

• Our lord and savior Yeshua of Nazareth for his Beatitudes, commandments, instructions and example.

4. And these: John Keats, William Blake, William Butler Yeats, the Blessed Mother Mary, Mary Oliver, Mary Oyer, John Oyer, John Howard Yoder, John Ruth, Jan Gleysteen, Jan Yoder my sister, the Sisters of Mercy, Leonard Cohen, Leonard Nimoy, Leonard Gross, everybody's Gross-daddies and mommies but especially mine, Mother Jones, Joan Baez, Bob Dylan, Dylan Thomas, Thomas Hardy, the Hardy Boys, Boy George, George Harrison, Jorge Luis Borges, Harrison Ford, *not* Henry Ford, Franz Kafka, Franz Fanon, Rudy Wiebe, Dallas Wiebe, Armin Wiebe, Katie Funk Wiebe and her beautiful lost daughter Christine. Et al.

Some Final Supplementary Notes

A. Surrealist Anabaptism intends to incorporate and embody all Anabaptist traditions and practices whether ordered, disordered, remembered, membered, forgotten, imagined or slanderous, including sexual anarchy, married monasticism, plain dress, cross dress, radical nonresistance, Peace Through Strength, the eschewing of all ornament, and tasteful piercings of and about the ears, nostrils, eyebrows and other sensitive tissues.

B. Surrealist Anabaptism trusts that the greatness of God's love and grace is so large that none shall be condemned to eternal torment, possibly excepting former members of the conference formerly known as General.

C. Anabaptist Surrealism knows which are the real Mennonite colleges and therefore sends its children to Taylor, Messiah, Brandeis, and Harvard.

D. Surrealist Anabaptism recognizes, believes, and acts on every verse of every hymn in the *Ausbund* and every line of the *Ordnung*, written and unwritten, especially in the face of irresolvable contradictions.

E. Anabaptist Surrealism accepts the words of its prophet, "Connoisseur of Chaos," and heretic Wallace Stevens that "A. A violent order is disorder; and / B. A great disorder is order. These / Two things are one. (Pages of illustrations.)" (Stevens 166). It has its own illustrations.

F. Anabaptist Surrealism is 1) dedicated entirely and absolutely to anti-sexism, anti-racism, anti-classism, anti-gay-bashing, anti-ageism, anti-baldism, and so forth, 2) too busy pursuing the True Cadence for any of that stuff, 3) helpless before all manifestations of beauty.

G. Surrealist Anabaptism has noted with mingled bemusement and despair that despite all its good intentions it becomes ever more spotted and wrinkled.

H. Surrealist Anabaptism simultaneously celebrates and forbids Anabaptist provincialism of all sorts, Anabaptist smugness of the left, right, and center, all ethnocentric, Eurocentric, PC-centric, Yoder-centric, Hauerwas-centric and pseudocentric complexes, all versions and perversions of excessive and insufficient pride and humility, arrogance and *Gelassenheit, Gemeinschaft* and *Gesellschaft, Hochmut* and *Demut*.

I. Surrealist Anabaptism expects to be martyred for any of a thousand transgressions and hopes only to be surprised by the day and hour.

J. Anabaptist Surrealism anticipates being praised and disparaged as radical, reactionary, patriarchal, feminist, ethnic, universalist, missional, socialist, postmodern, charismatic, atheist, and so forth, and will plead no contest in every case.

K. Anabaptist Surrealism seeks to perform itself by creating through poetic, artistic, mystical, transcendental, concrete practices a new growth of images of impossibly pragmatic grace, hope, faith, tenderness and generosity that will spring up like mushrooms from horse droppings across the stage, the town, the country, the planet and indeed the cosmos, so that those who taste and see will themselves be taken up with the spirit of justice, beauty, peace, love, poetry, music, wild hope and holy play that we learn from our teacher, guide, friend, and savior the carpenter of Nazareth. Hallelujah and amen.

NOTES

1. The literature on martyrdom and its meaning for modern Mennonites is voluminous and controversial. Among literary treatments, see Al Reimer 6-9 and Kasdorf, *The Body and the Book* 99-121 and passim. For one critical treatment of the martyr tradition, see Goering: "Martyrs project a clarity of belief, a sense of being correct against all odds. They are right and they know it, no matter the degree to which they are in a numeric minority. For those in agreement with them, their behavior shows courage and faithfulness. To those in disagreement, the behavior often shows an arrogance and a moral smugness" (13). This psychological dynamic and division of views applies in varying degrees to Mennonite writers and their reception by Mennonite readers.

2. The Illinois Mennonite Historical and Genealogical Society is the clearest visible sign of this renewed interest. The society has several hundred members, operates a historical center near Metamora, Illinois, and publishes the quarterly journal *Illinois Mennonite Heritage*.

3. For a fascinating account of "Fiction, Role-Playing and the Multifold Self" and "Family Plots: The Writing and Reading Community" see Detweiler 3-16.

4. The phrase "Mennonite/s writing," with the postmodern slash to complicate the first term, goes back at least to the conference on "Mennonite/s Writing in Canada" organized by Hildi Froese Tiessen at Conrad Grebel College in 1990, and was also used for the 1997 "Mennonite/s Writing in the U. S." conference at Goshen College organized by Ervin Beck and the 2002 "Mennonite/s Writing: An International Conference" held at Goshen with joint sponsorship by Conrad Grebel University College. I have omitted the slash, but am indebted to both Tiessen and Beck in this and many other ways.

5. For an excellent analysis of Herald Press's ill-fated effort to publish more serious fiction, see Zercher.

6. Thanks to Scott Holland for e-mail conversations in which he helped me to understand and formulate this distinction.

7. See Tiessen 237 for one useful definition of Mennonite literature and art as "work produced by individuals who were nurtured within a Mennonite community, who , . . had access to the inside of the Gemeinschaft."

8. Yoder's lightly fictionalized biography of his Irish Catholic-born mother, who was adopted into an Amish family in central Pennsylvania, is a best-selling Amish text—the recent Herald Press edition boasts of 375,000 copies in print. That edition includes many changes made by Herald Press editors, some of them quite significant, with only the scantest of indications; scholars will want to consult Yoder's original, self-published edition (Yoder).

9. See Wright, "*Community*", for an essay teasing out themes of community and theology in *Flatlands*, *Community of Memory*, and my earlier book of poems *Inquiries*.

10. The neatness of my scheme is disrupted, I hope not fatally, by Friesen's two pre-*Shunning* collections, *The Lands I Am* and *Bluebottle*.

11. For an account of the making of this piece see Weaver 116. Essays related to the conference are forthcoming; see Schmidt, Reschly and Umble.

12. Clearly there is no neat or airtight way to separate humility from other traditional Mennonite emphases such as community and nonresistance. I am more concerned with exploring the persistence and function of humility language and imagery in recent Mennonite literature.

13. I have also drawn on the other essays by Suderman cited in the bibliography.

14. Kliewer's *The Violators* is itself a somewhat controversial collection of short stories, set in an isolated religious community in Canada which bears striking resemblance to his home town of Mountain Lake, Minnesota .

15. Wiebe's *Sweeter Than All the World* marks his return to Mennonite themes and characters but was published well after this chapter was completed. See my "New Maps of the Territory" (*Georgia Review*, Winter 2003: 870-887) for a review of this book and four other books by Mennonite authors.

16. A series of such conferences were held at various Mennonite colleges between the mid-1970s and the early 1990s in conjunction with the preparation and publication of a four volume series on the history of Mennonites in the United States.

17. Written for an audience of Mennonite historians and academics who were, even in 1986, predominantly male, this essay is in its way a request for entry into that crowd, and it now seems to me to reflect (unconsciously, I hope) the largely male and patriarchal assumptions that Mennonite institutions are still trying to break free from.

When I finished reading this essay, I looked up to encounter the smiling face of one of the more prominent and conservative Mennonite historians, nodding enthusiastically. It did not take long for me to wonder whether I should be entirely pleased by his enthusiasm, but his reaction to later essays adequately balanced things out.

In her excellent response to this essay, delivered at the conference and reprinted in *MQR*, Shirley Showalter rightly pointed out that humility has been much less emphasized in the Russian Mennonite tradition. I stand behind my judgments, but I should have recognized more clearly that in reading Rudy Wiebe and Armin Wiebe, in particular, in terms of the humility motif I applied a somewhat alien (though I believe not irrelevant) standard to their work.

Showalter also notes rightly that "Humility can be both genuine and abused, even abusive" (25). Since writing this essay I have come to see more clearly the part that enforced "humility" has often played in the abuse of power within traditional, patriarchal, sexist communities. Mennonites, and others, have often used the rhetoric of humility as a means of enforcing submission and obedience. I did not mean to justify or rationalize such maneuvers, but I should have been more sensitive to that possibility. This essay's lack of attention to texts written by women, an oversight that I did not even notice at the time, is no doubt both a symptom of the limits of my thinking and a reason for my blindness about such matters.

I also oversimplified Hildi Froese Tiessen's views on Mennonite literature and aesthetics; were I writing now, I would be more generous and less eager to valorize Swiss communalism over Russian aestheticism. That dualism, and the dualism of individual vs. community, have come under increasing and well-deserved suspicion. Froese Tiessen's writing on such issues has developed and deepened significantly in recent years under the influence of postcolonial and postmodern literary theory. Her essay "Beyond the Binary: Reinscribing Cultural Identity in the Literature of Mennonites" is an excellent deconstruction of the language of "central" and "marginal" in Mennonite literature and criticism, and "Mennonite Literature and Postmodernism: Writing the 'In-Between' Space" offers many further nuanced insights into Mennonite literary issues.

With all its flaws, however, this essay still seems to me to be groping toward a humility that might be of considerable use to Mennonites—one that is not enforced by the strong upon the weak, nor preached by the powerful to the subservient, but freely and joyfully undertaken by an equal community of people who truly seek to serve each other and the world.

For reconsiderations of "humility" more representative of my current thinking, see Chapters 9 and 10.

18. For the history of American pacifism, see Brock, and Cooney and Michalowski.

19. For an introduction to Anabaptist history, see J. Denny Weaver, *Becoming Anabaptist*, and Snyder, *Anabaptist History and Thought*. The seminal modern Anabaptist work on pacifism and social ethics is Yoder, *The Politics of Jesus*.

20. Stitt 62. Another perplexed critic is Alan Feldman, who repeats this anecdote in reviewing Stitt's book to demonstrate that "Stafford remains more of an enigma" (669).

21. See Dickinson-Brown, Zweig, and Kramer for largely negative evaluations.

22. The Mennonite world conference in Winnipeg in 1991, had a full slate of readings by poets and writers. The 1994 Anabaptist Vision conference in Goshen and the 1995 "Quiet in the Land?" conference in Millersville, Pennsylvania also had high-profile creative readings and presentations in addition to more traditional scholarship. From all accounts the joint MC-GC conference at Wichita in 1995 did not have much such content, for reasons I am not prepared to explain.

23. Among the most prominent Canadian Mennonite poets are Patrick Friesen, Di Brandt, Sarah Klassen, Audrey Poettker and David Waltner-Toews. See especially the Canadian journals *Journal of Mennonite Studies, New Quarterly,* and *Prairie Fire* for poems, essays about, and interviews with them and others. The latter two published special issues on Mennonite writing, both ed. Hilde Froese Tiessen, in 1990.

Also see Al Reimer, *Mennonite Literary Voices*, for a survey of Mennonite poets and prose writers, mostly Canadian. Turnstone Press in Winnipeg, a literary publisher, has been the most important single outlet for Mennonite poets and short story writers in Canada.

24. See Suderman, "Mennonites, the Mennonite Community, and Mennonite Writers," for a more extensive summary and comparison of these views. Kasdorf's review of Reimer argues cogently that much of the difference between Reimer's Romantic view of the artist and Ruth's communal view may stem from geographical and historical differences. She suggests that the Dutch/Russian experience of migration and exile informs his image of the artist as "the gifted pioneer [who] blazes the way for the community," just as Ruth's more settled experience informs his: "Ruth continues to wrestle with ghosts on his ancestral farm along Skippack Creek in Pennsylvania, where Mennonites have been living for three centuries" (33). Also see my "Humility in Mennonite Literature," especially on Ruth.

25. See Levi Miller for a recent statement that makes an even more self-conscious effort to reassert a tightly controlled community and "strict, biblical Christianity" (304).

26. A happenstance anecdote on this point: while working on this essay, I happened to pick up the then-current *Mennonite Reporter*. There on page 10 was an article titled "Mennonite Writers Hold Literary Party in 'Heaven,'" describing a three-night festival at a Mennonite literary cafe in Winnipeg, with readings by numerous local writers, including most of the best-known Manitoba Mennonite writers: Di Brandt, Armin Wiebe, Sandra Birdsell, Patrick Friesen. Nowhere in the United States could such a thing happen; there just is no such a geographical concentration of Mennonites, let alone of Mennonite writers.

27. I have not done a careful study of creative writing instruction at Mennonite colleges, but Ervin Beck informs me that S. A. Yoder taught a yearly course in creative writing at Goshen for many years before Nick Lindsay's arrival in the late 1960s. Elmer Suderman taught Dallas Wiebe and Warren Kliewer at Bethel College, but only in literature courses. At Bluffton College, Lawrence Templin began teaching a creative writing course and advising the student literary magazine at least by 1962. Omar Eby began teaching a course in creative writing at Eastern Mennonite College in 1964.

28. Space limits force me to mention only some poets whose work I respect, including Elaine Sommers Rich and Ruth Naylor, both of them widely published and church leaders in other spheres as well; Lauren Friesen, whose primary work has been in drama; Suzanne Lawrence, by my lights perhaps the best poet publishing mainly in church journals; Naomi Duke, Barbara Esch Schisler and Barbara Keener Shenk; and (among more widely known writers with some Mennonite connections) William Stafford, Nicholas Lindsay, and Janet Kauffman.

29. Conversations with several people who knew Bender well (as I did not; I was ten when he died) have convinced me that the real Harold Bender did have a more capacious inner life than Keim's biography gives him credit for. The Bender I muse on here is the figure of the biography and Bender's public persona; given the continuing visibility and influence of that public figure, it seems legitimate to leave this

piece as it stands, while recognizing that it may not do justice to the private man.

30. See Sawin for an analysis of current moves to maintain identity through such markers as quilts, copies of *Martyrs Mirror*, and Mennonite literary texts.

31. Although neither the phrase "narrative theology" nor the term "narrative" appear in the indices of J. Denny Weaver's three books, a major emphasis of his historical/theological project is to construct a narrative of Anabaptist history that will function as the foundation for a contemporary Mennonite theology of nonviolence. In the conclusion of *Becoming Anabaptist*, a survey of early Anabaptism, he emphasizes this point: "The story told above has related the different origins and the diverse histories of the several early Anabaptist movements. In spite of this diversity, however, a kind of unity eventually emerged. . After some initial equivocation, nonresistance came to belong virtually by definition to the Anabaptist understanding of the Jesus way" (111). Weaver's *Keeping Salvation Ethical*, a survey of "Mennonite and Amish Atonement Theology in the Late Nineteenth Century," surveys the theological writings of eight Anabaptist church leaders of the period, concluding that "The foregoing analysis shows that the modern development of a systematic theology for Mennonites should begin with the specific aspects of the Mennonite tradition, rather than with a more 'universal' creed from another tradition. Such a stance does not call for a rejection of learnings from the Western creedal tradition. It means, rather, that Anabaptist-Mennonite assumptions about discipleship, community, peace, and nonviolence will shape the way Mennonites discuss the issues contained in classic statements" (Weaver 236).

32. Brandt's later books of poems do not merely repeat this critique, but expand and complicate her narrative of a modern woman's experience of and reflections on family, mothering, politics, and life. See Chapter 9 for a closer analysis of one poem from her second collection, *Agnes in the Sky*.

33. I am not exactly sure what Redekop means by "free rein," but I doubt this statement is true today, if it was in the late 1980s when Redekop was writing. Progressive but long-established congregations like my own, First Mennonite in Bluffton, have shown great tolerance for and considerable support of artistic expression, and urban churches like the Cincinnati Mennonite Fellowship, which sponsors a biannual arts weekend, have probably been even more supportive of Mennonite art and artists.

34. See Suderman, *"Mennonites"*, for a detailed comparison of Ruth and Reimer. Kasdorf's review of Reimer argues cogently that much of the difference between Reimer's Romantic view of the artist and Ruth's communal view may stem from geographical and historical differences. She suggests that the Dutch/Russian experience of migration and exile informs his image of the artist as "the gifted pioneer [who] blazes the way for the community," just as Ruth's more settled experience informs his: "Ruth continues to wrestle with ghosts on his ancestral farm along Skippack Creek in Pennsylvania, where Mennonites have been living for three centuries" (Kasdorf, "Review" 33). See also chapters two and five in this volume.

35. See my discussion of Di Brandt's work, and the need for multiple perspectives and narratives, in Chapter 9.

36. Julia Kasdorf informs me that folk communities use terms such as *humility* or

obedience instead of *Gelassenheit*. Whatever the exact terminology deployed, though, the concept remains similar enough. I use the term in this section partly because I have written so much elsewhere about humility, and partly because the alternate meanings of Gelassenheit I trace here seem important to the Mennonite imagination.

37. The next chapter will discuss these issues in some recent books of Mennonite poetry, including Kasdorf's *Eve's Striptease* and my *Rhapsody with Dark Matter*. Also see Pamela Klassen's fine essay on sexuality, embodiment, power, and spirituality in the poetry and fiction of Mennonite women, including Di Brandt, Julia Kasdorf, Anne Konrad, Janet Kauffman (Klassen 234).

38. I choose this book of Ratzlaff's to discuss rather than his *Across the Known World*, published later the same year, because the poems in *Man Under a Pear Tree* were written later; *Across the Known World* reprints a number of poems from the chapbooks *New Winter Light* and *Out Here*.

39. See "Separation and Transformation: Tradition and Audience for Three Mennonite Poets."

40. As I completed this chapter I received a copy of the Goshen College *Bulletin* with a student article entitled "How Julia Kasdorf Changed My Life" and a back-page editorial by President Shirley Showalter musing approvingly on "Flying Lesson," so it is safe to say that Kasdorf's name is hardly anathema at the college she left after two years.

41. See Kasdorf's recent biography of Yoder, *Fixing Tradition*.

42. I am greatly indebted to Julia Kasdorf, Scott Holland, Gerald Biesecker-Mast, Gay Lynn Voth, John Rempel, Tom Finger, and Rebecca Slough, and others at the Ritual in Anabaptist Communities conference held at Hillsdale College on June 26-28, 2003, where I read an earlier version of this piece. Their generous attention, questions, and suggestions were invaluable as I worked and reworked it. Responsibility for its extravagances and errors, of course, remains with me.

43. I use the term "heresy" in at least two senses here. Innovative ideas and expressions once labeled as heresies by their opponents sometimes come over time to be accepted as possible if not necessary elements of Christian belief. In other cases, popular ideas propounded by powerful figures pass largely unchallenged despite their heretical nature. This essay is obviously written to advocate the first and resist the second.

WORKS CITED

Barthelme, Donald. "Not-Knowing." *The Georgia Review* 55/56.1 (2001 Spring 2002): 170-83.

Bender, Harold S. *The Anabaptist Vision.* Scottdale, Pa.: Mennonite Publishing House, 1960.

Benjamin, Walter. *Illuminations: Essays and Reflections.* Ed. Hannah Arendt and Tr. Harry Zohn. New York: Schocken, 1968.

Bergen, David. *See the Child.* Toronto: HarperCollins, 1999.

Berlin, James A. "Contemporary Composition: The Major Pedagogical Theories." *College English* 44 (1982): 765-777.

Bloom, Allen. *The Closing of the American Mind: How Higher Education Has Failed Democracy and Impoverished the Souls of Today's Students.* New York: Simon & Schuster, 1987.

Bloom, Harold. *Agon: Towards a Theory of Revisionism.* New York: Oxford, 1982.

———. *Omens of Millennium.* New York: Putnam's, 1996.

Bly, Robert. *A Little Book on the Human Shadow.* San Francisco: Harper & Row, 1988.

Brandt, Di. Agnes in the Sky. Winnipeg: Turnstone, 1990.

———. *Dancing Naked: Narrative Strategies for Writing Across Centuries.* Stratford, On.: Mercury P, 1996.

———. *Jerusalem, Beloved.* Winnipeg: Turnstone, 1995.

———. *Mother, Not Mother.* Stratford, Ont: Mercury, 1993.

———. *Questions i Asked My Mother.* Winnipeg: Turnstone, 1987.

Brenneman, John M. *Pride and Humility: A Discourse Setting Forth the Characteristics of the Proud and the Humble.* Elkhart, Ind.: John F. Funk, 1869. 2nd ed.

Brock, Peter. *Pacifism in the United States from the Colonial Era to the First World War.* Princeton: Princeton University Press, 1968.

Bruffee, Kenneth. "Social Construction, Language, and the Authority of Knowledge." *College English* 48 (Dec 1986): 773-90.

Brunk, Juanita. *Brief Landing on the Earth's Surface.* Madison: University of Wisconsin Press, 1996.

Calvino, Italo. *Invisible Cities.* Tr. William Weaver. Harcourt Brace Jovanovich: New York, 1972.

———. *Six Memos for the Next Millennium.* The Charles Eliot Norton Lectures 1985-86. Cambridge: Harvard University Press, 1988.

Carlisle, Thomas John. "Whisperings and Stirrings." *Purpose* 5 May 1981: 5.

Carroll, Lewis. *Alice's Adventures in Wonderland and Through the Looking Glass.* New York: Airmont, 1965.

Clark, Olynthus. "Joseph Joder, Schoolmaster-Farmer and Poet 1797-1887." *Transactions of the Illinois State Historical Society* 36 (1929): 135-65.

Cooney, Robert and Helen Michalowski. *The Power of the People.* Philadelphia: New Society Publishers, 1987.

Davis, Todd. *Ripe: Poems.* Huron, OH: Bottom Dog, 2002.

Deleuze, Gilles, and Felix Guattari. *A Thousand Plateaus.* Minneapolis: University of Minnesota Press, 1993.

———. "What Is a Minor Literature?" Ed. David H. Richter. *Falling Into Theory: Conflicting Views on Reading Literature.* Boston: Bedford, 1994. 166-72.

Derksen, Wilma. "Winnipeg Writers Hold Literary Party in 'Heaven.'" *Mennonite Reporter* 25, 8 (Apr. 17, 1995): 10.

Derrida, Jacques. "Structure, Sign, and Play in the Discourse of the Human Sciences." *The Critical Tradition: Classical Texts and Contemporary Trends.* Ed. David S. Richter. New York: Bedford/St. Martins, 1989. 959-71.

———. "'The Purloined Letter' from *The Purveyor of Truth.*" *The Critical Tradition: Classical Texts and Contemporary Trends.* Ed. David H. Richter. New York: Bedford/St. Martins, 1989. 971-78.

Detweiler, Robert. *Breaking the Fall: Religious Readings of Contemporary Fiction.* New York: Harper & Row, 1989.

Dickinson-Brown, Roger. "The Wise, The Dull, The Bewildered: What Happens in William Stafford." *Modern Poetry Studies* 6.1 (1975): 30-38.

Dickinson, Emily. *Final Harvest: Emily Dickinson's Poems.* Ed. Thomas H. Johnson. Boston: Little, Brown, 1961.

Dillard, Annie. *Teaching a Stone to Talk.* New York: Harper & Row, 1982.

Dintaman, Stephen F. "The Pastoral Significance of the Anabaptist Vision." *Mennonite Quarterly Review* 59.3 (July 1995): 307-22.

———. "The Spiritual Poverty of the Anabaptist Vision." *Conrad Grebel Review* 10 (Spring 1992): 205-08.

Eliade, Mircea. *The Myth of the Eternal Return.* Princeton: Princeton University Press, 1954.

Eliot, T.S. *Selected Prose of T.S. Eliot.* Ed. Frank Kermode. New York: Harcourt, 1975.

Emerson, Ralph Waldo. *Selections from Ralph Waldo Emerson.* Ed. Stephen E. Whicher. Boston: Houghton Mifflin, 1957.

Estes, Steven R. "Flanagan Mennonite Church One of Those Painted Yellow." *Illinois Mennonite Heritage* 24.4 (Dec 1997): 83.

Feldman, Alan. "Review of Peter Stitt, *The World's Hieroglyphic Beauty.*" *American Literature* 58.4 (1986): 668-69.

Fell, Margaret. "The Testimony of Margaret Fox Concerning Her Late Husband." *The Journal of George Fox*, 1694. Http://www.qis.net/~daruma/foxfell.html 5 June 2003.

Fitzgerald, F. Scott. *The Great Gatsby*. New York: Scribner's, 1953. 1925.

Forché, Carolyn. Ed. *Against Forgetting: Twentieth-Century Poetry of Witness*. New York: Norton, 1993.

Foucault, Michel. "Panopticism." *Ways of Reading*. Eds. David Bartholomae and Anthony Petrosky. Boston: Bedford/St. Martin's, 1996.

Franklin, Benjamin. *The Autobiography and Other Writings*. Ed. L. Jesse Lemisch. New York: Signet/New American Library, 1961.

Fransen, Sharon. "In the meadow yellow with dandelions and croaking with crickets." Unpublished poem in the possession of the author.

Friesen, Duane. *Artists, Citizens, Philosophers: Seeking the Peace of the City*. Scottdale, Pa.: Herald Press, 2000.

Friesen, Gordon. *Flamethrowers*. Caldwell, ID: Caxton, 1936.

Friesen, Patrick. *Blasphemer's Wheel*. Winnipeg: Turnstone, 1994.

———. *Flicker and Hawk*. Winnipeg: Turnstone, 1987.

———. "I Could Have Been Born in Spain." *Why I Am a Mennonite: Essays on Mennonite Identity*. Ed. Harry Loewen. Kitchener, On. and Scottdale, Pa.: Herald P, 1988.

———. *The Shunning*. Winnipeg: Turnstone P, 1980.

Goering, Melvin. "Dying to Be Pure: The Martyr Story." *Mennonite Life* 47.4 (Dec 1992): 9-15.

Goertz, Hans-Jürgen. "The Confessional Heritage in Its New Mold: What is Mennonite Self-Understanding Today?" Eds. Calvin Wall Redekop, and Samuel J. Steiner. *Mennonite Identity: Historical and Contemporary Perspectives*. Lanham/New York: University Press of America, 1988.

Good, Phyllis Pellman. Personal Letter, May 5, 1982.

Grimes, Ronald L. *Deeply Into the Bone: Re-Inventing Rites of Passage*. Berkeley: University of California Press, 2000.

Gundy, Jeff. *A Community of Memory: My Days with George and Clara*. Urbana: University of Illinois Press, 1996.

———. *Flatlands*. Cleveland: Cleveland State University Poetry Center, 1995.

———. *Greatest Hits: 1986-2003*. Columbus: Pudding House, 2003.

———. "How to Write the New Mennonite Poem." *Mennonot* 1 (Fall 1993): 10.

———. "If Struck I Should Give Off a Clear Note: A Conversation with William Stafford." *Paintbrush* 17 33/34 (Spring/Autumn 1990): 39-51.

———. *Inquiries*. Huron, OH: Bottom Dog P, 1992.

———. *Rhapsody with Dark Matter*. Huron, Oh.: Bottom Dog, 2000.

———. "Separation and Transformation: Tradition and Audience for Three Mennonite Poets." *Journal of Mennonite Studies* 4 (1986): 53-69.

Haas, Craig, and Steve Nolt. *The Mennonite Starter Kit*. Intercourse, Pa.: Good Books, 1993.

Hanson, Ellis. *Decadence and Catholicism.* Cambridge: Harvard University Press, 1997.

Heard, Gerald. *The Human Venture.* New York: Harper & Brothers, 1955.

Hinz-Penner, Raylene. "Betrayals of the Body." M. F. A. thesis. Wichita State University, 1995.

Hirschfield, Jane. *Nine Gates.* Entering the Mind of Poetry. New York: HarperCollins, 1997.

Holland, Scott. "Communal Hermeneutics as Body Politics or Disembodied Theology?" *Brethren Life and Thought* 40.2 (Spring 1995): 94-110.

———. "Response to Gordon Kaufman." *Conrad Grebel Review* 14.1 (Winter 1996): 48-56.

———. "Theology Is a Kind of Writing: The Emergence of Theopoetics." *MQR* 71 (1997): 227-41.

Homan, Gerlof D. "Good or Bad Citizens: Illinois Mennonites and Amish in World War I." *Illinois Mennonite Heritage* 24, 4 and 25, 1 (Mar. 1997): 61, 77-82; 1, 11-18.

Hostetler, Sheri. *The Mennonite Religious Imagination.* Masters Thesis. Episcopal Divinity School, 1990.

Hudgins, Andrew. *The Glass Hammer.* Boston: Houghton Mifflin, 1994.

Hugo, Richard. "Problems with Landscapes in Early Stafford Poems." *Kansas Quarterly* 2.2 (1970): 33-38.

Hunter, Catherine. "Style and Theme in Rudy Wiebe's *My Lovely Enemy*: Love, Language and 'the Big Trouble with Jesus'." *Journal of Mennonite Studies* 4 (1986): 46-52.

Jalal al-Din Rumi, Maulana. *The Essential Rumi.* Trans. Coleman Barks. New York: HarperCollins, 1995.

Janzen, Jean. "Author's Statement." *Mennonite Life* (1991).

———. *Snake in the Parsonage.* Intercourse, Pa.: Good Books, 1995.

———. *Tasting the Dust.* Intercourse, Pa.: Good Books, 2000.

———. *The Upside-Down Tree.* Winnipeg, Man: Henderson Books, 1992.

Kasdorf, Julia. "A Poet is not a Bridge." Convocation address. Goshen College, 1999.

———. "A Thank You to Jean Janzen." *Festival Quarterly* 22.2 (Spring 1995): 15.

———. "Bakhtin, Boundaries and Bodies." *MQR* 71 (1997): 169-88.

———. *The Body and the Book: Writing from a Mennonite Life.* Baltimore: Johns Hopkins, 2001.

———. "Dissertation Proposal," 1994.

———. *Eve's Striptease.* Pittsburgh: University of Pittsburgh Press, 1998.

———. *Fixing Tradition: Joseph W. Yoder, Amish American.* Telford, Pa.: Pandora Press U. S., 2002.

———. Personal Letter, April 5, 1995.

———. "Review of *Mennonite Literary Voices Past and Present*." *Mennonite Life* 48.4 (1993): 32-33.

———. *Sleeping Preacher.* Pittsburgh: University of Pittsburgh Press, 1992.

———. "When the Stranger is an Angel." *Conrad Grebel Review* 12.2 (Spring 1994): 197-201.

Kauffman, Janet. *Collaborators*. St. Paul: Graywolf, 1993. 1986.

Kaufman, Gordon. "Mennonite Peace Theology in a Religiously Plural World." *Conrad Grebel Review* 14, 1 (1996): 33-47.

———. "Theologian Gordon Kaufman: Giving up Big Daddy." With Sheri Hostetler. *Mennonot* 2 (Spring 1994): 1, 8-12.

Keats, John. "Letter to George and Tom Keats, December 21-27, 1817." *English Romantic Writers*. Ed. David Perkins. New York: Harcourt, Brace & World, 1967. 1209.

Keim, Albert. *Harold S. Bender: 1897-1962*. Scottdale, Pa.: Herald P, 1998.

Kierkegaard, Søren. *The Concept of Irony: With Constant Reverence to Socrates*. Trans. Lee M. Capel. Bloomington: Indiana U P, 1965.

Klassen, Pamela. "What's Bre(a)d in the Bone: The Bodily Heritage of Mennonite Women." *Mennonite Quarterly Review* 68.2 (Apr 1994).

Klassen, William and Klasasen, Walter, trans. and ed. *The Writings of Pilgram Marpeck*. Kitchener, Ontario: Herald Press, 1978.

Kliewer, Warren. "Controversy and the Religious Arts." *Mennonite Life* 20 (July 1965): 8-11.

———. *The Violators*. Francestown, NH: Marshall Jones, 1964.

Kramer, Lawrence. "In Quiet Language." *Parnassus* 6.2 (1978): 108.

Kristeva, Julia. *Black Sun: Depression and Melancholia*. Tr. Leon S. Roudiez. New York: Columbia U P, 1989.

Kundera, Milan. *The Book of Laughter and Forgetting*. Trans. Michael Henry Heim. New York: Penguin, 1980.

Lacan, Jacques. "Seminar on 'The Purloined Letter'." *The Purloined Poe: Lacan, Derrida, and Psychoanalytic Reading*. Ed. John P. Muller and William J. Richardson. Baltimore: Johns Hopkins University Press, 1988. 28-54.

Lesher, Emerson. *The Muppie Manual: The Mennonite Urban Professional's Handbook for Humility and Success*. Intercourse, Pa.: Good Books, 1985.

Liechty, Joseph. "Humility: The Foundation of Mennonite Religious Outlook in the 1860's." *Mennonite Quarterly Review* 54 (1980): 5-31.

Lowell, Robert. *Selected Poems*. New York : Farrar, Straus and Giroux, 1976.

Mellard, James M. "Josephine Hart's *Damage*, Lacanian Tragedy, and the Ethics of *Jouissance*." *PMLA* 113.3 (May 1998): 395-407.

Merwin, W. S. *Selected Poems*. New York: Atheneum, 1988.

Miller, Elmer. "Marking Mennonite Identity: A Structuralist Approach to Separation." *Conrad Grebel Review* 3.1 (Fall 1985): 251-63.

Miller, Levi. "A Reconstruction of Evangelican Anabaptism." *Mennonite Quarterly Review* 69 (July 1995): 295-306.

Milosz, Czeslaw. *The Witness of Poetry*. Cambridge: Harvard University Press, 1983.

Munro, Joyce Clemmer. "Passing on the Torch." *Mennonite Quarterly Review* 60 (1986): 10-14.

Neufeldt, Leonard. *Car Failure North of Nîmes*. Windsor, Ont.: Black Moss, 1994.

———. *Raspberrying*. Windsor, Ont.: Black Moss, 1991.

————. *Yarrow*. Windsor, Ont.: Black Moss, 1993.

Nietzsche, Friedrich. *The Portable Nietzsche*. Ed. and trans. Walter Kauffman. New York: Penguin, 1954.

Nye, Naomi Shihab. *Never in a Hurry: Essays on People and Places*. Columbia: University of South Carolina Press, 1996.

Oliver, Mary. *American Primitive*. New York: Little, Brown, 1983.

Oyer, John S. "Ethics, Aesthetics, and Mennonites." Ed. Harry Loewen. *Why I Am a Mennonite: Essays on Mennonite Identity*. Kitchener, On. and Scottdale, Pa.: Herald P, 1988.

Pagels, Elaine. *Beyond Belief: The Secret Gospel of Thomas*. New York: Random House, 2003.

————. *The Gnostic Gospels*. New York: Random House, 1979.

Palmer, Parker. *To Know as We Are Known: A Spirituality of Education*. New York: Harper, 1983.

Pascal, Blaise. *Pensées*. Trans. W. F. Trotter. London: Dent, 1931.

Peachey, J. Lorne. "To See Ourselves as Others See Us." *Gospel Herald* 17 Jan 1995: 16.

Pinsker, Sanford. *Three Pacific Northwest Poets: William Stafford, Richard Hugo, and David Wagoner*. Boston: Twayne, 1987.

Pinsky, Robert. *Poetry and the World*. New York: Ecco, 1988.

————. *The Situation of Poetry*. Princeton: Princeton Princeton University Press, 1976.

Plato. *Great Dialogues of Plato*. Trans. W.H.D. Rouse. New York: Mentor, 1956.

Pound, Ezra. *Selected Poems of Ezra Pound*. New York: New Directions, 1957.

Ratzlaff, Keith. *Across the Known World*. Farragut and Parkersburg, IA: Loess Hills Books, 1997.

————. "Lies to Tell a Presidential Search Committee." *Mennonot* 4 (Spring 1995): 14-15.

————. *Man Under a Pear Tree*. Tallahassee: Anhinga P, 1997.

————. *Out Here*. Pitchford, NY: State Street P, 1984.

————. Personal Letter, September 29, 1985.

————. "The Poet as John Nachtigal." *Mennonite Life* 46 (Dec 1991): 22-23.

————. "Winterreise." Unpublished manuscript.

Redekop, Calvin. *Mennonite Society*. Baltimore: Johns Hopkins, 1989.

Redekop, Magdalene. "Through the Mennonite Looking Glass." Ed. Harry Loewen. *Why I Am a Mennonite*. Kitchener, On and Scottdale, Pa.: Herald P, 1988.

Reimer, Al. *Mennonite Literary Voices: Past and Present*. North Newton, Kan.: Bethel College, 1993.

Reimer, Margaret Loewen. "Mennonites and the Artistic Imagination." *Conrad Grebel Review* 16.3: 6-24.

Rempel, John. "Spirituality in Recent Mennonite Writing." *Mennonite Quarterly Review* 71.4 (1997): 594-602.

Rensberger, Eric. "Contention Against Shunning." *Journal of Mennonite Studies* 8 (1990): 108-09.

————. Personal Letter, Oct. 3, 1985.

————. *Standing Where Something Did*. Bloomington, Ind. : Ink Press, 1984.

Robinson, James M., dir. *The Nag Hammadi Library in English*. San Francisco: Harper & Row, 1977.

Rothenberg, Jerome. Joris, Pierre. Eds. *Poems for the Millenium: The U. of California Book of Modern and Postmodern Poetry. Volume One: From Fin-de-Siécle to Negritude.* Vol. 1. Berkeley: University of California Press, 1995.

Ruth, John. *The Earth Is the Lord's: A Narrative History of the Lancaster Mennonite Conference.* Studies in Anabaptist and Mennonite History No. 39. Scottdale, Pa.: Herald Press, 2001.

————. "Knowing the Place for the First Time: A Response to Hildi Froese Tiessen." *Mennonite Identity: Historical and Contemporary Perspectives.* Editors Calvin Wall Redekop and Samuel J. Steiner. Lanham, MD: University P of America, 1988.

————. *Mennonite Identity and Literary Art*. Scottdale, Pa.: Herald Press, 1978.

Said, Edward. "The Text, the World, the Critic." *The Critical Tradition: Classical Texts and Contemporary Trends.* Ed. David S. Richter. New York: Bedford/St. Martins, 1989, 1021-36.

Sawin, Mark Metzler. "Moving Stubbornly Toward the Kingdom of God: Mennonite Identity in the Twenty First Century." *Mennonite Quarterly Review* 75.1 January 2001 89-98.

Schell, Jonathan. "Reflections: A Better Today." *The New Yorker* 61 (3 Feb 1986): 47-8.

Schlabach, Theron. *Gospel Versus Gospel: Mission and the Mennonite Church, 1863-1944.* Scottdale, Pa.: Herald Press, 1980.

————. "Mennonites and Pietism in America, 1740-1880: Some Thoughts on the Friedmann Thesis." *Mennonite Quarterly Review* 47 (1983): 222-40.

The Schleitheim Confession. Crockett, Ky.: Rod and Staff Publishers, 1527; 5th ed. 1985.

Schmidt, Kimberly D., Steven D. Reschly, and Diane Zimmerman Umble. *Insider Outsider: Women of Anabaptist Traditions in Historical Perspective.* Boston: Johns Hopkins University Press, 2001.

Shetley, Vernon. "Brief Reviews." *Poetry* 152.2 (May 1988): 108-09.

Showalter, Shirley, "Bringing the Muse into our Country: A Response to Jeff Gundy's "Humility in Mennonite Literature." MQR (Jan 1989): 22-29

Snyder, Arnold. *Anabaptist History and Theology: An Introduction.* Kitchener, Ontario: Pandora Press, 1995.

————. "*Anabaptist History and Theology*: History or Heresy." *Conrad Grebel Review* 16.1 (Winter 1998): 53-59.

Stafford, William. *Allegiances*. New York: Harper & Row, 1970.

————. *Crossing Unmarked Snow: Further Views on the Writer's Vocation*. Eds Paul Merchant and Vincent Wixon. Poets on Poetry. Ann Arbor: University of Michigan Press, 1998.

————. *Down in My Heart*. Elgin, Ill.: Brethren Publishing House, 1947.

————. "Making Peace Among the Words." *Festival Quarterly* 17.1 (Spring 1990): 12-14.

————. Personal Letter, June 5, 1987.

————. *Stories That Could Be True: New and Collected Poems*. New York: Harper/Colophon, 1977.

————. *The Way It is: New and Selected Poems*. St. Paul: Graywolf, 1998.

————. *Writing the Australian Crawl: Views on the Writer's Vocation*. Ann Arbor: University of Michigan Press, 1978.

————. *You Must Revise Your Life*. Ann Arbor: University of Michigan Press, 1986.

Stambaugh, Sara. *I Hear the Reaper's Song*. Intercourse, Pa.: Good Books, 1984.

Stein, Kevin. *Private Poets, Worldly Acts: Public and Private History in Contemporary American Poetry*. Athens: Ohio University Press, 1996.

Stevens, Wallace. *The Necessary Angel: Essays on Reality and the Imagination*. New York: Vintage, 1951.

————. *The Palm at the End of the Mind: Selected Poems and a Play*. New York: Vintage, 1972.

Stitt, Peter. *The World's Hieroglyphic Beauty: Five American Poets*. Athens: University of Georgia Press, 1985.

Stolzfus, Phil. "Performative Envisioning: An Aesthetic Critique of Contemporary Mennonite Theology." *Conrad Grebel Review* 16.3: 75-91.

Suderman, Elmer. "Father Homesteads a Quarter Section on the Cherokee Strip: September 16, 1893." *Mennonite Life* 49.4 (Dec 1994): 8-10.

————. "Mennonites, the Mennonite Community, and Mennonite Writers." *Mennonite Life* 47.3 (Dec 1992): 21-26.

————. "Religious Values in Contemporary Literature." *Mennonite Life* 20 (Jan 1965): 22-28.

————. "The Mennonite Character in American Fiction." *Mennonite Life* July 1967: 123-30.

————. "The Mennonite Community and the Pacifist Character in American Literature." *Mennonite Life* 34 (Mar 1979): 8-15.

————. "Universal Values in Rudy Wiebe's *Peace Shall Destroy Many*." *Mennonite Life* 20 (Oct 1965): 172-76.

Swartzentruber, Elaine K. "Marking and Remarking the Body of Christ." Toward a Postmodern Mennonite Ecclesiology. *Mennonite Quarterly Review* 71 (1997): 243-65.

Thoreau, Henry David. *The Illustrated Walden*. Ed. J. Lyndon Shanley. Princeton: Princeton University Press, 1973.

Tiessen, Hildi Froese. "Beyond the Binary: Re-Inscribing Cultural Identity in the Literature of Mennonites." Eds John D. Roth, and Ervin Beck. *Migrant Muses: Mennonite/s Writing in the U.S.* Goshen, Ind.: Mennonite Historical Society, 1998. 11-21.

————. "Mennonite Literature and Postmodernism: Writing the 'In-Between' Space." *Biesecker-Mast and Gerald Biesecker-Mast 2000): 160-174. Anabaptists and PostmodernitySusan*. Eds Susan Biesecker-Mast and Gerald Biesecker-Mast. Telford, Pa.: Pandora Press U.S., 2000. 160-74.

———. "The Role of Art and Literature in Mennonite Self-Understanding." Mennonite Self-Understanding Conference, 1986.

———. "The Role of Art and Literature in Mennonite Self-Understanding." *Mennonite Identity: Historical and Contemporary Perspectives*. Ed. Calvin Wall Redekop and Samuel J. Steiner. Lanham, Md.: University Press of America, 1988. 235-52.

——— and Hinchcliffe, Peter, eds. *Acts of Concealment: Mennonite/s Writing in Canada*. Waterloo, On: University of Waterloo Press, 1992.

Trilling, Lionel. *The Liberal Imagination: Essays on Literature and Society*. New York: Scribners, 1950.

Wagner, Shari Miller. "A Capella." *Southern Poetry Review* (1996).

———. Personal Letter, Nov. 15, 1995.

Waltner-Toews, David. *The Impossible Uprooting: Poems*. Toronto: McClelland & Stewart, 1995.

Weaver, Carol Ann. "When Two Plus Two is More Than Four: A Saga of Collaborations." *Conrad Grebel Review* 16.3 (Fall 1998) 110-19.

Weaver, J. Denny. *Anabaptist Theology in Face of Postmodernity: A Proposal for the Third Millenium*. Telford, Pa.: Pandora Press U.S., 2000.

———. *Becoming Anabaptist: The Origin and Significance of Sixteenth-Century Anabaptism*. Scottdale, Pa.: Herald Press, 1987.

———. *Keeping Salvation Ethical: Mennonite and Amish Atonement Theology in the Late Nineteenth Century*. Scottdale, Pa.: Herald P, 1997.

———. "Personal e-Mail," 2001.

———. "Reading Sixteenth-Century Anabaptism Theologically: Implications for Modern Mennonites as a Peace Church." *Conrad Grebel Review* 16.1 (Winter 1998): 37-51.

Wiebe, Armin. *The Salvation of Yasch Siemens*. Winnipeg: Turnstone Press, 1984.

Wiebe, Dallas. "Can a Mennonite Be an Atheist?" *Conrad Grebel Review* 16.3 (Fall 1998): 122-32.

———. *Our Asian Journey*. Waterloo, Ont.: Mlr editions canada, 1997.

———. "Personal Correspondence," 1995.

———. *Skyblue the Badass*. New York: Doubleday/Paris Review Editions, 1969.

———. *The Kansas Poems*. Cincinnati: Cincinnati Poetry Review P, 1987.

Wiebe, Katie Funk. "The Mennonite Woman in Mennonite Fiction." *Visions and Realities: Essays, Poems and Fiction Dealing with Mennonite Issues*. Ed. Harry Loewen and Al Reimer. Winnipeg: Hyperion, 1985.

Wiebe, Rudy. *My Lovely Enemy*. Toronto: McClelland and Stewart, 1983.

———. *Peace Shall Destroy Many*. Grand Rapids, Mich.: Eerdmans, 1962.

———. *Sweeter Than All the World*. Toronto: Vintage Canada 2002.

———. *The Blue Mountains of China*. Grand Rapids: Eerdmans, 1970.

Wilde, Oscar. *The Critic as Artist*. Corpus of Electronic Texts Edition: E800003.007, 1907. Http://www.ucc.ie/celt/published/E800003–007/index.html.

Wright, David. "Community, Theology and Mennonite Poetics in the Work of Jeff Gundy." *Migrant Muses: Mennonite/s Writing in the U.S.* Ed. John Roth, and Ervin Beck. Goshen, Ind.: Mennonite Historical Society, 1998. 145-58.

——. *Lines from the Provinces.* Greatunpublished.com, 2000.

Wright, James. *Collected Poems.* Middletown, Conn.: Wesleyan University Press, 1971.

Yoder, John Howard. "Goshen College Convocation Address." October 22, 1973. *Goshen College Maple Leaf,* 1974. 5.

——. *The Politics of Jesus.* Grand Rapids, Mich.: Eerdmans, 1972.

Yoder, Joseph W. *Rosanna of the Amish.* Huntingdon, Pa.: Yoder Publishing Co., 1941.

Young, David. "The Bite of the Muskrat: Judging Contemporary Poetry." *A Field Guide to Contemporary American Poetry and Poetics.* Ed. Stuart Friebert and David Young. New York: Longman, 1980. 123-34.

Zercher, David L. "A Novel Conversion: The Fleeting Life of *Amish Soldier.*" *Mennonite Quarterly Review* 72.2 (Apr. 1998): 141-59.

Zinsser, William, ed. *Inventing the Truth: The Art and Craft of Memoir.* Boston: Houghton Mifflin, 1998.

Zweig, Paul. "The Raw and the Cooked." *Partisan Review* 41 (1974): 604-11.

THE INDEX

ACKNOWLEDGMENTS AND PERMISSIONS

CHAPTER 2

Passages from *My Lovely Enemy,* by Rudy Wiebe, reprinted by permission of the author.

Passages from Armin Wiebe, *The Salvation of Yasch Siemens,* 1984, pp. 155, 167-8, 176 © 1984 Armin Wiebe, reprinted by permission from *The Salvation of Yasch Siemens,* Turnstone Press.

Passages excerpted from *I Hear the Reaper's Song* by Sara Stambaugh. Copyright by Good Books (*www.goodbks.com*). Used by permission. All rights reserved.

CHAPTER 3

Passages from Patrick Friesen, *The Shunning,* 1980, pp. 19, 52, 63, 87, 90, 97, 98 © 1980 Patrick Friesen, reprinted by permission from *The Shunning,* Turnstone Press.

Passages from Patrick Friesen *Flicker and Hawk,* 1987, pp. 3, 23, 41, 45, 47, 49, 53, 70, 67 © 1980 Patrick Friesen, reprinted by permission from *Flicker and Hawk,* Turnstone Press.

W. S. Merwin, "For the Anniversary of My Death," © 1988 by W. S. Merwin, reprinted with permission of the Wylie Agency Inc.

CHAPTER 4

Passages from William Stafford, *Down in My Heart* and *An Oregon Message,* by permission of the Estate of William Stafford.

"Traveling Through the Dark," "Serving with Gideon," "Thinking about Being Called Simple by a Critic," "A Life, A Ritual," "A Memorial for My Mother," and

"An Oregon Message" © 1962, 1983, 1986, 1987, 1998 by the Estate of William Stafford. Reprinted from *The Way It Is: New and Selected Poems* with the permission of Graywolf Press, Saint Paul, Minnesota.

CHAPTER 5

Excerpts from "Mennonites," "Vesta's Father," "Green Market, New York," "When Our Women Go Crazy," and "Sleeping Preacher" from *Sleeping Preacher* by Julia Kasdorf, © 1992. Reprinted by permission of the University of Pittsburgh Press.

Excerpts from dissertation proposal and personal letter by Julia Kasdorf reprinted by permission of the author.

Two poems by Elmer Suderman reprinted by permission of *Mennonite Life*.

Three poems from *The Kansas Poems,* by Dallas Wiebe, reprinted by permission of the author.

114, 115, Leonard Neufeldt, *Yarrow*

"Chicken Guts" and "You Talk with Your Hands" are a part of the collection of poems, *Snake In The Parsonage*. Copyright © by Good Books (*www.goodbks.com*). Used by permission. All rights reserved.

"Lies to Tell a Presidential Search Committee" © Keith Ratzlaff, first published in *Mennonot*, reprinted by permission of the author.

"How to Write the New Mennonite Poem" from *Jeff Gundy: Greatest Hits* © 2003 by Jeff Gundy, reprinted, by permission of Pudding House Publications and the author.

"Rich Hill" by Raylene Hinz Penner, reprinted by permission of the author.

"Baptism" by Sheri Hostetler, reprinted by permission of the author.

"My Father's Hands" from *Brief Landing on the Earth's Surface* © 1996, reprinted by Juanita Brunk, by permission of University of Wisconsin Press.

"In the Meadow Yellow with Dandelions and Croaking with Crickets" © Sharon Fransen, previously published in *The Mennonite,* reprinted by permission of the author.

"Contention with Menno Simons" © Eric Rensberger, previously published in *Journal of Mennonite Studies*, reprinted by permission of the author.

"A Cappella" © 2003 by Shari Wagner, previously published in *Southern Poetry Review,* reprinted by permission of the author.

CHAPTER 6

Passages from "The Poet as John Nachtigall" © Keith Ratzlaff from *Mennonite Life*, reprinted by permission of the author and *Mennonite Life*.

"Cover Me" is a part of the collection of poems, *Snake In The Parsonage*. Copyright by Good Books (*www.goodbks.com*). Used by permission. All rights reserved.

Passages from *The Essential Rumi* © 1995 by Coleman Barks, reprinted by permission of the author.

CHAPTER 9

Di Brandt, "nonresistance, or love mennonite style," *Agnes in the Sky,* 1990, pp. 38-39, © 1990 Di Brandt, reprinted by permission from *Agnes in the Sky,* Turnstone Press.

Passages from *Our Asian Journey* © 1997 by Dallas Wiebe, reprinted by permission of MLR Editions Canada and the author.

CHAPTER 10

204 Italo Calvino, *Invisible Cities*
213 Naomi Shihab Nye, *Never in a Hurry*
"Seams" and "Knowing the Father," from *Flatlands,* © 1995 by Jeff Gundy, reprinted by permission of the Cleveland State University Poetry Center and the author.

CHAPTER 11

Excerpts from "Mural from the temple of Longing," "Rough-Cut Head," "Winterreise," "Oh," "Gospel," "Midmorning Glare," "My Students Against the Cemetery Pines," "Fitful Angel," "Forgetful Angel," and "Woman Flying" from *Man Under a Pear Tree* © 1997 by Keith Ratzlaff, reprinted by permission of Anhinga Press and the author.

The passages by Jean Janzen in Chapter 11 are from the collection of poems, *Tasting the Dust.* Copyright © Good Books (*www.goodbks.com*). Used by permission. All rights reserved.

Excerpts from "Sixth Anniversary," "Freight," "The Sun Lover," "Flu," "Ghost," "A Pass," "Bulbs," "Eve's Striptease," "Ladies' Night at the Turkish and Russian Baths," "Flammable Skirts Recalled," "Eve's Curse," "Thinking of Certain Mennonite Women," "Boustrophedon," "First Bird," and "Flying Lesson" from *Eve's Striptease* by Julia Kasdorf, © 1998. Reprinted by permission of the University of Pittsburgh Press.

Excerpts from *Rhapsody with Dark Matter,* © 2000 by Jeff Gundy, reprinted by permission of Bottom Dog Press and the author.

CHAPTER 12

"Evensong" from *Ripe,* © 2002 by Todd Davis, reprinted by permission of Bottom Dog Press and the author.

CHAPTER 13

THE AUTHOR

Jeff Gundy was born in 1952 on a farm near Flanagan, Illinois, and grew up among Mennonites, corn, soybeans, and chickens in the prairie country that remains his psychic home. In 1975 he graduated from Goshen College with a degree in English, and did masters work in creative writing and a doctorate in American literature at Indiana University in Bloomington. After teaching for four years at Hesston College in Kansas, since 1984 he has been at Bluffton University, where he is Professor of English and former chair of the English/Language department.

Among his books are four chapbooks (including the recent *Greatest Hits 1986-2003* from Pudding House Press), four full collections of poems—*Deerflies* (Word-Tech Editions, 2004) *Rhapsody with Dark Matter* (Bottom Dog Press, 2000), *Inquiries* (Bottom Dog, 1992) and *Flatlands* (CSU Poetry Center, 1995) and two books of creative nonfiction—*A Community of Memory: My Days with George and Clara* (Illinois, 1996) and *Scattering Point: The World in a Mennonite Eye* (SUNY, 2003).

His poems and essays have appeared in literary, scholarly, and religious magazines including *The Sun, The Mennonite, Witness, Shenandoah, Antioch Review, Poetry Northwest, Pleiades, Mennonite Life, Creative Nonfiction, Image, Mennonite Quarterly Review, Conrad Grebel Review*, and *Mennonot*. His work has been anthologized in *A Capella: Mennonite Voices in Poetry, Food Poems, Modern Poems of Ohio, Illinois Voices*, and several volumes in the yearly series *What Mennonites Are Thinking*.

He has served on the faculty of the Antioch Writers Workshop, the Language of Nature workshop, and led numerous other writing workshops and seminars.

Since 1992 he has written a series of essay-reviews of current nonfiction and poetry books for *The Georgia Review*, including an extended review of five books by Mennonite authors which appeared in 2004.

Other honors and awards include five Ohio Arts Council fellowships, seven Pushcart Prize nominations, and two C. Henry Smith Peace Lectureships.

He has been married to Marlyce (Martens) Gundy since 1973, and they are members of First Mennonite Church in Bluffton. They have three sons: Nathan, Ben, and Joel. Gundy's hobbies include playing guitar, jogging, and soccer.

Printed in the United States
60751LVS00003B/122

9 781931 038263